IN SEARCH OF DREAMTIME

RELIGION AND POSTMODERNISM/ A SERIES EDITED BY MARK C. TAYLOR

In

Search

THE QUEST FOR

TOMOKO MASUZAWA

of

Dreamtime

THE ORIGIN OF RELIGION

THE UNIVERSITY OF CHICAGO PRESS / CHICAGO & LONDON

The University of Chicago Press, Chicago 60637
The University of Chicago Press, Ltd., London
© 1993 by The University of Chicago
All rights reserved. Published 1993
Printed in the United States of America
02 01 00 99 98 97 96   5 4 3 2

ISBN (cloth): 0-226-50984-2
ISBN (paper): 0-226-50985-0

An earlier version of chapter 1 appeared in *The Journal of Religion* 69 no. 3, © 1989 by the University of Chicago. All rights reserved. An earlier version of chapter 3 appeared in *Representations* no. 23, © 1988 by the Regents of the University of California; permission granted.

Library of Congress Cataloging-in-Publication Data

Masuzawa, Tomoko.
    In search of dreamtime : the quest for the origin of religion / Tomoko Masuzawa.
        p.   cm. — (Religion and postmodernism)
    Includes bibliographical references and index.
    ISBN 0-226-50984-2. — ISBN 0-226-50985-0 (pbk.)
    1. Religion—Historiography.   2. Müller, F. Max (Friedrich Max), 1823–1900—Contributions in historiography of religion. 3. Durkheim, Emile, 1858–1917—Contributions in historiography of religion.   4. Freud, Sigmund, 1856– 1939—Contributions in historiography of religion.
    I. Title.   II. Series.
    BL41.M345   1993
    200—dc20   93-518
                                                          CIP

⊗ The paper used in this publication meets the minimum requirements of the American National Standard for Information Sciences—Permanence of Paper for Printed Library Materials, ANSI Z39.48-1984.

CONTENTS

ACKNOWLEDGMENTS

MORE THAN ONCE I have read nineteenth-century authors describe the task of acknowledgment as "a pleasant duty." I find it exceedingly difficult as well, for fear that one could never do right with one's creditors when it comes to the debt of this sort. With this caveat, it behooves me to carry out the duty.

The National Endowment for Humanities and the Institute for the Arts and Humanities at the University of North Carolina at Chapel Hill supported different stages of the research.

I thank Laurence Rickels, Walter Capps, and Rainer Nägele for everything they taught me. The extent of my debt to them seems to become clearer as my days at graduate school grow more distant. Meanwhile, five years of collaboration in the American Academy of Religion with Jay Geller, a true kindred spirit within the field of religious studies, have been the most significant factor in sustaining my aspiration for this particular work. I am indebted to him on account of his intelligence, his erudition, and his generosity in sharing interests (his and mine) as well as information. The graduate students in my seminars at the University of North Carolina, some from the nearby Duke University, have been sustenance for my conviction that critical theory can be brought profitably to bear on the problem of modern discourses on religion. Among them, Barry Saunders and Neal Keye also served ably as my research assistants. I thank Alan Thomas of the University of Chicago Press and the series editor, Mark C. Taylor, for the most constructive and felicitous relationship an author could hope to have with a publisher.

No one has waited longer for the completion of this book than my parents, Jotaro and Reiko Masuzawa; I thank them for their loving patience and for having taught me strength, independence, and love of scholarship. My husband, Donald Lopez, read the manuscript several times at different critical stages and, of course, helped me immeasurably, as he also helped me live with the project during the difficult time of writing.

Finally, I mention three friends whose extraordinary ability, commitment, and accomplishments in their own fields have long been a source of courage and inspiration to me: Rebecca Comay, Nicole Gordon, and Judith Farquhar. I dedicate this work to them in friendship and admiration.

IT HAS BEEN SOME TIME since the question of the origin of religion was seriously entertained. Today, there is little sign of the matter being resuscitated and once again becoming the focus of the lively debate of old. Looking back upon the bold speculations of their forefathers, contemporary scholars of religion seem to consider themselves to be in a new phase of scholarship, having learned, above all, not to ask impossible questions. Reputedly, those grand old ideas—the so-called theories of the origin of religion—were conceived by the powerful Victorian imagination in the lacunae of concrete data, and it therefore should be hardly surprising that they turned out to be stillborn. Such is the present-day assessment of these "theories," and if we still study these ideas today, it is supposed to be only in order to assist their more decorous—and more secure—second burial.

Still more serious than the paucity of factual grounding, however, it is the prerogative of origin itself that has come under suspicion in recent times, together with the assumption of the unity, simplicity, and self-identity of absolute beginning. In short, all of the pristine metaphysics of presence, permanence, and plenitude that the concept of origin is said to embody have been rendered problematic. In this connection, we have also come to see that the sovereignty of the author-originator over her text is as imaginary as any other assumption of a unitary origin.

In light of this overriding critique, it might seem a questionable endeavor to draw attention once again to the dubious exploits of those Great Books that so unambiguously set out in search of origins many decades ago, the books that are now laid to rest in the sepulchral category called "classics." While accounting for such venerable texts from time to time may be a respectful sort of activity, *reading* them is perhaps another matter. For, like an autopsy, reading can be an invasive procedure, which might, for that matter, induce some dead souls to a rude awakening. But if we are to encounter some unlaid ghost at the burial site of such "classics," there is a chance that the haunting spirit may tell us more than the dead author-master had intended or would have allowed.

What has prompted my return to some of those classic texts discussed in this book, however, is not simply a necromantic curiosity or, as it is usually and more respectably called, "historical interest." What first intrigued me, rather, was the incomplete state of their burial itself. And what strikes me as more peculiar still is the position of the contemporary scholar, who is perforce cast as a guardian of these tombs, obliged to stand at once venerating and condemning the dead. The singularity of

1

this post seems to be in no small part due to the very construction—
scaffolding? set-up?—of the contemporary study of religion.

•   •

   This, in effect, is the disciplinary setup an aspiring student of religion
is likely to find herself in at the threshold of a graduate school. First, presumably, there is something like an object called "religion," and this object, as it has been taught in the academy for the last half century or so, is
intricately graced with an imposing network of rules and regulations. By
and large these rules have to do with proper scholarly conduct. In addition to the usual litany of the general ethics of learning, which advises us
to "approach" the subject matter gingerly and not to be too eager to
"grasp" it, there is a remarkable profusion of warnings prohibiting *violation* and *reduction*. Concomitantly, there is an impression that this object
which the scholar—or "Western man," as the position of the observer has
been traditionally called[1]—seeks to examine, either historicoscientifi-
cally or hermeneutically, is something exquisitely "alive," or if not so at
present, at least it was once alive.[2] Be it a "religion," a "tradition," or a
"primitive society," this type of object, which we as scholars of religion
are duty-bound to understand, is said to possess integrity, a genius, and
"organic wholeness" all its own. In today's harsh world of invasive sciences, it is felt, this precious object stands in imminent danger of being
violated and reduced to a mere social fact, a mistake in grammar, a kind
of collective neurosis, or perhaps even to nothing.
   While this fear of sinning against the sanctity of "a living whole"
would no doubt offer a fitting occasion for starting a general investigation
into Western fantasies of global politics, I found one precept in particular
more startling than any other. This is the dictum, "Thou shalt not quest
for the origin of religion." It is as though our integrity as modern, factu-
ally responsible scholars of religion depended on our compliance with
this fundamental vow, or rather, disavowal. This is striking especially in
light of the fact that, together with this precept, we also learn that every
one of the "founding fathers" of our discipline stunningly violated this
rule and indulged and jubilated in the forbidden act. Hence, those great
forefathers are to be at once denounced and admired; for, after all, we are
told, they lived and wrote before there was any recognition of the prohibition. Apparently, they inhabited the prehistory of our discipline; indeed,
they must be our own primal fathers, roaming the earth before the Fall or,
at any rate, before reality set in, in such forms as the two world wars, the
collapse of colonial regimes, and other unpleasant events of this century.
Owing to these disappointments that irrevocably divided their era and
ours, the patrimony due us turned out to be rather meager. Whatever the
glorious exploits and putative discoveries of our forefathers may have

been, their fantastic bounty followed them to their graves and expired, so it seems, leaving virtually nothing that we the epigones could invest in the future of our "discipline." In effect, their precious bequest to us amounts to just this prohibition, this piece of wisdom: Deny yourself the liberty your forefathers took unrestrained; renounce the desire for the origin, give up the desire for the ultimate naming of the source, the essence, the Reality, or anything with capital letters—abandon all this for the sake of *Wissenschaft*.

It seems uncertain if someone in this far end of the twentieth century would spontaneously think of launching on such a quest for an origin if left unchecked by this well-publicized interdiction. However that may be, a number of compelling reasons not to do so have been frequently presented to the students of religion, and many of these reasons are surely deserving of attention. But what is even more noteworthy is the voice, the gesture, the pathos of this prohibition itself. There is at once a humble pride and a special poignancy in this self-denial, or renunciation, on the part of the latter-day representative of "Western man"; in some other circumstances one might be tempted to call such a demeanor "religious." But if I were to give into the temptation here, it would not be in order to discredit or diminish the authority of the voice of prohibition by calling it names. Rather, I am interested in raising another sort of question: Why should *this* particular renunciation of desire, *this* ascetic practice, be any less interesting, any less deserving of close analysis, than anything else in the world that is classified by "Western man" with the label "religion"?

Added to this singular practice of self-denial is another curious aspect of the modern study of religion: a sweeping assertion to the effect that religion itself, whether "primitive" or "highly developed," is preeminently concerned with origins. This notion can be elaborated in various ways. For instance, there is a recurrent claim among the scholars of religion that the quintessentially sacred myths are creation myths, and rituals are periodic recreation of those mythic times of beginning, or repetition of some "axial" event. This idea, which universally and uniformly valorizes the meaning of origins in religious beliefs and practices worldwide, first came into prominence with the myth-ritual school earlier in this century, and was immensely popularized by Mircea Eliade and others thereafter.

To be sure, there have been many strong cases made against this idea, and some of the most effective criticisms have come in the form of rigorous alternative interpretation of alleged creation myths and alleged reorigination rituals.[3] These criticisms notwithstanding, the fundamental "insight" of the myth-ritual school is still viable and continues to inform our sense of historicity, cultural diversity, and global plenitude—to the extent that we have not grown sufficiently suspicious of what is invested in these latter notions. This is another way of saying that, as post-

3

structuralist criticism has put it most succinctly, the logic of origination animates and dominates much of our discursive practice, in religious studies as in many other fields. The preeminence of origin lives on and articulates itself in different transmutations, and, unless we find good reasons to dismiss the post-structuralist critique in toto, we would be hard pressed not to keep on insisting that the effect of the origin-logic operative in the study of religion is limited to its most frankly obvious form manifest in the particular brand of "history of religions."[4]

At any rate, it is undeniably the case that the idea of religion as an origin phenomenon continues to hold sway in the popular imagination and that it remains pervasive in the academy, above all in pedagogy. Anyone who has occasion to teach "religious studies" in an undergraduate curriculum has likely found in the audience an alarming receptivity to the notion of religion as origin, source, or center related. The reception is immediate and virtually without resistance. And the array of introductory textbooks on the subject of religion does little else than to reinforce this "truism." In contrast, should one initiate a course with an admission that "religion" is first of all a discursive construct of the modern West, or that "spirituality" may be an entirely local idea without much currency on its own anywhere else, in no time it becomes palpable that such a suggestion painfully rubs against the grain of our audience's natural disposition.

4

If this prevailing depiction of religion and religious peoples as origin oriented or origin obsessed is brought to bear upon the equally conspicuous matter of *scholarly renunciation of origin quests* mentioned earlier, this conjunction offers an interesting analytic situation. There is a curious configuration of agencies here: "Western man," who gives up the desire for origins for the sake of science but also imputes to the ones who are positioned to be the objects of "his" study the unrestrained indulgence in this desire. The opposition of renunciation versus gratification thus sharply demarcates and separates the modern *scholar* of religion from the primitive *practitioner* of religion, the studying subject from the studied object. As always, the declaration of difference is pronounced from the point of view of the subject, against the object. At the same time, it would seem, the configuration also allows a kind of vicarious participation in the forbidden. For, according to this delineation of difference, those "primitive," "archaic," or "religious" peoples conveniently play out the suppressed desire of the observing scientist without endangering the latter's authority invested in the asceticism of "objective observation."

Is this too good to be true? Do these other people—call them "primitive," "archaic," or simply "religious"—exist?

. .

This question is not meant to be rhetorical, nor does it call for a merely empirical answer. Rather, it should call attention to itself, to its own grounds; for, the very question of the reality of the non-Western, nonmodern—in short, the other of "us"—arises from the prevailing discourse of "our science" itself, that is, from the grounds of the "Western" pursuit of knowledge, rather than from the incomplete state of this knowledge. But in addition to this recognition, of course, there are indeed many requisite questions to be asked if we hope to come to terms critically with the present state of our "discipline." The principal desiderata, no doubt, would be comprehensive and specific analyses of the works of some key figures in the field today, as well as sustained investigations of institutional—particularly pedagogical—practices. This book, however, is at once more modest in its immediate aim and less frontal in its strategy.

The focal point of the present study is the ambiguity—or, perhaps more properly speaking, the ambivalence—permeating the scene of incomplete burial of the classical masters. First, there is the ambivalence of the contemporary appraisal and of the attitude toward the dead: admiration and virtual veneration for their daring on the one hand, and condemnation of their hubris and naiveté on the other. Second, there is the ambivalence of the position of the contemporary scholar, qua "Western man," that "he" both does and does not renounce the quest for origins. This second ambivalence is constitutional to the basis of scholarship as "he" understands it, and makes possible the whole enterprise of knowledge.

Thanks largely to psychoanalysis, we have learnt to expect the presence of a rather complicated process called repression whenever we encounter a highly charged ambivalence. This may indeed be a case in point. If repression is suspected in the contemporary study of religion and, in particular, in its self-understanding of the position vis-à-vis its own past, it may be strategically expedient to apply a method that is neither merely phenomenological/observational nor surgical/invasive, but perhaps a method akin to psychoanalysis. This alternative strategy is, in brief, to invert and to reverse the self-claimed positioning of the scholarship by deliberately turning out the "wrong" side, and thus casting the whole problematic in an entirely different light. In other words, if the ambivalence embodied by the subject-object demarcation is intended to justify the (ambivalent) silencing of the past masters and the disallowing of their direct "influence," we may now turn this situation around, inside out, and suggest that *there may be something in those now-discredited origin quests of yesteryear that can threaten the very configuration of positions that legitimates "Western man's" occupation in science/knowledge.* It may be that, despite their manifest intentions, those classical authors did not so much identify an origin, even erroneously, but rather they hit upon

5

some monstrosity, a discovery which threatened to overpower the very basis of their origin quest; and it may be that those great forefathers, no less than their later critics and detractors, "failed to recognize"[5] the import of their prodigious discovery and therefore did not account for the implications their own speculative adventures brought forth.

Thus the task I set before myself is for the most part rereading of some of the best known classical texts. One might call it a monomaniacal reading, carried out, when necessary, against the sanctioned judgment by posterity, or even against the apparent will of the authors themselves. The choice of the three figures was not exactly premeditated. That is to say, there seems to me no reason a priori a fresh reading of J. G. Frazer, R. R. Marett, W. Robertson-Smith, Wilhelm Schmidt, or any others should not produce an equally volatile condition, equally serviceable for analysis by contemporary critical theory. Perhaps the virtue of the selection of the three here is in the diversity and multivalency of their legacy; for Emile Durkheim, Max Müller, and Sigmund Freud certainly represent divergent parameters of the (pre)history of the study of religion.

6   What may be expected from this rereading—with, admittedly, a potentially insurgent intent—is, at the least, gaining some ground, from which we may begin to challenge the position of the self-appointed "ascetic priest" (alias "modern scholar"), whose sanctimonious self-understanding seems to dictate unilaterally the entire configuration of the field of knowledge. What is sought here is a critique that departs fundamentally from the kind of vaguely narcissistic self-criticism within the confines of "ethics of science"—"Are we *fair* in our representation of the 'primitives'?"—which ultimately refuses to question the positional structure of the knowing and the known, and thus remains insistently blind to the question of power. What is called for instead is a critical inquiry about the practice of knowledge and power, about the politics of writing, as it pertains to the study of religion.

The outcomes of my reading of the three authors are not structurally uniform because their respective positions with regard to the contemporary study of religion vary greatly and because, partly owing to this divergence, my reading strategy is different in each case. This book is thus motivated less by a unifying principle than a singular intent. About this purpose I have already spoken to some extent in this introduction; but in the first chapter this will be given a more analytic and textual delineation. In the course of this delineation I will be also suggesting that the grounds for critical articulation—the space which contemporary critical theory seeks to materialize—is inextricably tied to a certain supplementary or appendant structure, a position signaled by such pervasive terms as *post-modern* and *post-structuralism*.

This is perhaps as good a place as any to accede that each of my readings of the three authors may be termed, though perhaps in a rather loose sense, post-structuralist. I have no reason to object to this designation, assuming that by a post-structuralist reading we do not understand—as those who are hostile to post-structuralism sometimes do—a new, upgraded version of formalist exercise,[6] or even more dismissively, an effete, formulaic reading that produces little else than torturously refined, but ultimately inconsequential results.

.   .

Early in Durkheim's *The Elementary Forms of the Religious Life*, one comes across an unexpected and largely unnoticed element: a strikingly radical statement concerning the sacred. Throughout the text subsequently, there are periodic resurgences of this element at some exceptionally critical junctures. This recurs in spite of the author's forceful argumentation in favor of another, more famous statement about the sacred, popularly rendered as "the 'sacred' is society," which is eventually made to triumph and thus becomes the master thesis by which Durkheim is remembered. The submerged thesis on the other hand—which is therefore a sort of *counterauthorial* thesis—defines "the sacred" stringently as "the absolute opposite of the profane," as a kind of *empty* category. "The sacred" in this sense is a figure for *difference* itself. Viewed in this light, *Elementary Forms* is not exactly a singular pursuit attaining the Q.E.D. at the end; rather, it is a record of a protracted battle between the two theses joined on the imagined continent of Australia. Admittedly, this is a strange battle to observe, for it is essentially the textual equivalent of shadowboxing. The "opponent" of the master thesis continually disappears and reappears; it does not really develop; it just keeps haunting the text. The strategy for reading here is therefore to assume the counterauthorial position and to give an account of the barely visible opponent so as to render various moves of the contenders intelligible.

Also notable is the curiously atavistic recurrence of this other, recessive thesis in the works of posterity. In contrast, the master thesis saw its decline immediately after the author's demise. The very notion of the Durkheimian "sacred"—predominantly associated with the master thesis, "the essential origin of religion is society"—became something of an embarrassment for those in the most direct lineage of the Durkheimian school, the reason being that the idea is either too fantastic or too vague. But the persistence of the other thesis does not amount to an exoteric legacy either. Rather, its very recurrence seems to take the form of a series of rejections—it recurs at each turn of innovation, at each point of departure from the predecessor. In circumstances such as these, it would be inadequate to say that what persists through the subsequent generations of (French) scholars is "the same idea." The inadequacy is acutely felt espe-

7

cially when we acknowledge the radically counterfoundational temper of what is thus shown to recur: something like "absolute difference."

•   •

When it comes to the case of Friedrich Max Müller, the ambiguity of his search for the origin seems to echo his own complex career as a philologist residing abroad who happened to become famous for what was for him essentially a hobbyhorse: speculations on the origin of mythology and the growth of religion. Though the notoriety remains, it appears that his books on these subjects are read very little today, and few among us would ever inquire seriously what his theory really looked like. What remains of him in the standard "history of the discipline" is an honorable mention as the first comparativist who gave the name *Religionswissenschaft* to the field that was yet to come into existence, and a few memorable phrases. Nor are we particularly bothered by the apparent incongruity within the standard shorthand description of his accomplishments: "He was a principal exponent of the 'nature myth school,'" on the one hand, *and* "he said: 'mythology is a disease of language' and *'nomina* became *numina,'*" on the other. What, exactly, was the origin of mythological gods according to Max Müller? The sun? Or mangled words? Do they amount to the same?

A presumed answer to this question runs roughly as follows. In the manner of the enlightened liberal intellectuals generally, Müller believed in the universality of religious truth, in the ubiquity of the most somber awareness of "the Infinite" among all humans. He assumed that this sentiment most readily found a form of expression in the majestic wonder of nature, especially the sun. On the other hand, mythology is a particular and primitive—that is to say, crude and corrupt—delineation of this primordial sentiment in the form of a narrative, and the specific nature of this delineation derives from accidental transmutations and transmigrations of words. This indeed must be the answer Müller would be prepared to give if asked squarely, and if he were to wish to appear roughly coherent. Nevertheless, this smooth rendition of his position works precisely by glossing over a certain gap which Müller himself found rather difficult to cross. This gap may be best measured by, though not to say causally ascribable to, the complex circumstances of his life, crossing over disciplinary as well as national boundaries.

Max Müller was German by birth and a philologist by training, two facts which he did not consider entirely coincidental. He lived more than half a century in a foreign land (in Oxford) where his sponsor/publisher was located. He did much to propagate the nineteenth-century German university culture and its brand of rigorous *Wissenschaft* amidst what, to him, amounted to Oxford's Anglican complacency and polite manners that passed as a good education. In his opinion, the British reading public did not know or understand properly philology as a science, and their attention was apt to be captivated by amateur topics of general cultural interest, such as mythology. In contrast, Müller himself reserved a pride of place for his scholarly, and therefore decidedly inaccessible to amateurs, endeavors, while ascribing a more or less incidental status to his own engagement with the question of the origin of religious tales, mythology, and folklore, which were but by-products of the history of languages. In assessing his career he claimed repeatedly that his essays on these subjects were so many scraps (or, in his words, "chips") issuing from his "German Workshop," where the really serious business of editing the *Rig Veda* went on for nearly thirty years.

The present reading of Max Müller, in effect, attempts to restore these fallouts to the vicinity of their original scene of production, his philological workshop. What comes to the fore as a result is an unexpected image of history, seemingly uncharacteristic of his time and of his profession: "history" not as an organic, continuous narrative of origin and development but as a series of casualties fraught with loss, decay, incidental conjunctions of foreign elements, and fortuitous and deviant aftergrowths. Such a history is anything but teleological; there is no font of plenitude anywhere in this history that guarantees its destiny. Above all, it is a history of going abroad and going astray.

9

•   •

Freud presents a very special case and a very special problem for the overall strategy of this book. To begin with, unlike Müller, Freud is avidly read today, in fact, read by a bewildering number of scholars and amateurs of all stripes. In comparison to Durkheim's case, the critiques of Freud are staggeringly multifarious, contested, and literally growing larger by the minute. Freud's is surely one modern corpus that can most effectively preempt the fantasy of mastery and completion; no sane person could possibly feel, or even imagine what it means to be in complete control of this voluminous and disputed legacy, or to arrive at a definitive interpretation.

But a structural problem of the Freud case specific to this book also stems from this diversity. On the one hand, he is accused—like Frazer, Müller, and Durkheim—of having engaged "naively" in the quest for the origin of religion and having come away with a rather outrageous result. On the other hand, he is credited, together with Nietzsche, to have done most to destabilize the whole question of origin radically, precisely, and polyvalently. It is on account of this latter achievement that Freud is so

widely and meticulously read today. Although the two parties representing these divergent views never seem to engage one another in conversa-
tion or in polemic, if they were to do so, the renowned account of the
parricidal moment of origination in *Totem and Taboo* no doubt would be
the fiercest battleground.

Like many others today, I have been deeply affected and profitably instructed by the second, more recent, so-called post-structuralist reading
of Freud (in its liberal sense, that is, which includes readings by Jacques
Lacan, J. Laplanche and J.-B. Pontalis, Nicolas Abraham and Maria
Torok, Gilles Deleuze and Felix Guattari, as well as Michel Foucault and
Jacques Derrida). Needless to say, this fact accounts for much of the design, or even the very topic, of this book.

The interpretive strategy employed here with respect to Freud is to
follow through certain directives that his texts provide. To begin with, he
says at the outset that *Totem and Taboo* should not prove compelling unless the reader is sufficiently informed both by the basic principles of psychoanalysis and by the (then current) ethnographical works on the
primitive and on totemism, because this work is an instance of *application* of psychoanalytic theory to a remote area of interest. As a disclaimer,
the statement seems, at least in principle, sensible enough, especially
when it comes to the directive to familiarize oneself with the rudiments of
the turn-of-the-century Australian ethnography. But in practical terms,
digesting the basics of psychoanalytic theory "sufficiently" is a rather tall
order, and one would wonder what Freud expected of his audience when
he published these highly volatile essays in the journal specifically intended for nonclinical, nontechnical, "human-scientific" discussions.
But once Freud's relation to "human sciences" [*Geisteswissenschaften*]—
especially history, archaeology, literature—is examined closely, one
would soon come to recognize that for Freud "application" and "remote
area of concern" (meaning, here, humanities in general) are anything but
what one would expect them ordinarily to mean. *Totem and Taboo* itself
is the best testimony to the fact that the outlandish world of the "savages"
is not an extraneous area of interest for Freud but in fact an indispensable
segment of the skeletal structure of psychoanalytic theory, or what he
calls metapsychology.

The sojourn into metapsychology naturally entails both a detour and
an enormous complication of the question that everyone seems to want to
know, the one about the primal parricide: Did it happen, or did it not?
Posed in this manner, it seems only natural that one would expect an unequivocal answer, or if not an answer at least a credible procedure that
can effectively do away with the question. Whereas more traditional, empiricist readers look for an answer, post-structuralist readers tend to opt
for a dissolution of the question. Short of declaring the whole thing non-

sense, however, it seems as though this vexing question could be dissolved or dissipated only rhetorically.

Ultimately, the present study is not concerned with either the solution or the dissolution of this cardinal question because its principal aim is not to find satisfaction and a conceptual place of rest at that particular juncture but rather to document the destabilizing effect of Freud's own pursuits. Many a Freudian quest was carried out in the name of some "origin"; at the same time, we might pronounce, lifting a phrase from Walter Benjamin, that "origin" for Freud "was almost always a flag under which sailed a cargo that could not be declared because it still lacked a name."[7] To give the most general description of this cargo, as many Freud readers have done, the Freudian origin, or originary *event,* is nonunitary, and it is structurally uncanny; in Freud, what is customarily compressed in the phrase "one day" in fact happens twice, so to speak.

As one retraces the course of Freud's pursuit of origins, the path becomes entangled with the problem of his association with Carl Jung. From the beginning Freud's psychoanalytic venture into the question of religion was closely related to the chronology of Jung's stimulation, support, dissent, and eventual defection. The strategy adopted here, however, is in a sense the converse of the one employed for the Durkheim reading in that Jung is not really granted a voice (which he and his sympathizers articulate well enough elsewhere in their own works) but he is accorded only the status of the negative contour of Freud's theory formation during its critical years (roughly 1909 to 1919), or what may be termed Freud's metapsychological decade. It was in those years—the years, it so happens, in which Freud analyzed, wrote, and finally published his celebrated case of the Wolf-Man—and in part in lingering quarrels with Jung that Freud came to articulate some of the most far-reaching psychoanalytic precepts concerning origination. The distinctly discernible but fundamentally interrelated parameters of Freud's origin question are the "origin and development" of infantile sexuality, the origin of sexual trauma, and the possible phylogenetic origins of the trauma.

Incidentally, Freud's insistence on the reality of infantile sexuality is not tantamount to claiming that sexuality is primordially "present" in the child. In point of fact, it is difficult to say if there is anything universally and timelessly "present" in the domain of psychoanalysis at all. Everything, to the extent that it comes into the view of psychoanalysis, is already constituted, *already derived; it has already taken place* somewhere, and, as a rule, it has taken place somewhere other than where it comes to appear; and it behooves psychoanalysis to discern, though perhaps never to *re-present,* this "elsewhere."[8] The question of origin in Freud has to do above all with this process of derivation rather than with some primary state before derivation. The origin is literally a "primal

11

fissure" *(Ursprung)*, not a primary *(primär)* state. Hence the contrast between Jung's outlook on religion and Freud's probe into its origin shows up in the constitutional difference between their objects of attention: on the one hand, universal archetypes and the mythic structure of the unconscious, and on the other, traces *(Spuren)* of what once took place. One calls for the contemplative gaze, the other, for reading.

ONE

Original Lost: Myth and Ritual in the Age of Mechanical Reproduction

IN THE INTRODUCTION TO *Reading after Freud,* Rainer Nägele portrays **13**
the life of a typical contemporary reader, living in a postindustrial society,
reading postmodern literature amid postmodern furniture and architecture, and turning out post-structuralist criticism. While we are certainly
familiar with this emblematic scene, we wonder all the more as to the
meaning of the curious appendage *post-.* Is this an extension—some kind
of an afterlife, perhaps, of what it qualifies *(structuralist, modern, industrial)?* Or does it indicate a reversal of some sort, an atavistic return of
what once was . . . a return of the *pre-?* These are rather nervous questions; as Nägele puts it, this *post-* sticking out of everything modern signals "a neuralgic spot in our contemporary experience of time and
history."[1] This is probably a more refined way of saying that, in our time
of the ubiquitous *post-,* the order of time itself has become somewhat
weird. We thought we were accustomed to living in terms of beginning,
middle, and end, and we thought we always traveled in a passage of time
as smartly arranged as the pages between two hard covers; but now it
looks like we are traversing a bad infinity which is, worse still, strangely
convoluted.

In fact one of the conceptual "perversities" often attributed to contemporary theory is its alleged tendency to expose the convolution of the
logical relation between origin and what was always thought to come after: repetition, reproduction, representation, copy. This inversion, however, is not a matter of simply reversing the priority and claiming that the
reproduction is prior to the original. For the question of priority, the question of which comes first, as well as the last-ditch declamation—"well it's
got to start somewhere, doesn't it?"—all this belongs to the repertoire of

traditional metaphysics, so it is said, to the apparatus governed by the prerogative of the absolute beginning. The voice that speaks in the name of the postmodern, on the other hand, speaks rather differently; this voice purports to put into question the pristine logic of origination as a whole. If we are to listen to this voice, then, "before" we could hope to ascertain the status of the dangling *post-* we would have to examine this inversion and convolution of the logic of origination.[2]

The principal concern here, however, is not so much to sort out the intricate ties and knots that situate postmodernism in relation to modernism, or to determine what does or does not constitute "postmodern conditions," or to ascertain the overall relevance, vis-à-vis the study of religion in general, of those debates multiply carried out in the name of postmodernism. Without being drawn into this endlessly engrossing territory of contemporary debate, the task at hand is to initiate a probe into the historical condition of what has come to be known as comparative religion or, more recently, the history of religion(s),[3] by devising a little experiment—that is, by bringing certain local, perhaps fragmentary voices of postmodernism debates within earshot of "religious hermeneutics," as the study of religion is finally called by Mircea Eliade. This experimental approximation may produce a variety of consequences. It may, eventually, alter how we feel we ought to go about cataloging and interpreting religious narratives, rituals, and so on, in short, everything that is routinely construed as raw data, or primary objects of investigation. But more immediate to my present concern than the question of the so-called methodological alternatives, again, is the prospect that this experiment may effectively throw into relief the specific ways in which the modern scholarly discourse on religion is constituted and situated.

As rehearsed in the introduction, the scholar of religion stands in a rather complicated, if not to say convoluted, relation to the question of origin and origination. On the one hand, it is said that history of religions, or *Religionswissenschaft,* as a scholarly practice is founded upon a voluntary renunciation of the pursuit of origin; as Eliade repeatedly instructs us, this scholarship now deems unscientific any endeavor that purports to identify once and for all the origin, source, or cause of religion, or any attempt to plot religious development in terms of an evolutionary scenario, be it progressive or regressive. According to the Eliadean orthodoxy, then, anyone with a scholarly pretention in this field would have to be prepared to say that the question of the origin is of no concern, for "the historian of religions knows by now that he is unable to reach the 'origin' of religion. What happened in the beginning, *ab origine,* is no longer a problem for the historian of religions, though conceivably it might be one for the theologian or the philosopher."[4]

On the other hand, the same "science" admits, or rather presumes, that the question of origin is of the utmost concern for some other people, and those others include not only theologians and philosophers but a far greater number of people in the world. Let us recall that the brand of *Religionswissenschaft* professed by Eliade customarily imputes an irrepressible desire for origins, and a veritable claim for origins, to all religions and religious peoples. With a remarkable consistency, religion is said to be essentially concerned with origins and with the need to represent—and thus making it *present again*—an absolute beginning. Hence the prominence in the field of topics such as myths (understood as narratives of origin), ritual (repetition, reenactment of an original event or paradigmatic order), and tradition (concern for the transmission of an essential, original "truth" through time). Seen from the perspective of the modern scholar, then, it is precisely the difference in the management of the desire for the origin—that is, whether to embrace this desire and to form a whole system of beliefs and practices around it, or to renounce this desire and to build science at a critical distance from it—is what distinguishes the subject (the scholar, or "Western man," as Eliade calls "him" explicitly) and the object (the religious person, "the premodern," "the archaic," "the primitive") of this scholarship.

A reading of postmodern criticism, inasmuch as it puts into question the logic of origination as such, can make us confront this aspect of the contemporary study of religion and by so doing expose the covert operations of its metaphysical assumptions. Most significantly, these assumptions have allowed the scholar to advance and to occupy the position of critical articulation, a discursive position at a certain distance from his object of study, his other—that is, the archaic, the religious. To be sure, even under the most radical postmodern interrogation, some myths may never cease to be a narrative about some "axial episode" any more than certain rituals can stop repeating themselves. Yet whether all this narrating and repeating amounts to cosmic nostalgia and a universal craving for an absolute origin on the part of the religious premoderns, as Eliade claims it does, is quite another question. Is the ritual repetition necessarily a reproduction of some occurrence (real or imagined) which is itself not a repetition but a singular, originary event? Does a typical myth represent and re-actualize a pristine moment which is itself outside of time? Or, to put the matter most generally and pointedly, do repetition and representation presuppose an absolute origin and the concomitant logic of origination? Could repetition and representation be conceived, or performed, in some other way?

It should not be surprising if questioning of this sort has not risen most readily in religious studies or traditional ethnography, fields where the particular concern has been to document the disappearing "primitives" and "archaics," an industry geared toward capturing the last traces

15

of the dreamtime. Meanwhile, some serious probes into the logic of origination has been launched in other areas. It has been a compelling topic, for instance, in certain quarters of art history, where issues such as original versus reproduction and the originality of the artist and its domain of influence have forced the question of origin into a particularly interesting corner.

· ·

Already in 1936, Walter Benjamin—who perhaps could be called a postmodern theorist *avant la lettre*—set the stage for the questioning of the origin in his now renowned essay, "The Work of Art in the Age of Mechanical Reproduction."[5] With an irony of fate rather difficult to describe, this essay has become a *locus classicus* of contemporary discussions on the disappearance of the authority of origin, original, originality. Written under a fresh "influence"—namely, that of his new Marxist friend, Bertolt Brecht—much to the irritation of his "more dialectical" Marxist friend, Theodor Adorno, and to even greater consternation on the part of his messianic kabbalist friend, Gershom Scholem, this essay resolutely acknowledges, and in the last analysis celebrates, the irrefragable arrival of modernity, which ushered in entirely new modes of material production, new shapes of collective and individual experience, a new psychology of perception, and hence new conditions for art and the new possibilities for its politicocritical role.[6]

In order to mitigate the vertiginous impact of his characteristically condensed, multivalent argument, I shall tug at one particular strand and focus on one issue: the advent of photography and its implications for the economy of origination and reproduction. According to Benjamin, the invention of this new technology marks a turning point in the general history of art; with it, a certain long-term, increasingly accelerated development reaches its climax and is at last exploded.

The underlying general theory of the history of art seemingly implied here may seem at first glance too schematic, and certainly not very novel. It is a common enough idea: art originated in the context of magical-religious cult practice, and only gradually did its aesthetic value proper (that is, its exhibition value) come to overtake and replace the initially dominant cult value. This is a familiar historical scenario depicting the process of secularization, in the course of which religion goes underground, or rather, becomes entrenched in the aesthetic.[7] What is more characteristically Benjaminian, however, asserts itself at this point. With the appearance of the new technological modes of production and reproduction, he suggests, this erosion of the cult value is all but complete; what has been thus diminishing and is now at the point of demise he calls "aura." As regards this portentous term—which reappears and functions in much the same, weighty, and taciturn fashion in his other essays—he chooses to give only a laconic definition, with no more than these enigmatic words: "We define the aura of [natural objects] as the unique phenomenon [*Erscheinung*, appearance] of a distance, however close it may be. If, while resting on a summer afternoon, you follow with your eyes a mountain range on the horizon or a branch which casts its shadow over you, you experience the aura of those mountains, of that branch" [222–23].

If this is not entirely illuminating, its association with the cult practice can be instructive. Like Durkheim and Freud, Benjamin believes that the fundamental defining characteristic of the cult object is that it is marked by prohibition; it is that which "sets itself apart," and aura may be understood as the forbidding atmosphere of invisible distance surrounding the object, even at the time one enjoys the most intimate ritual encounter with it. In fact, Benjamin confirms this more explicitly in a footnote:

> The definition of the aura as a "unique phenomenon of a distance however close it may be" represents nothing but the formulation of the cult value of the work of art in categories of space and time perception. Distance is the opposite of closeness. The essentially distant object is the unapproachable one. Unapproachability is indeed a major quality of the cult image. True to its nature, it remains "distant, however close it may be." The closeness which one may gain from its subject matter does not impair the distance which it retains in its appearance. [243]

17

But how does a technological development such as the invention of photography precipitate the loss of aura? By "substitut[ing] a plurality of copies for a unique existence" [221], and by bringing the object ever "closer," and destroying the "distance" that surrounds it. Photography, like other forms of mechanical reproduction, responds to "the desire of contemporary masses to bring things 'closer' spatially and humanly" [223]; by "pry[ing] an object from its [auratic] shell" [223], photography lets the object circulate in a new system of economy. In contrast, the traditional art work, with its aura emanating from its "unique presence" [*Hier und Jetzt*] and guaranteeing its authenticity, wholly controls the authorizing power of its transmission. Traditionally, that is to say, the unique presence of the object sets up what may be called the originary[8] economy of dissemination. As Benjamin puts it, "the authenticity of a thing is the essence of all that is transmissible from its beginning, ranging from its substantive duration to its testimony to the history which it has experienced. Since the historical testimony rests on the authenticity, the former, too, is jeopardized by reproduction when substantive duration ceases to matter.

And what is really jeopardized when the historical testimony is affected is the authority of the object" [221]. When a copy is made of a traditional, auratic artwork, the relation between the original and the copy is forever that between the real thing and an imitation—a fake, a mere copy. The original gives up none of its unique (read "setting itself apart") authenticity, it alone remains authoritative (read "original") [220]. Photography upsets this originary economy through a radical alteration in the material relation between the original and the reproduction. This alteration may be examined in two aspects.

First, photography, as a new medium of reproduction of other art forms, cuts deeply into the authorizing and controlling power of the original for the reason that, in photographic reproduction, the "copy" acquires a certain autonomy and independence from the original. This is above all due to the fact that photography, with no more than a mere movement of a finger, can capture, literally in an instant, what may easily escape the naked eye. Although the camera is guided by an eye looking through the lens and hands directing its aim, in an important sense the photographic process bypasses altogether the servitude implied in the traditional mode of reproduction, that is, what is involved in the long labor of drawing hands and studying eyes. It does not reproduce what the human body learns to experience, but offers something different, a view taken by surprise. No matter how prolonged and laborious the preparatory staging of the shot, ultimately it is a swift, violent capture; every photograph is in the last instance a *snapshot*. Moreover, photography can, as can a phonograph, disseminate this captured image on a massive scale, that is, in prodigious quantity and into a great distance, and it can be made to reach where the original could never travel. Once the reproductions proliferate and scatter about in the world, these countless simulacra do not leave the original alone in peace but, as Benjamin puts it, they "reactivate" the original. Indeed, we are familiar with such a phenomenon: an artwork worn out and made into a cliche through innumerable reproductions invariably affects our experience of the "real thing" when we finally encounter it. Perhaps a curious embarrassment—a far cry from the solemnity of ritual encounter—comes to be mingled in our enjoyment. At any rate, the photographic reproduction partially but significantly moves out of the reach of the original, liberates itself from the economy of origination and dissemination; it circulates on its own terms, and in turn co-opts the original into its own economy.

Secondly, photography as an art form in its own right reveals another aspect that threatens the authority of the original. For this is an art form which has reproducibility already built into it; it produces from the beginning an indefinite number of reproductions but no original, save the one that is, literally, a *negative*. Or, as the French would have it, the photographic "original" is a *cliché*. To be sure, one might say that to a certain extent this is true also of lithography, or even of woodcut printing. But what makes the case of photography historically decisive is this very question of the extent, which is so prodigious as to be incalculable.

In sum, according to Benjamin, the advent of photography establishes, over and against the traditional auratic economy of origination, a new, independent system of circulation which deeply affects the former to the point of completely overriding it; and in the process desiccates the last residue of the cult value of art.

This conclusion might seem somewhat surprising when we consider how photographs participate in numerous cultic observances in our own lives, albeit mostly secular ones. Who among us does not admit to a little cult of the photographic image, placed at one's desk or carried in one's wallet, a monument erected to assure the auratic power of the unique presence behind the image, a special person, a special place? Benjamin certainly knows something of this latter-day cultish behavior associated with photography, but for him this amounts to a momentary intensification of the dying aura, its last ray. "Cult value does not give way without resistance. It retires into an ultimate retrenchment: the human countenance. It is no accident that the portrait was the focal point of early photography. The cult of remembrance of loved ones, absent or dead, offers a last refuge for the cult value of the picture. For the last time the aura emanates from the early photographs in the fleeting expression of a human face. This is what constitutes their melancholy, incomparable beauty" [225–26]. **19**

The intense illumination of those faces, made somber by the prolonged stare into the early photographic apparatus, is hardly detectable, it is true, in the present-day version of the cultic photographs, embellished as they are by glossy colors and the smiles and gestures abundantly quoted from the products of the culture industry; ours are unquestionably impoverished in their auratic aspect. All the same, we still treasure this bit of fetishism.

It is also in accordance with this phenomenon—that is, impoverishment of aura, retrenchment of the dying cult value, desiccation of its residue into fetishism—that some of the modern movements in art, nostalgic or futuristic, may be best understood. Benjamin seems to consider the cult of beauty, *l'art pour l'art,* as something of a death rattle of auratic art, in which, in the total absence of religious significance, the exhibition value itself has become a peculiar form of cult value. And again, there is a rampant fetishism of objects in the art industry today, wherein the uniqueness proper to the auratic object is simply replaced by the overvaluation of the empirical singularity of an object, that is, the ascription of extravagant values to an object, a rather Spartan attachment to the object on the meager basis of the fact that it is it, and nothing else is, or that it is executed by X, and no one else legitimately occupies the identity of X but X herself.

It is instructive to locate Dada in this context, a movement whose historical intentions, according to Benjamin's understanding of the matter, are the exact opposite of the ones just mentioned. For Dada's very raison d'être is in its committed and active aggression against such retrenchment and fetishism. Of those contentious vanguards, Benjamin writes that "their poems are 'word salad' containing obscenities and every imaginable waste product of language. The same is true of their paintings, on which they mounted buttons and tickets. What they intended and achieved was relentless destruction [*rücksichtlose Vernichtung*] of the aura of their creations, which they branded as reproductions with the very means of production" [237–38]. In other words, Dada contrives to produce the same effect that photography achieves quite naturally; it executes this, mainly, through a systematic degradation of the traditional art forms, that is, by defrauding their formal structure.

Some Dadaists went so far as to attempt to reverse the original-copy relation in order to muddle and confound the hierarchy implicit in the configuration. Consider, for instance, Marcel Duchamp's art consisting of ready-made objects. He simply (re)produced a "model," that is, (re)presented a "real thing," an already manufactured object—say, a snow shovel. But it turns out that this object is already a kind of a copy; it most probably refers to some drawing in a book of instruction for industrial arts, the sort of books that were commonly available at the turn of the century.[9] What underlies Duchamp's method here is the knowledge that the tyrannical economy of origination that has governed the tradition of art in all of its aspects is at bottom commensurate, nay, identical, with the economy of consumerism and with what Marx aptly termed "fetishism of commodities." By "lifting" a mass-produced quotidian object out of the shop window and endowing it with a lopsided status as an artwork representing an item in a manual for industrial drawing, Duchamp wrests this ordinary commodity out of its normal circulation, not in order to resurrect its aesthetic value—it has none—but in order to render inoperative the furious general economy surrounding it. This is why his art resembles vandalism; the result is a priceless public scandal.

Hardly less bold and celebratory than the ill-behaving Dadaists, Benjamin, too, pronounced more or less the last word on the fate of the auratic art while he also expressed his studied optimism for the postauratic future of art, which he envisioned as an essentially political one. Exactly where he went from here is another story, and it would be a long story indeed. For the purpose of the present discussion, we shall have to leave him at this point, for we must now return to our *post-*.

•   •

From this end of the twentieth century, one may get the impression that the loss of origin, or more precisely the internal collapse of the economy of origination, is a sign of the times. As we saw in the previous section, an instance of this collapse has been deftly plotted by Benjamin with regard to the advent of photographic technology. But in the meantime, what in that instance seemed characteristic primarily of photography and of a few other mechanically reproducible media is now vastly generalized; it is insidiously and ubiquitously affecting the way one produces and views other more traditional forms of art, such as painting. The result is that the conceptual framework with which we have hitherto understood artistic representation and its historicity has become deeply problematic; for this framework itself has become predicated on the premise of the economy of origination.

This, however, is neither to mistake nor ignore the fact that much of the scholarly industry of art history to this day—as in many other historical disciplines—consists of the same laborious productions based on the traditional economy. For example, identifying the authorship, distinguishing the original from a forgery or false attribution, determining the historical value of the work in terms of originality, innovation, sources, influence—in short, art history is, now as ever, writing developmental histories. Yet the well-nigh oxymoronic juxtaposition of this dominant scholastic attitude on the one hand and some of the most prominent aspects of contemporary practice of art since the beginning of this century on the other seems to have opened a new space for criticism. In this space, contemporary critic Rosalind Krauss offers an astute outlook on the present state of affairs, which is now often called—though not necessarily with common consent—*the postmodern condition*.[10]

Indeed, a critical articulation such as Krauss's—which questions the obsessive preeminence of the problem of origin among both scholars and artists—must be in part the effect of this incongruous juxtaposition realized only today. For is it likely that throughout history it has always been so consistently believed as it has been in recent times that behind every representation lies a unitary origin? Is it not rather a recent postulate that the truth of every representation must be redeemable at its origin, whether the point of origin be the true meaning, the essential being, the real thing, or the genius of the author-creator? Admittedly, it was long ago that we heard the phrase "art imitates nature." And this from Plato, reputedly the most original philosopher of all time, on whose founding act, some suggest, all subsequent philosophy amounts to one long commen-

21

tary. Yet it seems doubtful that this venerable phrase was always taken at face value, if indeed it ever had such a value. Rather, it could have been tacitly known, to judge from the practice of art itself, that art does not imitate nature, that it mainly quotes from the multiplicity of cultural products, including, of course, art itself.

In this regard, readers of Henry James may recall a charming story, "The Real Thing," in which an impoverished bourgeois couple, Major and Mrs. Monarch by name, turn up at the narrator's studio in hopes of getting themselves employed as models for the illustration of some drawing-room novel. The artist, who happens to have just such a commission at hand, is willing to oblige, more or less out of charity. But as he soon finds out, while the couple can be, or rather, they *are* themselves—a gentleman and a lady—they simply cannot represent themselves. In fact, they—who are the real thing, taken "directly from nature"—are totally unrepresentable. We are not told what they look like in the few attempted drawings except that they are stately and that, try as the artist might, they always come out colossal, upward of seven feet tall, as if, here, art itself were attempting to break out of its own frame in order to emulate their real stature in life. Disappointed, the artist resolves to resume his usual practice and ends up employing a cockney woman and an Italian street vendor who can represent, with a help of a few theatrical props, anything that they are not.

Much of modern art has turned its wrathful back against this act of faking. As James's story reveals, this is a two-fold fake, for in the first place it imitates and copies the real thing from nature and from life, but secondly it turns out that this model in nature, insofar as it is representable at all, is not a genuine article but a copy, a pretense. To put this more art-historically, we might remember the rumor that the delicate foliage that surrounds many of Thomas Gainsborough's portraits was not painted directly from real trees in nature but from clusters of broccoli. Or, as E. H. Gombrich famously argued, no one ever draws or paints "directly from nature," but one always solicits styles and conventions available in the art of one's own time and place; one draws from culture, if you will.[11]

But if modern artists turn against this double faking and its myth of the original, their intentions are far from obliterating the economy of origination itself. In fact, they have a vested interest in this economy, being the vanguard, the ones at the front, who have only the future and no past. A new birth without parentage, art at its absolute beginning, radical originality—such are the watchwords of the avant-garde, which Krauss appropriately terms "the discourse of originality" [157]. With this singular preoccupation with the question of originality, the avant-garde artist divests everything that has hitherto claimed priority of its power, and reinvests it, in toto, in the very moment of his own creation, that is, in the *Hier und Jetzt* of the avant-garde artist himself, and in the ground zero of his creation—for instance, in the pictorial surface. Regarding this axiomatic stance of the avant-garde, Krauss's discussions on the grid—a quintessentially modern form and subject matter—helps us understand this reinvestment project, their discursive practice, as well as what this discourse glosses over.

First, she observes historically, "the grid is an emblem of modernity by being just that: the form that is ubiquitous in the art of our century, while appearing nowhere, nowhere at all, in the art of the last one. . . . By 'discovering' the grid, cubism, de Stijl Mondrian, Malevich . . . landed in a place that was out of reach of everything that went before. Which is to say, they landed in the present, and everything else was declared to be the past" [10]. The avant-garde, eager to disown every claim placed on them by what supposedly comes *before*, almost universally favors this form, the grid, which carries with it no precedents or tradition, no authorship or copyrights that might threaten the present with the nightmarish weight of the past. The grid is a form existing at large, without a determinable point of origin; it is everywhere without beginning.

23

More importantly than this ubiquity, the pristine structure of the grid is emblematic of the absolute present, for this structure shuts out the possibility of a prior origin—what comes before—and it denies any notion of some model preexisting in nature. Put differently, the grid refuses representation after nature by referring only to, while being physically fused with, the pictorial surface itself:

> The absolute stasis of the grid, its lack of hierarchy, of center, of inflection, emphasizes not only its anti-referential character, but—more importantly—its hostility to narrative. . . . No echoes of footsteps in empty rooms, no scream of birds across open skies, no rush of distant water—for *the grid has collapsed the spatiality of nature onto the bonded surface of a purely cultural object.* With its proscription of nature as well as of speech, the result is still more silence. And in this new-found quiet, what many artists thought they could hear was the beginning, the origin of Art. [158; emphasis added]

But an irony is already disturbing this quiet, as Krauss soon notes. First, since the grid is a form without an author and is in the public domain instead, what this enactment marks is a moment of repetition, but repetition without any fixed point of reference which might determine the inception of a series. What is evoked in the name of absolute originality is therefore, in reality, absolute repetition, that is to say, repetition without the first time.

Second, if the grid refuses representation after nature by insisting on pure *self-reference*, it nonetheless *represents* this pictorial surface rather than being self-identical with it. "The canvas surface and the grid that scores it do not fuse into that absolute unity necessary to the notion of an origin. For the grid *follows* the canvas surface, doubles it. It is a representation of the surface, mapped, it is true, onto the same surface it represents, but even so, the grid remains a figure, picturing various aspects of the originary object: through its mesh it creates an image of the woven infrastructure of the canvas; through its network of coordinates it organizes a metaphor for the plane geometry of the field; through its repetition it configures the spread of lateral continuity" [161]. Structurally speaking, then, the origin of art in the form of a grid is in the doubling implicit in the structure of representation.[12] First there is nothing, then suddenly, there are two, or rather, there is this doubling, which poses as an absolute (univocal) origin.

Even the most faithful representation—for instance, a word-for-word transcription of a text—would by no means be identical with that which it repeats. This point, too, has been already suggested by a poet, Jorge Luis Borges, author of "Pierre Menard, Author of Don Quixote."[13] In this story, the narrator remembers, in the exemplary manner of men of letters, an early twentieth-century French author, Pierre Menard, who *wrote* Cervantes's novel by the same name. While this twentieth-century novel corresponds exactly and literally to the seventeenth-century "original," they are obviously not identical. The comic effect of Borges's story is due above all to the narrator's highly refined and pedantic persuasion; the narrator argues that the task must have been incomparably more difficult for Menard than for Cervantes, and the result infinitely more subtle. Cervantes, being a seventeenth-century Spaniard and generally just being what he was, naturally, that is, almost inevitably, produced a perfect seventeenth-century novel, *Don Quixote*—work equal to his genius, natural to his circumstances, and so on; whereas for Menard, a twentieth-century Frenchman, to produce a seventeenth-century Spanish novel must have presented unfathomable difficulties. As a matter of fact, we are told, his novel remained incomplete; he managed to finish only a few chapters after more than a decade of dedicated labor.

Aside from being an acerbic joke on the profession of literary history, this story raises a serious question about representation. Menard did not merely, mechanically, copy Cervantes's novel; rather, he *wrote* it, *authored* it. (Otherwise, he certainly would have completed the job in a short while.) Nor did he attempt, the narrator claims emphatically, a modern adaptation of the "original" novel; rather, he meant to write, word-for-word, line-by-line, *Don Quixote*, nothing more, or less. In short, this was to be a *representation* of Cervantes's novel at its most perfect. It *follows* Cervantes's novel by repeating it; yet it does not originate in, or derive from, the latter; for its distinct character, that is, its unusual identity as a seventeenth-century Spanish novel written by a twentieth-century French author, arises from this doubling itself. The word-for-word correspondence (complete similarity) does not indicate a relation of descent, which might be assumed in a case of perfect resemblance between the father and the son. Representation as such does not establish identity either through resemblance or by the logic of descent; rather, the story suggests, representation is a function of difference, of repetition without a unitary origin.

But the repetition is precisely what *covers* this doubleness and makes it invisible. Krauss observes this point, to go back to our grid, immediately following the passage quoted above: "The grid thus does not reveal the [pictorial] surface, laying it bare at last; rather it veils it through a repetition." Yet this veiling that poses as laying it bare is essential to what she calls the "discourse of originality"; for this discourse operates on the assumption of the absolute origin, and the concomitant occultation of the corresponding other, namely, absolute repetition; in other words, this discourse is based on a repression [162].

To sum up, the grid repeats without originating, both spatially and temporally. The originality of the avant-garde predicated on this figure lies in repetition, in the absence of origin. Upon this reality of repetition stands, or rather, is overlaid, the modus operandi of the avant-garde. And this overlaying in turn repeats the veiling by repetition which the grid so stunningly performs.

The discerning eye that sees through this veiling and overlaying situates Krauss in the position of the *post-;* that is to say, she seems to be in line with some of the art of the postmodernists, which is supposed to open up, without fear, to the groundless (originless) repetition which at once underlies and undermines all representation.[14] But this, too, is another story, which I shall have to leave for another place.

•   •

Although Benjamin himself already suggested some serious implications that the notion of repetition without origin may have for the question of religion, it might still seem that I am taking the matter very far afield were it not for the fact that the almost diametrically opposed view of repetition—that is, the metaphysically conservative view of repetition grounded in the belief in the absolute origin—has been so immensely influential in the study of myth and ritual to this day. In light of this glaring contrast, there is a sense of urgency with which that particular, ironic, discerning eye of postmodern art and criticism may be turned toward the modus operandi of the study of religion. Such a turn would not only initiate its reexamination, but it also opens up a space for critical articulation by allowing us to identify the modern historian's unacknowledged repetition and vicarious participation in the quest for origins.

The extent of the modern historian's preoccupation with the question of origin may be measured by the number of formidable assumptions operative in the field of the history of religions as well as much of the ethnography focused on religious phenomena. We may for the time being set aside the notorious search for the origin of religion, which brought many an early armchair anthropologist into ill repute. The modern historian of religion or ethnographer would condemn this line of investigation characteristic of the previous era as "unscientific" or "presumptuous." On the other hand, while a modern scholar might consider this renunciation of the desire for the origin of religion as a major scientific triumph over musty metaphysics steeped in hubris, modern scholarship as a whole is far from renouncing the powerful logic of origination. In the abode of learning generally, the origin-obsessed principles still hold sway: the preeminence of cosmogonic myths (that is, the myth of creation as the most paradigmatic of all myths), the notion of ritual as a repetition and reactualization of axial (mythic) events, or, more sociologically, ritual as representation of the ideal social paradigm projected into a mythic narrative. In short, all these notions are predicated on the economy of origination and its correlative, the ideology of representation, which the foregoing postmodern criticisms have put into question and exposed, precisely, as mythic and probably repressive.

In order to begin to measure the possible impact of such a criticism to the study of religion, for the remainder of this chapter I shall take up a text by Mircea Eliade, who must be judged one of the most influential representatives of the scholars of myths and rituals. Specifically I shall discuss his *The Myth of the Eternal Return*, which, in 1958, the author called "the most significant of my books."[15] Eliade began to write an essay under the title "Cosmos and History," but when the manuscript was completed it bore the title "Archetypes and Repetition." His French publisher persuaded him to change it yet again to "The Myth of the Eternal Return." The original title refers to the fundamental difference between premodern and modern man, which is "the essential theme" of his investigation, that is to say, "the chief difference between the man of the archaic and traditional societies and the man of the modern societies with their strong imprint of Judaeo-Christianity lies in the fact that the former feels himself indissolubly connected with the Cosmos and the cosmic rhythms, whereas the latter insists that he is connected only with History" [xiii–xiv].

But his interest in the two types—archaic and modern—is not symmetrical; his focus is on the former of the pair, which justifies his second title, "Archetypes and Repetition," as these terms most succinctly and essentially characterize the "archaic" frame of mind. The book, in short, is an exploration of archaic man's relation to time, and the very different kind of "history" implied in it. Their "history" is a " 'sacred history,' preserved and transmitted through myths. More than that, it is a 'history' that can be repeated indefinitely, in the sense that the myths serve as models for ceremonies that periodically reactualize the tremendous events that occurred at the beginning of time" [xiv].

This characterization of archaic society is axiomatic for Eliade; it is not so much argued for as it is presented as something that has "especially struck" him in the course of his investigation [ix]. His book comprises so many instances of this striking feature, arranged so as to persuade us to the same effect. By marshalling example after example, the author seeks to impress upon us the "revolt against concrete, historical time" of archaic societies, their "nostalgia for a periodical return to the mythical time of the beginning of things" [ix], and their "need . . . to regenerate themselves periodically through the annulment of time" and "through repetition of an archetypal act, usually of the cosmogonic act" [85].

Eliade's presentation is masterful, after a fashion; his mode of argumentation stands in a marked contrast with that of Benjamin, or of Krauss, for that matter. Benjamin's discourse—as if deeply suspicious of the traditionalist argumentation which is structured as a singular pursuit of mastery over multiplicity, the kind that always strives to arrive at where it begins: *quod erat demonstrandum*—tends to proceed as if it were an episodic or even casuistic traversal over disparate and oddly particular object domains rather than as a single-mindedly pursued argument presented with high seriousness. His purpose is to achieve, through collage-like cumulation and discriminating elaboration, an absolutely compelling image.[16] Eliade, on the other hand, at all times strives to subsume every example, even every potential anomaly, under an all-encompassing rubric: "the archaic" and their alleged obsession with the moment of origin.

In Eliade's view, every cult practice ultimately refers to cosmogony. The transformation of the dead into ghosts, for example, is a case of the cult of the origin insofar as this "signifies their reidentification with the impersonal archetypes of the ancestors" [47]. The ritual exchange, potlatch, which Marcel Mauss has analyzed to quite different effect,[17] is called "only the repetition of a practice introduced by the ancestors in mythical times" [34]. The structure of matrimonial rites is "not merely a question of imitating an exemplary model, the hierogamy between heaven and earth" but "the principal consideration is the result of that hierogamy, that is, the cosmic Creation" [24]. "The annual expulsion of sins, diseases and demons is basically an attempt to restore . . . mythical

27

and primordial time . . . of Creation" [54]. The dead return at the New Year season, when the original creation is repeated, because it is the moment when the world returns momentarily to chaos and the demarcation between the living and the dead is annulled [62]. It would be pointless—as Eliade often remarks as he interrupts his long list—to try to exhaust the "endless variety" of this phenomenon.

What is assumed and displayed in the form of enumeration of discrete examples, yet never demonstratively argued, is that a cult always presupposes a certain narrative of the beginning of time, and this narrative organizes, justifies, and gives meaning to ritual behavior and all other types of behavior, insofar as they are "meaningful." Identity, reality, and the meaning of an event are felt by archaic man, it is claimed, only to the extent that they refer to the stock of paradigmatic narratives [5], and everything else will fall into the sea of chaos, that dangerous, unformed region without reference [9]. Of course, Eliade admits, there are cases where a certain ritual seems to have existed prior to any mythic narrative. But even this does not prevent him from positing a yet-to-be-articulated originary myth. "If the myth sometimes followed the rite, the fact in no wise lessens the sacred character of the ritual. The myth is 'late' only as a formulation; but its content is archaic and refers to sacraments—that is, to acts which presuppose an absolute reality, a reality which is extrahuman" [27].

It is certainly a striking picture of the "archaic" person. Reading Eliade we are duly struck by the image of the archaic man's violent conservatism—his "revolt" against the unprecedented occurrence, his demand for the "abolition" of nonparadigmatic temporality, his "refusal to accept himself as a historical being . . . refusal to grant value to memory and hence to the unusual events . . . that in fact constitute concrete duration" [85]. The image of the archaic's paradisiac confinement is also striking: he is "imprisoned within the mythical horizon of archetypes and repetition" [156]. Even as he dwells in the "paradise of archetypes" [75], archaic man forever suffers from cosmic nostalgia; his life is an endless series of ceremonials performed on the brink of chaos. Terrorized by the continual threat of the new and the meaningless, he resorts to compulsory and compulsive repetition; through birth, marriage, war, commerce, healing, death, and mourning, he repeats, and he refers, time and time again, to the self-identical beginning.

Given, on the one hand, that contemporary theorists on the whole are in the habit of designating the nostalgic yearning for the absolute beginning—in fact, any assertion of the univocity and centrality of origin—as "theological," and given also, on the other hand, that these "archaic societies" are supposed to be in all respects premodern and monolithically religious, there appears to be no immediately available space for the student of religion to voice skepticism and to protest, regarding this truly striking picture of archaic man, or, regarding the sharp contrast that is presumed to exist between the archaic and the modern. How are we to raise a question, and on whose behalf, when we are told that archaic ontology consists of Platonic mimesis and, concomitantly, "the abolition of time through the imitation of archetypes and the repetition of paradigmatic gestures" [35]? Or that "the desire felt by the man of traditional societies to refuse history, and to confine himself to an indefinite repetition of archetypes, testifies to his thirst for the real and his terror of 'losing' himself by letting himself be overwhelmed by the meaninglessness of profane existence" [91–92]. Is this true?

I am not prepared to address this question at this particular moment or to open a general discussion concerning the adequacy of the historical or ethnographic study of religious rites. I raise this question here in order above all to claim that it is indeed a question, and that it is probably not of the kind that can be settled by a competition in producing examples and counterexamples. I also suggest, as a kind of open insinuation, where the space for such a questioning might open up: most invitingly, in the purported "gap" between the archaic and the modern, which is so crucial to Eliade's method of representation.

The archaic, the other of the modern, is at once the other of us, the contemporary scholars of religion. But the other of oneself is always a double of oneself, a mirror image, a picture in reverse, a representation that doubles and couples the self and the other. This other—the archaic—is presented as peculiarly marked by a singular obsession with the moment of origin. What does this reflect vis-à-vis the modern scholarship on myth and ritual, the scholarship, that is, that rather emphatically denied itself the quest for the origin of religion some time ago? This scholarship is peculiarly marked by its obsession with cosmogony, paradigms, and archetypal narratives—in short, a preoccupation with the question of origin. Does this not signal a certain displacement, a certain shifting that repeats and veils—which is a telltale sign of repression—a displacement of that very desire which we once renounced and continue to deny ourselves?

Repetition veils. This tradition of scholarship caught up in the repetition compulsion of the originary economy is yet to be struck, yet to be disturbed from its own dreamtime, by the cacophony of postmodern debates. Or it is perhaps more accurate to say that the impact of such disturbances is at the present moment barely kept at bay, for there are indeed multiple voices hovering above our scholarly sanctuary. One may name and classify them as one pleases: critical voices within the Eliadean legacy, voices from a range of critical politics, including feminist criticism, postcolonial criticism, and so on. But in the last analysis one may come to suspect that the persistent disquiet is due above all to the fact that the voices issue forth not only from outside the field, or just from inside for that matter, but from nowhere, or, to be precise, from that strange place—is this a spatial equivalent to the neuralgic *post-?*—that puts the anxiety-ridden demarcation of inside and outside itself into question.

I shall single out one of those voices, in whose repercussion I began this discussion. This voice—sounding very much like an umbrageous echo of the Viennese physician—seems to be telling us what we always suspected, namely, that ghosts keep coming back not only to be immortalized in the archetypal *illo tempore,* but also to haunt us so as to be forgotten. The voice, in other words, insinuates thus: Ought we not know, after Freud, that we do not repeat only to make present again a past irreparably lost, but we repeat and remember, so that we may be released from the grip of our memory?

.   .   .

I have spoken of "repression," even though this term, which harks back to the highly contested authority of psychoanalysis, may be deemed too loosely metaphoric, or worse, taken as a term of easy abuse. But it is precisely of repression that is useful to speak here, however licentious, figurative, or derivative the designation may seem. For what is repression if not a kind of absence, or disappearance, of the grounds for articulation, as a result of which any query that suspects an alliance or complicity between "here and now" and "long ago" comes to seem immaterial, or even delusionary?

The Eliadean brand of "religious hermeneutics" purports to decipher, from the very patterns of rich traditional encrustations, essential human endowment of "the religious," be it universal (as Eliade himself apparently believes) or culturally specific (as many of his detractors believe). In either case, these modern hermeneuts carry out their interpretive tasks by drawing the line between the past and their own present, whether this past refers to the remote region populated by strange peoples or to their own recent predecessors.[18] This line of temporal demarcation is upheld even, or especially, at the moment when the contemporary scholars dutifully acknowledge many valuable lessons learnt from the (essentially negative) examples of the past masters.

As for Eliade, he sees "Western man's" transformation occurring in his own days—the transformation from the intrepid metaphysical quester of origins to the clear-eyed, globally conscious historian—as another providential moment of awakening. This turn of event, in other words, is by no means accidental for him, and he says as much: "So it appears that the Western man's longing for 'origins' and the 'primordial' forced him finally into an encounter with history."[19] Eliade goes on to suggest that this moment of encounter marks "the grave crisis" which entails "a profound humiliation for the Western consciousness," because this "discovery of the universal historical conditioning" implicates "Western man" himself, relativizing his universe of values.[20]

It remains to be seen whether this "humiliation" has turned out to be as humbling as he warrants; we shall have occasion in the last chapter to return to the issue. For the moment, let it suffice to note the mordant irony: this attitude of renunciation—"after more than a century of untiring labor, scholars were forced to renounce the old dream of grasping the origin of religion," he says[21]—repeats, rather than disengages, the grand surrendering gesture of the ascetic priest, the paramount practitioner of the Judeo-Christian piety, the follower of its proscription against the direct naming of God. This negative axiom, this sublime humility of the ascetic priest, as Nietzsche's caustic portrayal reminds us, has always done "Western man" proud.

If we come to conclude that the "new" historicohermeneutical pursuit of "the religious" in the mode advocated by Eliade seems suspect because its proud asceticism too closely resembles a traditional religious posture, or because it is predicated on a disavowal too ambivalent, it is tempting for us contemporary—that is to say, even newer—scholars of religion to disclaim, quickly and decisively, the whole Eliadean legacy as yet another episode belonging to the past. As in all other disciplines that have come under critical historical scrutiny, the disclaimer is a typical reflexive response from the scholars of today. With or without Eliade, we feel, we have been hard at work in "a field," trenchantly confronted as we are by the inescapable historicity of our own disciplinary formation; and, with the promptness of a vanguard summoned to a new mission, we often declare: *that* was *then* (for example, nineteenth-century evolutionism, easy optimism of prenuclear age, heyday of the Chicago School, and so on), and *we* don't do that sort of thing anymore. On such occasions, nothing is more comforting than the knowledge of the limits and the specificities of one's own research area, of which each accomplished scholar is supposed to be a master and custodian, however modest the territory may be. For the chastily finite claim to mastery on our part seems to assure a safe haven from any guilt by association with the grand masters of yore, from the ever growing domain of the "past errors," in which Eliade is now also implicated. Do we escape, at last, from repetition and from affinity with the past?

It is hard to ignore the element of disavowal here, the same anxious declaration of a swift, unilateral, and irreversible severance from the past. Thus we, too, are caught red-handed, it seems, while attempting a hasty exit from the old workshop, whose air has become too thick not so much with errors and hidebound ideas but with the sheer weight of its historicity. We are all tempted by this exit, or more accurately, by the fantasy of

31

such an exit. Unfortunately for us, what really disappears from our sight in this process of getting away is not the old workshop but, rather, the highly tenuous and volatile space where questions about historicity itself can arise—above all, questions about all those imagined processes of escape that purport to locate us on the clean slate of the present, where there is nothing but "the real data" to confound us.

Obviously, there is a strong compulsion at work here. (As psychoanalysis helps us understand, one tries to allay guilt typically by admitting it and repudiating it at the same time.) But if we could let up the pressure of this compulsion a little, it may be possible to investigate, historically and critically, those crucial imaginings that constitute our sense of *Hier und Jetzt,* which is to say, our own situation beyond Eliade and his imaginings.

. .

For this general reason, my intention is to linger at this hypothetical threshold, this imagined spot that is the hinge of a past and a present. Or, to revert to my earlier metaphor, I will conduct my reading project at the crypt of some of the past great masters whose viability at the moment is uncertain—the crypt being the domain of the undead.

The result of such a reading, it is hoped, will not be a mere realization of some curious convolution of time, a banal appreciation for the way in which what we thought was old and past in fact contained something new and current or, conversely, what we thought was fresh and our own belonged to a past by some unrecognized line of descent. All too often this kind of effete wisdom is associated with the name *postmodern.* The "postmodern" is also frequently extolled as a liberation from the "modern," while the "modern" becomes the ensign for much of the mess that mires, or rather constitutes, the present.

Whether or not such characterizations are justified, I did not wish to evoke *postmodern* with these intentions. Rather, if I continue to equate the strange status of *post-* with that of the critical discursive space that is to open up—not once and for all, but time and time again—through rereading projects of this kind, it is because of another import germane to the *post-.* This is the sense of *postmodern* associated with, or rather posthumously ascribed to, Walter Benjamin. Benjamin's sense of the present—a *Hier und Jetzt* that no longer can be translated as *immediacy* of here and now—is not a surgical point demarcating the past from the virginal future. It is where a legacy of the past is felt not so much as a weight but, rather more ominously, as a claim. Like the evanescent place of *post-,* the Benjaminian *Hier und Jetzt* signals the radical temporality of all points of critical articulation. As was the case with Proustian surge of memory, Benjamin demonstrates, these moments of articulation are

32

places and spaces crisscrossed with time.[22] Concomitantly, it brings us
face to face with the ultimately hallucinatory status of the conceptual devices which we use to manage and distance the past/other from present/
us—those devices, in Benjamin's own words, that enable "historicism"
to turn the past into an indolent tale told by stringing a sequence of events
"like the beads of a rosary."[23] Under the sign of Benjaminian *post-*, then,
the revisiting of the classics would be carried out not with an aspiration to
rise above the past or with a hope of gaining a new vantage point unen-
cumbered by past prejudices. Instead, we hope, it will let us venture a little
further into the present epistemic mire, into our own time.

Society versus Difference:
Durkheim's Shadowboxing

34   PERHAPS NOT A LITERARY MATCH for the purple prose of J. G. Frazer's *The Golden Bough,* but Émile Durkheim's *The Elementary Forms of the Religious Life* is counted among the masterful performances of the speculative search for the origin of religion. The book is touted as "Durkheim's most ambitious work."[1] The year was 1912; the objective: the excavation of the origin of religion; and the general context of discussion: totemism, which the author estimated to be the "more fundamental and more primitive" of all the known forms of religion.[2] In the course of several hundred pages, the author locates, names, and identifies an origin and claims its identity to be ultimately simple. That such an essentialist quest for the sine qua non of all religions was indeed the authorial design of this book seems hardly contestable. Upon rereading, however, an unassuming reader might be struck by curious equivocation just on this cardinal point. Notwithstanding the palpably single-minded intent of its author, the argument takes a rather convoluted course. While the author claims that there is one origin of religion and it is simple, the text also demonstrates that it is not so, that origin as such is something disjunctive. In due course, the reader comes to recognize a certain unnamed and unacknowledged element that continually interrupts and obfuscates the authorial writing. In effect, this unauthorized "voice" silently criticizes the metaphysical quest that motivates the text, and in time induces some muffled confessions concerning the disparity that inhabits every assertion of origin. What is to follow in this chapter is an attempt to lend an ear to the late arrival of this posthumous voice, the dissonant echo that does not finish with the book.

A return to the text may not necessarily amount to resuscitating a

SOCIETY VERSUS DIFFERENCE

dead idea, and probably not even to rewriting the history of scholarly fashions; but it may put into question the authority of the history already written, which is in part predicated on the authorial—and repressed—reading of the Durkheimian corpus. Above all, our rereading will induce rethinking of an old idea, "the sacred," which has been strangely neglected, depreciated, or even trivialized in the assessment of Durkheim hitherto, not only by his functionalist descendants such as A. R. Radcliffe-Brown but also by Claude Lévi-Strauss, who said of the Durkheimian sacred that it was an incompletely analyzed, vague notion.[3] The present reading will show how, on the contrary, this idea of the sacred assumes its proper—if unstable—position as the principal subject matter of the text. As a matter of fact, as we follow this subject with some degree of insistence, what comes to the foreground is the *signifying function of difference,* which is precisely the point that Lévi-Strauss assumes as his point of departure from and against the Durkheimian theory of "so-called totemism," that is to say, against the classical ethnography obsessed with identity and the logic of the same. As we shall see, however, already in this "prestructuralist" text by Durkheim, it is not only the drive and strife for identity but the work of difference that is operative under the name of the sacred. And the complicated discursive movement of the text, in its ponderous pursuit of an origin, simulates the rubric of the sacred, the wayward protagonist of this speculative masterpiece.

35

Two Theses on the Sacred

From the outset the ambiguity of the textual movement in *The Elementary Forms of the Religious Life* shows itself in two seemingly irreconcilable statements concerning the sacred, which we shall call, for the reason of convenience, theses.

The first thesis on the sacred in its most frugal form states, "Anything can be sacred" [52]. Seemingly innocuous, the statement is nevertheless rigorously qualified by the paragraphs surrounding it. A little earlier, it is said that "all known religious beliefs, whether simple or complex, present one common characteristic: they presuppose a classification of all the things, real and ideal, of which men think, into two classes or opposed groups, generally designated by two distinct terms which are translated well enough by the words *profane* and *sacred*. This division of the world into two domains . . . is the distinctive trait of religious thought" [52]. Then, a little later: "Up to the present we have confined ourselves to enumerating a certain number of sacred things as examples: we must now show by what general characteristics they are to be distinguished from profane things" [52]. But soon he concludes that "there is nothing . . . with which to characterize the sacred in its relation to the profane except their heterogeneity. However, this heterogeneity is sufficient to characterize this classification of things and to distinguish it from all others, because it is very particular: it is absolute" [53].

In sum, having observed that the sacred-profane distinction is the universal characteristic of all religions, Durkheim maintains that the sacred itself is without any determinable characteristic; in fact, the only possible determination of the sacred is that it is absolutely heterogeneous with its opposite, the profane. This characterization is of course purely formal, semantically empty. Yet the very lack of substantive determination and the absoluteness of the heterogeneity renders this particular opposition distinct from all other oppositions, and therefore *defines* it.

To underscore further the singular characteristic of this absolute heterogeneity, it is stated that, unlike other pairs of opposites, the sacred-profane opposition has no general category or class under which the two extremes are subsumed. "In all the history of human thought there exists no other example of two categories of things so profoundly differentiated or so radically opposed to one another. The traditional opposition of good and bad is nothing besides this; for the good and the bad are only two opposed species of the same class, namely, morals, just as sickness and health are two different aspects of the same order of facts, life" [53–54].

Normally, *opposition* does not imply "absolute heterogeneity" but on the contrary designates a particular type of relation by virtue of which the two extremes are encompassed as a kind of totality, as the same order of facts. This, says Durkheim, is not the case with the sacred-profane. "The sacred and the profane have always and everywhere been conceived by the human mind as two distinct classes, as two worlds between which there is nothing in common. The forces which play in one are not simply those which are met with in the other but a little stronger; they are of the different sort" [54]. Thus this "opposing pair" alone is logically untotalizable.[4]

The second thesis is the better publicized of the two. It is punctiliously introduced prior to the main exposition, announcing in advance what is to be expected in the way of a "general conclusion of the book," namely, that religious ideas represent society [22]. In a more popular phrasing this reads, the sacred (alias God) is society [237; discussed below]. In this second thesis, the identity of the sacred is clearly defined, even though the first thesis asserts that the sacred lacks any such definitional determination. Moreover, the hidden identity of the sacred turns out to be something eminently unifying, namely, social sentiment, or more famously, "collective effervescence," which, being the power uniting individuals into a group, designates the very essence of society, according to Durkheim. Even more important in this connection is his contention that this societal unity serves as the concrete model of a more general (but also ontologically deeper) notion, totality.[5]

The contrast between the two theses is therefore doubly marked: while the first thesis asserts the sacred as untotalizable heterogeneity, the second asserts it as effervescent unity and totality; while the first announces the sacred's lack of identity, the second identifies it. In retrospect, it might be construed that the author's whole enterprise was aimed at the triumph of the second thesis over the first; it is therefore not surprising if such a tendentious authorial attitude dictated how the "Durkheimian theory of religion" was to be understood by posterity.

Totalization—the Development of the Second Thesis

Immediately, however, the situation is obscured as the asymmetrical disjunctive contrast between the two theses is displaced by another oppositional theme, namely, the apparent dichotomy between unity and plurality (or diversity, multiplicity). The terms of this "dichotomy" already suggest an obvious solution; predictably enough, Durkheim seeks to subsume and control this pseudoconflict by means of the language of "part-whole":

> When a certain number of sacred things sustain relations of coordination or subordination with each other in such a way as to form a system having a certain unity, but which is not comprised within any other system of the same sort, the totality of these beliefs and corresponding rites constitutes religion. From this definition it is seen that a religion is not necessarily contained within one sole and single idea, and does not proceed from one unique principle. . . . *it is rather a whole made up of distinct and relatively individualized parts.* . . . there is no religion, howsoever unified it may be, which does not recognize a plurality of sacred things. [56; emphasis added]

And for the next two hundred pages or so, the diversity and internal multiplicity of totemism is abundantly illustrated.

Meanwhile, the author remains unperturbed; this is because, as the above passage betrays, he assumes that to be related is roughly the same as to be unified, and that *system* means more or less the same as *totality*. His penchant favoring unity over difference comes to the foreground as of book 2, chapter 6, where a sudden shift in perspective comes into effect and the argument becomes entirely sub specie totius: "As the analysis which we have just made of [totemism] has resolved it into a multiplicity of beliefs which may appear quite heterogeneous, before going farther, we must seek to learn what makes its unity" [216].

Evidently, its "unity" is to be taken for granted, but this unity is no longer a matter of systematicity of difference but the kind of totality that is claimed to emanate from a common source, an original and originating principle.[6] To be sure, this is a mere preamble to the next chapter, where totemism will reveal its ultimate source, society. Meanwhile, Durkheim is paving the way to that assertion by extending a series of equations.[7]

The final identification of the sacred and society is brought about rather casually. The pivot of this operation is the totemic emblem by virtue of the fact that the emblem symbolizes both the totemic principle and the clan. "So if it is at once the symbol of the god and of the society, is that not because the god and the society are one? How could the emblem of the group have been able to become the figure of this quasi-divinity, if the group and the divinity were two distinct realities?" [236]. Finding it impossible to resist this suggestion, Durkheim completes the equation and moves on. But once this end of the equation is accomplished, the argument begins to run backward. Durkheim now returns to the specific features of totemism mentioned earlier, and retroactively explains them. In light of the newly acquired "knowledge" that the essence of totemism is a ubiquitous and totalizing "force," he explains why the sacred is contagious, whence comes the radical heterogeneity of the sacred and the profane, why emblems are more sacred than the objects they represent, and so on.

Roughly speaking, the explanation runs as follows. In the beginning is the experience of excitement in the midst of some collective activities. Since this state of effervescence is in such striking contrast to the everyday drudgery of individual life, whatever is associated with it is conceived as wholly different, as something owing to an extraordinary power over and above nature and individual life. Thus, the "absolute heterogeneity" is explained [249–50]. During such collective excitement, it might very well happen that there arises an "instinctive tendency" in people to inscribe "almost automatically" a design on their bodies in order "to bear witness to the fact that a certain number of individuals participate in the same moral life." The design may ostensibly represent some specific object, but what that object is is unimportant, for the very significance lies in the fact that the same mark is borne by all of the people concerned. Thus the primacy of the emblem over what it represents—that is, the reason why abstract inscriptions of the totem occupy a more prominent place in the hierarchy of sacredness than the totemic species themselves—is explained [264–65]. Furthermore, the anonymity and indeterminacy of the collective force accounts for the peculiar character of the sacred objects: because this force is impersonal and is not entrenched in the particularity of

the object/person it happens to inhabit, it can readily escape and transfer to another object. Thus, contagiousness of the sacred is explained
[362–63].

What is decisive in these explanatory operations is that logical priority is granted to totality, over against the multivalence of difference; in
fact, "difference" is treated here merely as apparent relation of the
"parts," whose logical function is to constitute a "whole."

• •

Yet there is more to the master thesis—the god-is-society thesis—
than this explanation. For the thesis conveys more than just the notion
that religion represents collectivity; it also implies that religious ideas (or
representations) are modeled after social structure, that is, after the particular modes of social *differentiation*.

It is precisely on account of its conformity to social divisions, our author claims, that religion proper is to be distinguished from magic.[8]
Magic denotes those religious forces gone astray, that is, fallen out of the
social organization; hence, magic forces "do not belong to any special   **39**
portion of the tribe in particular . . . . These are vague forces, specially
attached to no determined social division" [266]. Or, even more explicitly, Durkheim noted earlier that

> while the properly religious forces do not succeed in avoiding a cer-
> tain heterogeneity, magic forces are thought of as being all of the
> same nature; the mind represents them in their generic unity. This is
> because they rise above the social organization and its divisions and
> subdivisions, and move in a homogeneous and continuous space
> where they meet with nothing to differentiate them. The others, on
> the contrary, being localized in definite and distinct social forms,
> are diversified and particularized in the image of the environment in
> which they are situated. [227]

In this remarkable passage, Durkheim assigns to religion the image of social divisions as a matter of definitional necessity.

But this is not all. Durkheim also contends that religious forces
proper—as opposed to magical ones—conform to the divisions and sub-
divisions specifically in such a manner as to promote the unity of the
group.[9] People belonging to a group, having the same beliefs and partici-
pating in the same rites, says Durkheim, constitute a "church." In contrast, "there is no church of magic"; belief in magic may be pervasive and
universal but it "does not result in binding together those who adhere to
it, nor in uniting them into a group leading a common life" [60].

In short, the assertion that religion is social seems to comprise two
disparate senses: on the one hand, that the essence of religion is a kind of

collectivity and therefore a unifying factor, and on the other hand, that it conforms to social divisions. The duplicity of this claim becomes more pronounced when we ask what is meant by *group*. If totemism proper is at issue, the group in question—the group that constitutes a church—certainly must be the clan. But the clan is not a society, it is a subdivision of it. In point of fact, Durkheim designates by *society*, first and foremost, the tribe.[10] He also makes an explicit mention of the fact that there is no single-clan tribe as far as we know [195]. This implies that a society is always divided, and what he calls group could be any one of those divisions. He then observes that totemism proper is the affair of the clan, never of the tribe as a whole [181, 226].

One might wonder why this is the case. If religion serves to unify a social group, why should its exclusive concern be with the unity of a subdivision rather than with that of the "whole" society? Why does "collective sentiment" not express itself as a sense of tribal unity rather than that of the clan? Or, does it?

On the whole, Durkheim's answer is ambiguous.[11] He manages the situation by suggesting that the very fact that "a single totem is not repeated twice in the same tribe" indicates a mutual agreement among clans [180–81]. In the same vein, he says a little later, "the carefully regulated way in which the totems and subtotems are divided up . . . obviously presupposes a social agreement and a collective organization" [205].

He obviously assumes that this agreement provides unequivocal evidence of the tribal sense of unity, and also forms the basis for its "collective organization." He valorizes the fact of agreement at the expense of what is presumably agreed upon: methodic *divisions*. Because of this partiality, he virtually effaces the fact of division when he concludes with the familiar tag, that the multiple cults celebrated in different clans are "only the parts of a single whole, the elements of a single religion" [180]. Accordingly, "since all the clans are only parts of one and the same tribe, unity of the tribe cannot fail to make itself felt through this diversity of particular cults" [320]. The motley particulars of totemism are thus made into a totality. "Totemism [is] not the work of isolated clans, but [is] always elaborated in the body of a tribe which [is] to some degree conscious of its unity. It is for this reason that the different cults peculiar to each clan mutually touch and complete each other in such a way as to form a unified whole *[un tout solidaire]*" [333].

As much as Durkheim looks towards the sentiment of unity as the basis of this "agreement," the "unified whole" illustrated here does not suggest anything like primordial indistinction. Rather, one is "united" with another through the recognition of their proper distinctions. While the author's vision of the social unity is dominated by the sense of merger and totalization, the text displays quite another method of alliance, namely, *systematic relation based on the pronouncement of difference.*

Ultimately, of course, the author's totalizing vision holds sway over the entire textual progression, and the argument steadily moves towards the anticipated conclusion, even though, strangely enough, this crowning point of the authorial argument is relegated to the position of a footnote, which reads, "At bottom, the concept of totality, that of society and that of divinity are very probably only different aspects of the same notion" [490 n. 18].

In sum, the contrast between the first and the second theses—between the sacred as heterogeneity and the sacred as totality—is repeatedly deflected and displaced by another issue, that is, by the apparent dichotomy of unity and plurality. This latter "dichotomy" is easily sublated by means of the part-whole rhetoric. The result of this deflection and sublation is therefore in the interest of the second thesis; for through overdetermination (that is, through the totality-society-sacred complex), this notion of "all" triumphs and eclipses the fact of absolute heterogeneity. But in truth, absolute heterogeneity cannot be accommodated by this logic of part-whole; as we shall see in the following section, it operates according to quite another kind of logic.

41

Production—The Development of the First Thesis

Toward the end of the book, the argument begins to run in an almost opposite direction, that is, toward proliferation. The initially proclaimed objective of the book was to identify the origin of religion, but for Durkheim, origination is less a process of a temporal beginning than a process of proliferation or, more precisely, continual duplication of systems of *representations;* in his terminology, religious belief, objective thought, and language itself are all systems of representation.

There are more layers to this duplication of systems, however. What Durkheim has been variously calling "society," "social phenomena," "collective life," and so on—this "social reality" itself has a dual constitution at its very origin. This is because society, if it is for Durkheim an empirical fact, is an empirical fact *of consciousness:* "For a society is not made up of the mass of individuals who compose it, the ground which they occupy, the things which they use and the movements which they perform, but above all is the idea which it forms of itself" [470].

In a sense the actual, materially realized society before our very eyes is only half of what he means by *society,* the other half being its own conscious idea/ideal of itself, projected and superimposed upon the former. Society therefore consists in an "ideal" society being "added to" the "real society" [469–70].

This turn of the argument is a crucial point leading to the confirmation of Durkheim's general theory of religion. It establishes that the dual constitution of society exactly corresponds to—hence underscores—the sacred-profane duality, which has been already ascertained as the essential characteristic of religion. His phrasing at this juncture noticeably echoes a passage some two hundred pages earlier, where he states that the reality of the sacred is none other than our inner collective sentiment projected externally and "added to," or "superimposed upon," material objects [261]. The analogy could not have been more explicit.

Yet this is more than an analogy. For if the duality of religion is analogous to the duality of society, it is presumably because the latter somehow *accounts for* the former [469]. The relation between these two dualities, however, is far from that of unilateral causation. For neither side of this relation is primordially simple; everything calls for a counterpart, the real implies the ideal, and the sacred, the profane. And there is much inner entanglement in the relation of these doubles. To begin with, the doubles are not neatly separable. "The ideal society is not outside of the real society: it is a part of it. Far from being divided between them as between two poles which mutually repel each other, we cannot hold to one without holding to the other" [470]. This sticky situation stems from the fact that, according to Durkheim, the genesis and the sustenance of the "real" society is in an important sense dependent on its "ideal" representation [400–401].[12] In sum, if religion represents society, this "representation" is not like an object casting its own image upon a mirror. The priority is almost the reverse: for the "real" object (the actual/material society "before our very eyes") is being produced at the very moment in which its ideal image is being (re)produced.

To recapitulate, religion consists in sacred-profane duality, while society consists in real-ideal duality; the relation between these two dualities is both one of origination and one of representation (that is, one originates from another, and one represents the other). But when religious sentiment is identified with collective sentiment, this identification in turn undermines the initial set of dualities. The corresponding dualities do not really fall into place, nor is the analogy finally settled; instead, another series of doubles has taken their place. For by identifying religion and society, Durkheim in effect implies that religion as a whole is an ideal representation of society [see 469–70]. This would lead us to understand that the duality of the real and the ideal society corresponds not only to the sacred-profane duality but also to the religion-society duality. On the other hand, the sacred itself would not remain identified only with the ideal society (and the profane with the real society); for in yet another rendition of the dichotomy, Durkheim identifies the sacred sphere with the *social* life, whereas the profane is equated with the *individual* life [28–29]. Here again, a new duality—that of collective versus individual—has slipped into the scene, further confounding the analogy of the sacred-profane versus the real-ideal.

.   .   .

The indeterminacy of dual opposition and the extreme mobility of the line of difference—thus the "shiftiness" of this text—has much to do with the aforementioned "absolute heterogeneity" that Durkheim's first thesis asserted as the only "determinable" characteristic of the sacred. In point of fact, one could conceivably argue that the "logic" of this instability can be deduced from the logic of "the absolute heterogeneity lacking in identity," even though as far as Durkheim's text is concerned this conversion in logic is passed over in silence, or perhaps better, its deliberation remains unconscious. Briefly, this conversion of logic runs as follows.

If the sacred lacks any determinate characteristic, its heterogeneous other (the profane) is also without determination; but if the sacred and the profane are equally without determination *and* at the same time opposed to each other, then they are each nothing but "the other end of the other." This means that they are actually *equivalent,* while they cannot—owing to the ineradicable line of difference—be identical; there is always "a sort of logical chasm" between these (otherwise indiscernible) "opposites" [55]. Moreover, if the sacred and the profane are both "the other of the other," the sacred is at once itself (on account of self-identity) and the other of itself (on account of equivalence); thus is established the system of exchange. What is equivalent is not ultimately identical but, at most, mutually substitutable, or *interchangeable;* and the system of exchange thus established makes *conversion*—not unity—possible.[13] To assert the absolute difference in the manner of our "first thesis" therefore amounts to claiming *the nonidentity of the equivalent,* or conversely, *the equivalence of the nonidentical.*[14]

The heterogeneity that marks the sacred-profane duality is a double marking, for it is both internal and external to the opposition—external because it demarcates this "opposition" from all other pairs of opposites and internal because, of course, it is the only thing that marks the difference between the sacred and the profane in the first place. But what exactly is "inside" or "outside" here, where the "distinguishing mark" draws its own internal line as well? Because there is nothing else that *substantiates* the sacred-profane distinction, the line of difference is capable of shifting in and out;[15] the line itself constitutes the determination of its difference. Consequently, while it is unerasable, the line is extremely unstable.

This anticipates the question of contagion. That the sacred qua difference leads to the problem of contagion is easily inferred from the logic of absolute heterogeneity, which we have just articulated. According to this elaboration of logic, the sacred contains within itself its own other, or perhaps more properly, it contains an *internal* line of difference. The danger of contagion is the danger of this internalized difference; the very use of the epidemic metaphor suggests this. A person who has contracted a contagious disease becomes "after a fashion and to a certain degree" the disease itself [55]; it is now he who is the disease, who threatens others. Yet he is not identical or cosubstantial with the disease, but he is in the state of being invaded by something other than himself. The line marking the self and the other is now inside him. This erosion of the proper place of distinction, this shifting of the line of difference, leads to a state that is an acute danger internally (to himself), as well as externally (to others).

The actual route of Durkheim's discourse confirms this logical development. It is probably no accident that, immediately following the initial statement of the first thesis [52–53], he proceeds to intimate the peculiar nature of the "passage" between the sacred and the profane, between what he has just called "two worlds between which there is nothing in common," when he states, "This is not equivalent to saying that a being can never pass from one of these worlds into the other; but the manner in which this passage is effected, when it does take place, puts into relief the essential duality of the two kingdoms. In fact, it implies a veritable metamorphosis" [54]. The "passage" that joins the two worlds also marks their separation. Admittedly, that is characteristic of any passage: it at once connects and separates two places. However, what is peculiar about this particular passage is that it is not a road but a break of the road, a chasm. Moreover, for the very reason that the two worlds are "of a different sort," one and the same object can and must transform its nature from one sort to the other, as it traverses the line of difference.

The same point is repeated a little later, when he suggests that it is "quite impossible" for the profane being to enter into relation with the sacred, "unless the profane is to lose its specific characteristics and become sacred after a fashion and to a certain degree itself. The two classes cannot even approach each other and keep their own nature at the same time" [55].

As if one had no immunity from the other, it immediately contracts the nature of the other, and becomes of that quality, "after a fashion and to a certain degree"—that is to say, not entirely. By this contraction the profane being becomes, in a sense, *relatively* more sacred; but there is more to this transformation than mere relativizing; the line of distinction has been not erased but dangerously internalized.

The topic of contagion is merely anticipated in this passage, yet this anticipation is eventually borne out in a later passage [357–58] when the same theme returns and introduces the discussion of contagion more explicitly.[16]

Rereading Totemism—Contagion and Prohibition

Let us now examine the question of contagion from the negative side, that is, from the side of its management, namely, prohibition. The member of the totemic society identifies himself by asserting his identity with a totemic animal but his identity also obliges him to respect a certain demarcation line: one should not touch, and should not introduce into one's own body, the corporeal substance of the totemic animal. Thus the line is drawn in the form of a *prohibition against contact* and internalization of the eponymous species so as to prevent the undue intermingling of two essentially similar substances.[17] This observation, however, may seem contrary to the more familiar assumption that the religious interdiction marks a separation between radically different sorts of things. Our task at hand, then, is to ascertain to what extent the religious interdiction institutes a separation between things of "different sorts" and to what extent a separation between things that are "the same." The still deeper question is whether, in fact, these two modes of separation are contrary.

To begin with a general observation, Durkheim remarks that religious interdictions can be classified into two categories: those separating what is sacred from what is profane, and those separating "two sacred things of different species." The latter refers to the interdiction between the purely sacred and the impurely sacred, or the propitiously sacred and the unpropitiously sacred. The necessity of the latter type of interdiction, says Durkheim, stems from "the fact that there are inequities and incompatibilities between sacred things" [340]. But because these interdictions differentiate not the sacred from the profane but one sacred thing from another sacred thing, "they do not touch what is essential in the idea of sacredness" [340] because the religious interdiction par excellence is still defined as the regulation of the sacred-profane distinction. In fact, the sacred-sacred interdictions are *secondary*, not simply in the sense that they are less paradigmatic or less important, but above all in the sense that they are *derived* from the primary (sacred-profane) interdictions. Thus, "many of the interdictions between sacred things can be traced back, we think, to those between the sacred and the profane . . . . the more sacred repels the less sacred; but this is because the second is profane in relation to the first" [340–41 n. 7].

But this derivation of the secondary type from the primary type is, in an important sense, a deviation; for the secondary/derivative type of interdiction operates according to a principle different from the one govern-

45

ing the primary/original type. To take Durkheim's argument at face value, the sacred-profane distinction implies a radical "break of continuity" [see 54–55] such that the sacred and the profane cannot be made into a whole, into a totality stretched between two relative opposites. In contrast, the secondary (sacred-sacred) interdiction implies *relative degrees* of sacredness, which—insofar as we take seriously Durkheim's insistence to the effect that the sacred and the profane are completely separate classes—seems to be an impossible idea. Our author is apparently well aware of this difficulty, so that by way of a footnote—in fact, at the end of the last quoted—he sets up two distinct classes of interdictions: "the interdictions between the sacred and the profane, and the purely sacred and the impurely sacred" [341 n. 7]. But more complications ensue.

Not only does he distinguish between the primary and the secondary religious interdictions, he also separates religious interdictions as a whole from so-called magical interdictions. But he is once again moved to qualify this polarization in a footnote, though the import of the qualification this time is considerably more obscure. "This is not saying that there is a radical break of continuity between the religious and the magic interdictions: on the contrary, it is one whose true nature is not decided. There are interdicts of folk-lore of which it is hard to say whether they are religious or magic. But their distinction is necessary, for we believe that the magic interdicts cannot be understood except as a function of the religious ones" [339 n. 5]. The intent of this note (especially the last sentence) becomes somewhat less cryptic only in light of a later passage, where he argues that magic is derivative of religion *and not vice versa,* and that this asymmetry of their unilateral-derivative relation accounts for their difference.[18]

So it seems that the fact of unilateral derivation is the fundamental basis for the categorical distinction between magic and religion; hence this difference is a purely formal one.[19] In fact, it is not even a matter of temporal priority; Durkheim adds yet another footnote to that effect, lest this "derivation" be mistaken for a question of historical sequence:

> We do not wish to say that there was ever a time when religion existed without magic. Probably as religion took form certain of its principles were extended to non-religious relations, and it was thus supplemented by a more or less developed magic. *But if these two systems of ideas and practices do not correspond to distinct historical phases, they have a relation of definite derivation between them.* This is all we have sought to establish. [405 n. 26; emphasis added]

The statement reinforces the fact of difference qua derivation without any new specification; the difference is still without any substantive determination. This "difference by asymmetry of derivation" merely implies,

46

first, that the two parties are identical in their original essence,[20] but, second, that since one issues from the other the derivative product has differentiated itself from the original one such that it now constitutes a separate class. The purely formal structure of the difference confronts us here simply as a given fact, just as plainly as the identity of their original essence is posited as a fact. Between these two facts, nothing seems to mediate, so that "the origin" and "the development" are agape before our eyes, presenting an improbable—or is it just an interminable?—tale of derivation.

This peculiar relation between religion and magic is isomorphic to the relation between the primary and the secondary religious interdictions mentioned above. In the case of the difference between the primary and the secondary, however, the principle operative in each of the two classes is seemingly well defined: one is based on the notion of the sacred as absolute heterogeneity (the sacred distinct from, and incommensurable with, its opposite), while the other is based on the notion of the relative degree of sacredness (the sacred continuous with its opposite).

Durkheim further attempts to incorporate these apparently incompatible principles in the following arrangement: the purely sacred and the impurely sacred are subclasses of the sacred in general, and the sacred in general, of course, stands in "absolute opposition" to the profane:

47

> So the pure and the impure are not two separate classes, but two varieties of the same class, which includes all sacred things. There are two sorts of sacredness, the propitious and the unpropitious, and not only is there *no break of continuity between these two opposed forms, but also one object may pass from the one to the other without changing its nature. The pure is made out of the impure, and reciprocally.* It is in the possibility of these transmutations that the ambiguity of the sacred consists. [458; emphasis added]

The secondary interdictions make distinctions inside the house, so to speak, preventing family disputes among the sacred, whereas the primary interdictions sharply mark the inside and the outside of the realm of the sacred. In sum, this is Durkheim's solution to the confusing situation: the sacred is sacred regardless of whether it is pure or impure; there is *no break of continuity* between the pure and the impure, and one thing *can* pass from the impure to the pure (and vice versa) without changing its nature [457]; in contrast, as we remember, between the sacred and the profane *there is a break of continuity,* and one thing *cannot* pass from one to the other without suffering a metamorphosis of its nature [54–55]. For the moment, therefore, it appears as though he had adequately accounted for the difference between the internal relation (purely sacred-impurely sacred) and the external relation (sacred-profane).

However, as the last sentence of the passage just quoted already indicates, Durkheim chooses to derive the essential nature of the sacred (that is, ambiguity and, ipso facto, contagion) from the transmutability of the pure-impure. The result—it seems inevitable—is the erosion once again of the line demarcating the two types of interdiction.

This same erosion is even more readily visible from the other direction. As seen in the aforementioned development of logic, contagion is only a converse of the peculiar relation of the sacred and the profane: as soon as a profane being approaches the sacred domain (or a sacred being approaches the profane), the being inevitably begins to change its nature, and the result is a state of *partial* transformation, or contamination, whose effect is at once consecration and profanation [360]. But what else could have been meant by "impurely sacred" if not this condition of being contaminated, of suffering a partial transformation of its nature, of becoming sacred "after a fashion and to a certain degree"? Contagion, therefore, actually explains not only the sacred-profane relation but also the phenomenon of the impure; but if so, this contagion factor not only bridges the two types of interdiction by explaining the derivation of one type from the other type, but in fact undermines the typological distinction itself. If the absolute sacred *induces* the relative/partial sacred, such a power of transformation, such fluidity would not leave unscathed the demarcation line between the two types of interdiction. Is there really a class difference between the sacred-profane interdicts and the sacred-sacred interdicts? Is the absolute sacred, after all, really so absolute, if it so easily— indeed, "by its very nature"—slips into the relative sacred?

Our critical inquiry would be short-circuited, however, if we were merely to conclude from this that contagion somewhat obscures the sacred-profane difference. For, rather than obscuring anything, it makes the ambiguity of the difference all the more pronounced.

Admittedly, at this juncture we are about to take another definitive step away from Durkheim's own line of analysis. Durkheim, for his part, explains the ambiguity of the sacred and the phenomenon of contagion in terms of the supposed fact that the general class of the sacred comprises two subclasses, the pure and the impure, which are apparently, but only apparently, heterogeneous. Specifically, he attributes the ambiguity to the interchangeability of the pure and the impure, and in turn this interchangeability to the commonality of their origin. "Since these two sorts of forces have a common origin, it is not at all surprising that, though facing the opposite directions, they should have the same nature, that they are equally intense and contagious and consequently forbidden and sacred. From this we are able to understand how they change into one another" [459].[21]

This, however, is tantamount to repeating, on the one hand, that there is an opposition between the two things having the same origin, and on the other that these opposing forces readily interchange. Despite the assertion that this pure-impure relation is distinct from the sacred-profane relation, as it appears, what is reenacted here is the same ambiguity, the same duplicity of difference endemic to the sacred-profane distinction. It is dictated by the two-way paradox of contagion, namely, even though there is a radical break of continuity, this chasm does not in the least prevent something from passing from one domain to the other; or, *conversely,* that this extreme communicability does not in the least erase the radical line of difference.

This leads us further to suspect that the ambiguity of the demarcation cannot be dispelled, nor is the nature of difference univocally determined, whether we, or Durkheim, designate a particular relation of difference as continuous or discontinuous, or whether we say one thing does or does not change its nature in transition from one side to the other. What matters, and matters crucially, is that there is an unerasable line, an untotalizable difference, *and* that there are traversals over that line. The ambiguity therefore is a function of the line of difference itself rather than an inherent characteristic of the things on the one side of the line, that is, the sacred entities.

But if so, is every line of difference—not just the one demarcating the sacred and the profane—equally affected by this same ambiguity? Such a generalization of the ambiguity would, no doubt, threaten the very basis of our own inquiry, for we too began with an assumption of a certain difference. We began, together with Durkheim, with an understanding that the sacred-profane "opposition" is unique and different from all other types of oppositions. But upon reflection, it now appears that we have nothing at hand to prevent the pervasive ambiguity from infecting our own demarcation line as well. This is in fact in keeping with Durkheim's own observation on the precariousness of typological demarcation. At the end of his main exposition he says, "This ambiguity, moreover, is not peculiar to the idea of sacredness alone; something of this characteristic has been found in all the rites which we have been studying" [460].

Here he is referring to the fact that many varieties of rites, which he has so carefully distinguished and classified, often defy such distinction and suddenly seem to appear identical; or that one variety appears in a wrong context; or that one substitutes for another of a different category.[22] If the basic interest of scholarship is to make proper distinctions and to clarify various relations of "facts," what Durkheim is intimating here is rather disconcerting inasmuch as it seems to imply that the instability and the ambiguity affecting the religious life of primitives is somehow haunting our own scholarly mark of distinction as well. As for Durkheim, even as he generalizes the condition of ambiguity in this man-

49

ner, he is already under the sway of the ambiguous double-crossing of difference. So he hurriedly adds that "of course it was essential to distinguish
[the varieties of rites]; to confuse them would have been to misunderstand
the multiple aspects of the religious life. But, on the other hand, howsoever different they may be, there is no break of continuity between
them. Quite on the contrary, they overlap one another and may even replace each other mutually" [460–61]. He believes he needs to draw the
line, so he does, yet he cannot help crossing the line, so he endlessly draws
upon "transmutation," "metamorphosis," and other such shifty ideas.

Ultimately, however, he does not remain wavering. In his exemplary
fashion, he manages to channel this confusing movement entirely to the
benefit of the totalizing argument of the master thesis. "Howsoever complex the outward manifestations of the religious life may be, at bottom it is
one and simple. It responds everywhere to one and the same need, and it is
everywhere derived from one and the same mental state" [461].

Thus, in the last analysis, violation of the line ceases to be a problem
for Durkheim because all are essentially the same. This marks a moment
of violent triumph of the second thesis over the first. As we have noted in
other instances as well, with this totalizing solution the author sublimates
difference. But again, here as elsewhere, he copiously keeps producing
distinctions. Time and again, he declares that two things are separate and
discontinuous, or that they are continuous; that one is derived from the
other and vice versa, or that one is derived from the other but *not* vice
versa; that they are kindred, that they are *not* kindred but antagonistic,
and so on. What is he doing by exact repetitions of these seemingly empty
phrases?

Of course, he is *specifying* the difference. And in each case, his specification is set in terms of its formal structure. The difference between the
primary and the secondary types of interdiction is paradigmatic. Their
relation consists in, first, the affirmation of the commonality of origin,
second, the denial of the commonality of the operative principle, and third,
the lack of rapport between the affirmation and the denial. Durkheim's
totalizing conclusion, the triumph of the second thesis, is deceptive not
because it denies diversity and difference—it never does—but because it
pretends to cancel this lack of rapport.

•　　•

We have explored the fundamental ambiguity of difference by focusing on the topic of contagion. The absoluteness of "absolute difference"
does not imply the impossibility of trespassing. The opposite is indeed the
case; there is abundant traversal over the line, and the traversal can be
controlled only by means of the most meticulous interdictions and ar-
duous scruples. And those interdictions are so many ways of specifying

50

the difference, or more precisely, of specifying the formal structure of difference. In effect, the first thesis on the sacred reverses the order of determination and specification: there is no qualitative/substantive difference that precedes and predetermines the difference between the sacred and the profane; "specific" differences (as *specified* by means of "totemic *species*," for instance) are merely formal categories employed in order to articulate the identity/difference of the "religious" kind, which is primary. And if these incidental and specific categories of differentiation are taken away, we are left with, precisely, nothing. And this nothing, as we remember, is indeed that very distinguishing mark of the sacred and the profane.

This is part and parcel of the absoluteness of the difference in question here; it refers to the total absence of the semantic content. There is no prior determination that accounts for the difference; it is the primary difference. This line of difference marks the difference of the otherwise indistinguishable, the difference of the same.

Origin

Finally, we come to the question of origin. The question of the origin of religion is, as announced at the beginning of the book [20], the foremost objective of *The Elementary Forms*. But the question is immediately made problematic, as we have just observed that *origination* could be but a shorthand for an improbable story of derivation bridging two irreconcilable states. If *origin* at once means the original entity from which something else is derived *and* the process of this derivation, such an origination actually deviates from, thus is extrinsic to, the origin itself. In fact we have observed a few instances in which such an irreducible duality is already dwelling at the origin—the dual "origin" of society as Durkheim has explained it, the origin of magic from religion, and the derivation of the secondary interdictions from the primary ones. In neither of these instances is the origin simple; it is always found to be already split.

To make the matter more unsettling, Durkheim reiterates the assertion that the notion of origin is to be distinguished from the question of temporality. Origination cannot be delineated in terms of successive stages or chronology. This atemporality of origin, according to Durkheim, holds true also with regard to the question of "the origin of religion":

> The study which we are undertaking is therefore a way of taking up again, *but under new conditions,* the old problem of the origin of religion. To be sure, if by origin we are to understand the very first beginning, the question has nothing scientific about it, and should be resolutely discarded. There was no given moment when religion began to exist, and there is consequently no need of finding a means

of transporting ourselves thither in thought. Like every human institution, religion did not commence anywhere. [20]

The origin, which never *begins* any place or any time in particular, is that which is *always there*. Hence, "what we want to do is to find a means of discerning the *ever-present cause* upon which the most essential forms of religious thought and practice depend" [20; emphasis added].

On the other hand, in another page nearby, he specifies "the duty of science" as knowing "how to go underneath the symbol to the reality which it represents and which gives it its meaning" [14]. By merging the notion of the atemporal origin and the notion of the reality beneath the symbol we finally arrive at a familiar rendition of the Durkheimian quest—in short, he is in search of the *essence* of religion.

And what is the true origin/identity/essence of religion? Society. But we understand now that this answer is only deceptively simple. The unresolved weight of the book actually hinges on a deeper question, which we might as well pose here and now. Does this answer dutifully meet the demand of the author's question—What is the origin, what is the truth behind religion?—in which case it provides a closure to the inquiry; *or* does it perchance amount to a monstrous discovery, a treacherous answer, whose duplicity ultimately undermines the very ground of the question and the questioner?

Let us now consider both these possibilities. As might be expected, Durkheim gives his authorial prerogative to the first of these two. Thus it is confidently announced in advance that "the general conclusion of the book which the reader has before him is that religion is something eminently social. Religious representations are collective representations which express collective realities; the rites are a manner of acting which take rise in the midst of the assembled groups and which are destined to excite, maintain or recreate a certain mental state in these groups" [22]. Here, the true content of religion is proclaimed as "collective realities"; and implicitly but unmistakably these "realities" are allotted their proper seat of governance in "certain mental states." Society is a definitive, if multiplex, *content* of religious representations, and, as remarked earlier, this content is called, ultimately, simple [461].

On the other hand, the second possibility opens with a no less quintessentially Durkheimian proclamation: "Society is a reality *sui generis*" [28]. This primordiality of society is expressed in terms of the irreducibility of the difference between it and whatever is not it. "It has its own peculiar characteristics, which are not found elsewhere and which are not met with again in the same form in all the rest of the universe. The representations which express it have wholly different contents from purely individual ones" [29].

52

As Durkheim tries to locate the grounds for this differentiation, however, he seems to find nothing but more variations of the same duality to which we referred earlier. Here, inquiring into the source of so radical a difference separating collective representations from individual ones, he looks into the nature of man and finds that "man is double. There are two beings in him: an individual being which has its foundation in the organism and the circle of whose activities is therefore strictly limited, and a social being which represents the highest reality in the intellectual and moral order that we can know by observation—I mean society" [29].[23]

If man is double, Durkheim complicates the point even further, one of the two aspects of his double nature, his social nature, cannot be merely a result of some propensity on the part of each individual, even if such propensity proves to be generic and universal. To attest to this point, he claims that in order for collective representations to come into existence, not merely a collection of individual minds but "a synthesis *sui generis*" of such individual consciousness is necessary [471].

That the synthesis itself should be sui generis is a far reaching claim. For without this claim it might be possible to assert that, since there is no society where there is no individual, a collection of individual men and women *is* the originary basis of society. But with this new claim, society seems not to originate constructively through association of individuals but to come into being *synthetically* in one fell swoop, precisely at the moment in which the entire synthetic structure eradicates itself from individuals and establishes its facticity on the basis of this eradication. This indeed seems to be the undercurrent of Durkheim's thought when he says, "Now this synthesis has the effect of disengaging a whole world of sentiments, ideas and images which, once born, obey laws all their own. They attract each other, repel each other, unite, divide themselves, and multiply, though these combinations are not commanded and necessitated by the condition of the underlying reality" [471].

To which point in time does this *once* of "once born" refer? Given the earlier assertion that human institutions do not *begin* to exist anywhere or any time in particular, it would seem that this "disengaging," too, cannot be of temporal order. Rather, one may have to call it synchronic or structural, or, by following Durkheim's own practice, "ever-present" disengagement. Therefore, the synthesis sui generis, which is at the core of social reality, implies *systematic eradication and continuous disengagement of origin from temporality.*

Now, this peculiar movement of disengaging is also what characterizes the itinerary of the quest for the origin of religion as understood by Durkheim. Durkheim cannot dissociate the quest for the origin from the realm of historicity; on the contrary, he insists that, even though the temporal "beginning" is not the same as the essential "origin" that he seeks, the only appropriate mode of investigating the origin is in the temporal; the question of "the origin of religion" can be approached only by means of "historical analysis" [15]. But at the same time the truth that this historical search reveals—the origin of religion—is not a historical one; this truth continually liberates its significance from the temporal.

•   •

With this first and last question of origin, we are again faced with the same two options, the same two directions for thought, namely, the first and the second theses on the sacred. Choosing to abide by the god-is-society thesis is one way of dispelling the mystery from the paradoxical dictum that the ahistorical origin be sought historically. For if a singular, permanent essence is at last *identified,* the apparent opposition of temporality versus permanence becomes a moot point because such "identity" is precisely what *persists* through time, and time is external to it; or, to put it in a formula used from of old, it is *in* time, not *of* time. In fact, is it not the voice of this venerable tradition that speaks in Durkheim as the author-master, the voice that has claimed for itself an eternal origin, an ever-present authority? And by this right of authority, it tells its own uninterrupted tale of origin and development.

But the other, counterauthorial thesis, to which we have sought to lend voice, repeatedly draws our attention to the irreparable rift that splits the origin from the development or rather, splits the origin itself. Origin as a break, as disengaging—this train of thought proceeds not according to the logic of identity and permanence but according to another one, the logic of difference and eradication. But even this submerged logic, in a way, tells its own story, inasmuch as it is *its* silent presence amidst the dominant voice of the author, *its* insurmountable difference from the master's voice, that betokens its own truth. For the truth thus told is none other than the reality of the originary difference, difference unaccounted for, difference beyond mastery.

Descent

In the seventy years since the death of the master, his remains have become the basis of, or rather a founding bequest for, a new tradition of scholarship. In fact, more traditions than one have come to consider themselves in some way Durkheim's progeny. On the other hand, what we have observed here is that among the same textual remains haunts another voice, which seems so far to have found no acknowledged position in the official legacy. This "other voice" speaks the unfamiliar tale of difference, at once dissembling and betraying the design of the master plot. If I have sought to articulate this unauthorized voice of difference and juxtapose it with the authorial one at this point, my intent is not merely to confuse any aspect of his legacy, or to nail down the ghost at last to the grave, and least of all to find a way of assimilating the other to the master. Rather it is to suggest how a certain obscure symbiosis obtaining between the two voices anticipates what is to be fully realized only in later generations.

What message, then, could we discern amidst the palpable discord between the master thesis (sacred equals society) and the subversive subplot (sacred equals difference)? The former ascribes to the sacred the fullest signification, "totality/society," whereas the latter completely hollows out the sacred until it is but a pure, empty sign of difference. But if one insists on attuning these conflictual and contradictory signals without attenuating the discord, it might occur to one, What could such a compelling, dominating, yet utterly indeterminate signifier be but a figure for signification itself, that is, the signifier of signifiers, the signifier that is at once everything and nothing? As a matter of fact, in a manner already affected by this hidden symbiosis, Durkheim himself characterizes the sacred-society-totality compound as a category par excellence, the category of categories; except that the master, as always, imagines that the category must be rather full than empty, and all this is in accordance with his astonishing monolithic belief that "the function of the categories is to dominate and envelop all the other concepts" [488]. Such a startling claim has the virtue of awakening our disbelief, instructing us to mistrust the univocity of the textual intentions, and thus inviting us all the more to read something else in the text, or else to turn to another text. **55**

It is customary to credit Marcel Mauss, Durkheim's own nephew and heir, for initiating an important turn of the (French) Durkheimian legacy toward social semiology, which has since proven to be as decisive as it was fructifying for this line of descent. With Mauss, "society" is no longer an abstract, pseudometaphysical entity as it is generally believed to be for Durkheim, but instead it is a "total social fact," as he demonstrates with expert deliberation in his 1925 essay, *The Gift*. The factual specificity of each aspect of social life constitutes a currency for exchange and conversion, and this transaction—which is "economic" in the sense that Freud used the term—constitutes the very mechanism that produces so-called meaning. In other words, without openly contesting the avuncular authority but rather by carrying it further, Mauss has shown that the total fact is signification, and "society" has become something *legible*.

Only a generation later, Lévi-Strauss "completed" this semiological turn by making Mauss's principle explicit, with a propitious infusion of Saussurean linguistics, thereby fathering structuralism. The rest is history. In fact, Lévi-Strauss helps us set the history straight by delineating the credit line, typically in the following fashion:

Even in his boldest proceedings, Mauss never felt that he was straying from the Durkheimian line. Today we can, perhaps, perceive better than he how, without betraying an oft-affirmed loyalty, he simplified his great predecessor's doctrine and rendered it more tractable. This doctrine has not ceased to astonish us by its imposing proportions, its powerful logical framework, and the vistas it opens onto horizons where so much is yet to be explored. The mission of Mauss was to complete and fit up the prodigious edifice conjured from the earth at the passage of the demiurge. He had to exorcise a few metaphysical ghosts who were still trailing their chains there.[24]

No doubt, Lévi-Strauss assumes that among the ghosts thus purged was that embarrassing, obscurantist idea, "the sacred." To be sure, the term *sacred* hardly appears in Mauss's text, in sharp contrast to its ubiquity in Durkheim's. Yet there is in Mauss's text another term that assumes virtually the same function as the sacred (qua difference), namely, *mana*. (We remember that for Durkheim this native Melanesian term is equivalent to the sacred.) This is duly recognized by Lévi-Strauss, although it does not seem to have occurred to him that this *mana* might have anything to do with one of Durkheim's ghosts:

Taking as our guide Mauss's precept that all social phenomena can be assimilated to language—we see in *mana, wakau, oranda* and other notions of the same type, the conscious expression of a semantic function, whose role it is to permit symbolic thought to operate in spite of the contradiction which is proper to it. In this way are explained the apparently insoluble antinomies attached to this notion . . . . At one and the same time force and action, quality and state, noun and verb, abstract and concrete, omnipresent and localized—*mana* is in effect all these things. But is it not precisely because it is none of these things that *mana* is a simple form, or more exactly, a symbol in the pure state, and therefore capable of becoming charged with any sort of symbolic content whatever?

This passage, actually, is here being quoted by Jacques Derrida, and in this context of quotation it proffers to set the historical record beyond Lévi-Strauss himself. For Lévi-Strauss's text then goes on to speculate further on the interminable shifting of the empty signifier, or "symbol in the pure state," and explicates it by employing yet another term, a term that has since acquired currency among us but bearing another trademark, even though at this particular juncture the patent holder—who happens to be the one quoting the passage—simply underwrites the term by underscoring it. Let us therefore continue to quote Derrida quoting Lévi-Strauss: "In the system of symbols constituted by all cosmologies, *mana* would simply be a zero value, that is to say, a sign marking the necessity of a symbolic content *supplementary* to that with which the signified is already loaded, but which can take on any value required, provided only that this value still remains part of the available reserve."[25] Thus evolves the discourse on *mana*, shifting and sliding slightly, but eventually to congeal around another term, unfolding the crux of signification as that which is at once a lack and superfluity.

Of course, the full story of this descent will have to be told in some other place than in the confines of the present context. If I nonetheless evoke here a series of names from Durkheim, Mauss, Lévi-Strauss, to Derrida, it is less for the purpose of insinuating that something like "the same idea" persists or transforms itself through these names, than to underscore the remarkable repetition of substitution witnessed at every turn, and the concomitant forgetfulness as to where the credit is ultimately due. Some kind of forgetting seems to attend every juncture of the transmission, beginning with, of course, Durkheim's own amnesia: he does not remember, at times, what his text says. But most probably this shortness of memory is an indication of something other than mere atrophy.[26] As might be the case here, forgetting of names could also occasion an atavistic resurgence of some kind; in point of fact, is it not precisely such substitution resembling usurpation, such forgetting, that constitutes the arcane method of this transmission?

•　　•

This gives me pause, as I have situated myself as the latest receiver of this transmission, the last in line for the moment, insofar as I have the task at hand of closing the text. Assuming, then—though not with any measure of confidence—that this forgetfulness itself could on occasion suffer a momentary lapse, let me announce quickly, with a phrase lifted from Lévi-Strauss, "Today we can, perhaps, perceive better."

Today, that is, we can perhaps perceive and remember better, from the far end of the twentieth century, how Durkheim instructed us, with an obscure gesture that he himself probably did not recognize, that "the sacred" is but an empty signifier, thus the most powerful; that "society" is signification, thus something to be read.

Accidental Mythology: Max Müller in and out of his Workshop

Words strain,
Crack and sometimes break, under the burden,
Under the tension, slip, slide, perish,
Decay with imprecision, will not stay in place,
Will not stay still.

58   T. S. Eliot, *Burnt Norton*

IT IS DIFFICULT TO SAY exactly when and who initiated the habit of honoring Friedrich Max Müller as the founder of comparative religion. This honorary designation seems to have been well established by the turn of the century if we are to judge from the account of Louis Henry Jordan, author of the first comprehensive history of the discipline, *Comparative Religion: Its Genesis and Growth* (1905).[1] Evidently, Max Müller's name at that time was preponderant enough that he is discussed not only in the "Prophets and Pioneers" chapter but also under the category of the "founders and masters" in the next chapter; he is, moreover, accorded by far the greatest number of pages. As a historian, however, Jordan found it necessary to qualify Müller's singular-founder designation, and he warned that to suggest that the science of comparative religion might have originated with one individual would be unduly simplistic and therefore misleading. Somewhat less scrupulous about such matters than Jordan was Joachim Wach—Max Müller's compatriot and himself another German émigré—who reaffirmed Müller's founder status fifty years later. Wach's last work, *The Comparative Study of Religions* (1955), opens with these definitive words: "There can be little doubt that the modern comparative study of religions began with Max Müller, about a century ago."[2] The same commemorative gesture was repeated by Mircea Eliade, the successor to Wach's chair at the University of Chicago, who began his own brief retrospective essay, "The 'History of Religion' as a Branch of Knowledge" (1959), with much the same assessment of Müller's position.[3] More recently, Eric Sharpe's oft-adopted textbook history, *Comparative Religion: A History* has a preface which commences with a quotation from one of Müller's pronouncements about the "science of religion," whose time, according to Müller's own estimation in 1870, had come.[4]

Although there are certainly exceptions,[5] this nearly ritual evocation of Max Müller's name as the founder of the new science in ceremonial opening pages of so many historical accounts is remarkable. All the more so because, by the beginning of the twentieth century, many of his principal assertions had been either discredited or their significance reduced. In truth, he is hardly read these days and, so far, no one has urged that he should be. At the same time, in such eulogic words of recognition recurrent in many historical accounts, and in many other comments about him repeated to this day, one often detects a certain presumption, or a tacit suggestion to the effect that it was somehow significant that "the founder" of comparative religion was this particular individual with these particular attributes—German émigré, philologist, orientalist, Oxford professor who never left the great libraries of Europe to experience in his own person "the real India"—if only for the reason that these qualifications should set him apart from more recent generations of scholars. It is as though this figurehead had been hoisted partly in veneration but also partly in order to mark how *we* should like to differ, how we do our business differently, how we have come a long way from that point of origin.

Whether the significance of this pioneer is finally substantial or merely symbolic, the simultaneous investment and divestment of interest, this giving and withholding of credit regarding the historical person of "the founder," is perhaps indicative of the general ambivalence felt by the subsequent generations toward the early days of the disciplinary history. There is, however, some peculiarity worth noting about Müller's case. Unlike Durkheim and Freud, who are regarded as definite innovators who brought the whole enterprise of the origin quest to new playing fields and, inadvertently, demonstrated its own limits, and whose repercussions therefore continue to be felt to this day,[6] this long-departed founder of the discipline is placed securely in his venerable position because he is truly fossil, dead beyond controversy.

To reopen his case, it thus seems, is not unlike trying to revive the memory of what Eliade called *deus otiosus,* the exulted sky god so ancient and lofty that he has long been irrelevant. Put differently, we begin with an impression that what we have in the figure of Max Müller is a scholarly legacy that is no longer viable, and thus structurally resembling a dead language or, perhaps better, an extinct animal species. If his science of religion can be said to be the ancestor of the contemporary study of religion in some way, there does not seem to be a direct line of descent but

59

perhaps something more akin to the "descent" of modern humans from Cro-Magnon or some other prehistoric primates. At least that is the way Eliade, for instance, would choose to represent the situation. Essentially, according to this school of thought, Max Müller's was a scholarly undertaking that went astray, ran aground, and left behind nothing but a formidable heap of conceptual wreckage. As Eliade puts it, "the discipline of comparative Indo-European mythology has been hopelessly discredited by the improvisations of Max Müller and his followers," much to the consternation of subsequent generations of worthy scholars such as Georges Dumézil, who happened to venture into the same territory.[7]

• •

Two things, or rather two incongruities, seem most remarkable about Müller's legacy, such as it is today. First, his voluminous work and his international renown during the last century, juxtaposed with his well-nigh total oblivion today. In addition to founding "comparative religion," Müller was regarded a leading scholar in nineteenth-century Indo-European philology. A man of great erudition, his scholarly achievements include: the first critical edition of the *Rig Veda* with the Sayana commentary,[8] some two dozen volumes of essays and lectures on the subjects of religion, mythology, and language,[9] a two-volume anthology of German literature, an English translation of Kant's *Critique of Pure Reason,* which is still highly praised by many, and the general editorship of the epoch-making fifty-volume compendium, *The Sacred Books of the East* (1879– 1910). According to the latest count, "all in all, he wrote and edited more than one hundred books."[10] Despite these prodigious accomplishments and the immense prestige and popularity he enjoyed in his own time, his work is now almost entirely forgotten except for a few memorable phrases quoted in textbooks, such as, "Mythology is a disease of language," "Mythology is the dark shadow which language throws upon thought," and "*Nomina* (names) become *numina* (divine beings)."

This leads us to the second incongruity. The present-day textbook assessment of Müller invariably holds him responsible for the so-called nature myth theory, that is, the once-popular opinion that all religions began as a primitive and prescientific contemplation of natural wonders and the subsequent personification of those natural phenomena, above all, the sun. But such an opinion accords rather badly with the aforementioned phrases, which are often quoted, presumably, to illustrate his characteristic views. For clearly the focal point of Müller's interest expressed in these emblematic passages is not the primitive's fascination with nature, but certain mischiefs attendant upon the practice of language.

Such inconsistencies in Max Müller's reception are by no means a recent phenomenon. In 1912 Durkheim discussed Müller's theory under the rubric of "Naturism" in his *Elementary Forms,* although it should be duly remembered that Durkheim was comparatively more attentive to the linguistic aspect of Müller's theory than many of the more recent commentators.[11] On the other hand, in *Totem and Taboo,* also published in 1912, Freud classified Müller's as a case of "nominalist theories."[12]

These apparent discrepancies are seldom recognized as such, no doubt, in part because his legacy is not one of those hotly contested areas, and perhaps also because Müller's own prose is exceedingly smooth and beguiling when he is making certain leaps. Here is an example of his rhetorical move: "Deification . . . does not mean the application of the name and concept of god to certain phenomena of nature. No, it means the *slow and inevitable development of the concept and name of God out of these very phenomena of nature*—it means the primitive theogony that takes place in the human mind as living in human language."[13] In the manner of many nineteenth-century romantic theories of the origin of language, he envisions language slowly but directly growing out of nature. His narrative advances and at once recalls "language" back into the fold of "nature"; the reader is never made to experience a jolt when it passes from nature to language, or vice versa.

61

To document and to account fully for these narrative crossings in Müller's texts would no doubt require a comprehensive analysis of his corpus in relation to various scholarly traditions of his time and thereafter, and of course such a task would exceed the limits of the present study. However, I hope to contribute something to this end by reexamining some of his works expressly with this hitherto neglected linguistic emphasis in mind,[14] and by accentuating some of the interstices and disjunctures in his work. In the course of it I will be suggesting that the easily traversed yet ultimately unreconciled aspects of his professional career— his philological work on the one hand and the reception of his public lectures on the other—can be seen as a structural analog to the way in which his theory of mythology itself is constructed.

In his private writing, Müller acknowledges with surprising frequency the essentially alien status of his philological endeavor in the context of the English "reading public," which was his immediate audience. And this alien status continued to hold also in the context of the English anthropological-ethnographic tradition, within which we have come to locate his legacy.[15] His overwhelming popularity and, in turn, his own appreciation of "free England" notwithstanding, even at Oxford where he lived for more than half a century, Max Müller the philologist seems to have been a curious foreign body, and thus he remains to this day.

•   •

We will begin with a letter, which he addresses to a fellow philologist in his native Germany. In this letter, as in many others, Müller mixes his terms of endearment with his complaints about Oxford. "My Dearest Friend," he writes to Jacob Bernays,[16] to whom he is about to dedicate one of his books,[17] "I had long looked forward to giving you a public recognition of my friendship and gratitude. Though our meetings have not been frequent of late, yet they have left the memory of many beautiful and stimulating hours, and I hope indeed that a lucky star will perhaps once more bring us close to each other for a longer period. What I miss most here in Oxford is stimulating intercourse in literary and scientific circles. That is entirely wanting, especially in my special branch of study."[18]

By the year 1867, when he wrote this letter, the project of editing and publishing the *Rig Veda,* the task to which Max Müller had devoted himself since his early twenties, had kept him in England already twenty-one years, and the project was still seven years away from completion. If he chose to stay in England all those years, it was certainly not on account of the English public's superior judgment regarding the true value of the literary treasures of their Asian colony, and even less, we might surmise from letters such as this, because of an intellectual climate conducive to serious philology.[19] In fact, on this latter subject, the best Müller could say about Oxford was that it left him alone. In another letter written eight years later, he ruminated in a similar vein. "Oxford has been, and is still, in a state of hibernation; I expect nothing for some years to come. It will wake after a time, but I doubt whether much is gained by disturbing its slumbers for the present. My only comfort at Oxford is that one can work on quietly there, without anybody taking the slightest notice of one. In all other respects I feel that one is perfectly useless there."[20]

At any rate, he knew why he was there. England offered him the two things that he had sought most earnestly and desperately through his early years of hardship: a place to work and a publisher—Oxford University Press—to print his *Rig Veda.* This rather costly venture was jointly subsidized by the French government, the Prussian government, and finally, after much persuasion on the part of the influential German diplomat Baron Christian Bunsen, the East India Company. In short, the intellectual isolation in a foreign country was a price he willingly paid; it was a sacrifice he offered to the *Veda* project which, for that very reason, could be rightly called his lifework.

Philology as such, or more precisely, scientific or comparative philology as he understood it, was by nature a Continental science—born in Germany and nurtured in France, and virtually unknown, as it appears, at Oxford.[21] Hence Müller was a foreigner by blood and by trade, and he named his own philological library "a German workshop," from which some "chips" would fall from time to time in the form of occasional essays; in the course of time, *Chips from a German Workshop* became a five-volume work. In the preface to the first volume, Müller recalls the circumstances which, in the end, brought about these collections:

> More than twenty years have passed since my revered friend Bunsen called me one day into his library at Carlton House Terrace, and announced to me with beaming eyes that the publication of the Rig-veda was secure. He had spent many days in seeing the Directors of the East India Company, and explaining to them the importance of this work, and the necessity of having it published in England. At last his efforts had been successful, the funds for printing my edition of the text and commentary of the Sacred Hymns of the Brahmans had been granted, and Bunsen was the first to announce to me the happy result of his literary diplomacy. "Now," he said, "you have got a work for life—a large block that will take years to plane and polish. But mind," he added, "let us have from time to time some chips from your workshop."
>
> I have tried to follow the advice of my departed friend, and I have published almost every year a few articles on such subjects as had engaged my attention, while prosecuting at the same time, as far as altered circumstances would allow, my edition of the Rig-veda, and of other Sanskrit works connected with it. . . . And now while the two last volumes of my edition of the Rig-veda are passing through the press,[22] I thought the time had come for gathering up a few armfuls of these chips and splinters, throwing away what seemed worthless, and putting the rest into some kind of shape, in order to clear my workshop for other work.[23]

63

In writing these pieces, Müller evidently had in mind as his audience the nonphilological, non-German, "reading public."[24] And, without a doubt, it is on account of these occasional essays and the popular public lectures that he gave at various institutions in England and Scotland that his views on religion and related matters are known to most of us, and not—with the probable exception of some Sanskrit scholars—through his very philological and, as he himself admits rather apologetically, very German and hardly readable works on the *Veda*.[25] In his characteristic prose, rich in metaphors, Müller often depicts his philological workshop as a dark, nearly subterranean place of obscurity, from which he, as a virtual ward of the English society, bore a certain obligation to the public to deliver at a regular interval some enlightening piece of wisdom or, at least, some useful information.[26]

Yet this polarity of the philological master work versus the incidental chips of essays begins to blur somewhat when we take into account Müller's own understanding of philology as a sort of "gathering of chips," a kind of linguistic geology, or archaeology of language, whose first and foremost task is to gather up and sort out the odd fragments of the obliterated language formations of the past which are half-buried in the languages of today. The interest of the one who studies languages, moreover, goes well beyond the mere curiosity of the antique collector, even though a language is indeed a veritable "museum of antiquities" which possesses objects that are "older than the oldest things from any part of the ancient world."[27] The philologist's work may be tedious, but it will allow him, ultimately, to read more than mere words: "The study of words may be tedious to the schoolboy, as breaking of stones is to the wayside laborer; but to the thoughtful eye of the geologist those stones are full of interest;—he sees miracles on the high-road, and reads chronicles in every ditch."[28]

If we ourselves are therefore to produce such a philological reading and subject Müller's "chips" to an "archaeological" study—even though at the moment these pieces may seem to be buried and preserved in history only as relics of nineteenth-century armchair anthropology and are, on that account, better passed over in silence—these chips may yield some hitherto unsuspected meaning. Then we, too, may be able to read another kind of history.

The "chips" that my discussion here will cover range from the early to middle stages of Müller's career. Especially pertinent are the essay entitled "Comparative Mythology," published in 1856,[29] the second series of lectures on the "science of language" given in 1863,[30] and another lecture, "On the Philosophy of Mythology," delivered in 1871.[31] By this last date, Müller had already held the Chair of Comparative Philology at Oxford University for some time, a position specially created for him as a belated recompense for having denied him the Boden Chair of Sanskrit some years before. That denial was in part due, it was generally believed, to his foreign origin, and to his questionable Christian orthodoxy, at least according to the appraisal given from the Anglican standpoint.

As it appears, his disappointment had a fateful significance for the rest of his career: it marks the beginning of the shift in his professional identity from that of a more or less orthodox Sanskritist to whatever it was that was yet to be named. As a way of retrospect, Müller's widow and editor of the two-volume posthumous publication, *The Life and Letters of the Right Honourable Friedrich Max Müller,* Georgiana Grenfell Max Müller offers this observation: "Had he been successful [in attaining the Boden chair], he must have devoted his great powers almost exclusively to Sanskrit, and by doing so would no doubt have remained . . . 'the first Sanskrit scholar in Europe.' It was the Chair of [Comparative] Philology, founded some six years later specially for him . . . that led him on from the Science of Language to the Sciences of Thought and Religion." Be that as it may, his disappointment at the time was palpable, as he wrote to his mother: "I was sorry, for I would gladly have devoted all my time to Sanskrit, and the income was higher."[32]

The same sense of regret for the missed opportunity still attended his decision eight years later, this time a decision *not* to leave Oxford for a more academically traditional Sanskritist position elsewhere. It was in 1868, when the prospect of a chair of Sanskrit at Cambridge University arose; but, again, according to Georgiana Max Müller, "Six years sooner he would have felt no doubt on the question, but he had now turned his attention more to general philology and the problems of mythology," and he eventually decided against announcing his candidacy.[33]

Later in the same year there came a semiofficial offer from Germany, communicated through his aforementioned philologist friend Jacob Bernays, of what appeared to be a modest but respectable position either at the University of Bonn or Berlin, where he could devote his life thereafter entirely to philological occupation.[34] But this offer, too, he declined, with a similar tone of melancholy resignation. Thus he wrote to Bernays, "What **65** you mentioned about the German plans the other day has occupied me much, but as I told you before, it seems to me best to remain in Oxford for a few more years. I do not deny that I should like to spend the evening of life in German air, but I stopped long ago wishing for certain things and making plans" [359].

What is striking in this passage above all is that, by this time, he had virtually abandoned both the strictly philological career and the immediate prospect of returning to Germany, or, perhaps more profoundly, all such definite plans. Within a year, he was offered the Oxford position in comparative philology, which, liberally understood, was to define the rest of his career.

By 1870s his theory of myth was already quite well known, so much so that he had a string of disciples as well as an army of opponents, and at least one witty parodist, who contributed an article to a journal published at Trinity College entitled "The Oxford Solar Myth." This latter treatise purported to demonstrate, through the most meticulous application of the philological method, that "Max Müller" was a solar deity.[35]

In point of fact, this left-handed attack was well aimed if for no other reason than that, in the last analysis, it was indeed the fame of "solar mythology" that eclipsed almost everything that ever was philological about Müller's theory. In the shadow of this reputation—and thanks also to the fame of the *Sacred Books of the East*[36]—the very work with which he wished to identify himself, namely, the *Rig Veda* edition, his only incontestably celebrated work, is now hardly mentioned except in passing.[37] By moving from the shadow of language to the daylight of nature—which was underwritten by the move from his dark philological workshop to the limelight of public lecture halls—his theory lost its native ground and Max Müller lent his name to a peculiarly naive and hardly novel idea, the "nature myth theory."

• •

Let us remember at this point the oft-voiced lament of the renowned mythologist of our time, Mircea Eliade. He regarded as a great misfortune for the students of myth the fact that, for the European intellectuals generally, the myth par excellence has always been the Greek myth, that is to say, the dead myth, whose cultic context has been long lost and forgotten, and which had already been proclaimed a "fiction" by the very carriers of the tradition, the Greeks themselves. As Eliade puts it, "It is true that only in Greece did myth inspire and guide epic poetry, tragedy, and comedy, as well as the plastic arts; but it is no less true that it is especially in Greek culture that myth was submitted to a long and penetrating analysis, from which it emerged radically 'demythicized.'"[38] According to Eliade's opinion, then, not only the long accumulation of the Greeks' great literary and artistic gifts but also the works of their overly philosophic minds ultimately spoiled their myths for the modern myth analysts; for in the course of their illustrious history the Greeks somehow lost their ritual practice, the original life-world of their now-petrified gods. Perhaps Max Müller was just the sort of Greek-obsessed mythographer that Eliade had in mind when he summarily criticized that branch of scholarship.

On this particular point, however, it so happens that Eliade is merely repeating the opinion voiced long before him. George Foucart, in his 1909 publication of some repute entitled *La Méthode comparative dans l'histoire des religions*, advised that Greek myths were of little use for comparativists because "the literary tradition furnishes nothing but myths that are disfigured and obscured [*défigurés et obscurcis*] by the fantasies of the poets or artists, no less by the speculations of philosophical systems."[39] Here there is little doubt that the point of criticism was directly aimed at our solar mythographer cum comparative philologist. Foucart continues immediately by observing how unenlightening all those theories of Greek religions have been—they do nothing but increase the darkness (*ténèbres*), he said—because those theories have been "based, for a century, on [romantic theory of] symbolism, solar myths, or comparative philology." Moreover, Foucart goes on to contend, half of the Greek deities were actually of foreign origin. Consequently, he opines, "Far from illuminating the history of religions [in general], it is the Hellenic religions themselves that are in need of being illuminated by comparisons with other, more ancient, and less mixed up religions."[40] Who indeed except the most blinded, he seems to say, would seek an original myth, paradigmatic myth, or myth par excellence, in ancient Greece? Interestingly, Foucart himself opted to examine Egypt, which was known to be, if not to say less *mélangée*, at least considerably older than Greece.[41]

But if the region of Greek religion is thus not pristine but of mixed descent, if their myths are dark, dead, and disfigured by excess imagination, perhaps Max Müller had good reason to turn precisely to this area for his theory formation. It is certainly true that such a disjointed and petrified nature of myth was the beginning point, or rather the very basis, of Müller's theoretical speculation. For in the last analysis Müller understood decay and loss not merely as an incidental misfortune that might befall some myths from without; on the contrary, he believed, such a vicissitude was constitutional to myth itself, it was a hidden trope of myth.

Above all, for Müller myths are strange stories whose elements are curiously misshapen and unnatural. The unnaturalness of myth resembles the unnaturalness of a dismembered body, or perhaps better, that of a broken fragment of a fallen statue, dislocated in a strange landscape, overgrown with the life of another century indifferent to its ancient meaning. As poetic as such a grotesquerie might be, myth in this view would be necessarily a macabre formation, a monstrosity resulting from a process which is at once fortuitous and inevitable: loss, displacement, and subsequent symbiotic growth.

It is on account of this constitutionally grotesque nature of myth, moreover, that he sharply distinguishes the domain of mythology from religion proper. Religion, according to his unshaken assumption, has to do with pure, unconditional adoration of the Infinite—this latter understood, to be sure, in a rather turgid Kantian fashion. Thus defined minimally, religion is for him a universal human propensity that is truly transhistorical and transcultural; it is essentially incorruptible by time and history, though it may become disguised and made invisible by cultural processes and their encrustations such as the ones just described.[42] Müller would therefore categorically disallow, and call blasphemous, the idea held by some Christians of his time who maintained that classical myths are in some way a corruption or misinterpretation of the original and universal (that is, biblical, proto-Christian) revelation. Concerning some of the typical Greek myths, such as "the story of Uranos maimed by Kronos,—of Kronos eating his children, swallowing a stone, and vomiting out alive his whole progeny," Müller has this to say:

Among the lowest tribes of Africa and America we hardly find anything more hideous and revolting. It is shutting our eyes to the difficulties which stare us in the face, if we say, like Mr. [George] Grote, that this mythology was 'a past which was never present;' and it seems blasphemy to consider these fables of the heathen world as corrupted and misinterpreted fragments of a divine revelation once granted to the whole race of mankind—a view so frequently advocated by Christian divines. These myths have been made by man at a certain period of history. There was an age which produced these myths.[43]

In fact, he was to observe sometime later, "the more we admire the native genius of Hellas, the more we feel surprised at the crudities and absurdities of what is handed down to us as their religion."[44] For Müller, the true spiritual zenith of the Greeks was to be sought elsewhere than their mythology. Mythology is *by nature historical, accidental,* thus not essential to the Greek genius.[45] The patent absurdity and immorality of the Greek gods is hardly commensurate with the celebrated principle of reason, *ratio,* which champions the nonmonstrous and proper proportion that is supposed to typify the classical sensibility. Perhaps it could be suggested that it is precisely in the Greek example that we see most clearly how mythology is a quasi-pathological growth protruding from the dark side of thought, in the shadow of monumental language of rationality. Mythology was a nightmare of Greek philosophy—just the sort of things Plato was intent on expunging from his utopian Republic.

68

Yet there is another train of thought recurrent in Müller's discussion that further privileges Greek myth despite its hideousness. If the Greek examples most readily reveal the essential nature of mythology, this is not because of their original purity but precisely because they are derivative and already "late." As such, they refer back to something older and prior, if not to say more pristine. The anterior of Greek mythology is not only a different geographic locale, but also a subtly different human sphere; this other place is India (before Greece), and this other sphere is language (before mythology). Thus, even though he often commences a discussion on mythology with a mention of these well-known stories concerning the strange goings on between Uranos, Kronos, and Zeus as depicted by Hesiod or Homer, the truth of the matter, he claims, is that the account by Hesiod is "a distorted caricature" of something more original. He thus goes on to say that "the real Theogony of the Aryan races" is to be found not in Greek myths but in Vedic hymns, for the latter have better preserved the traces of the gods' *names,* which is the key to the mystery of mythology. The Greek myth is "exemplary" on account of its already "diseased" character; it is a perfect embodiment of myth as constitutionally *derivative,* as something going awry and growing monstrous.

In sum, the birth of a god is a linguistic process; such a birth story does not really pertain to the body, either human or divine, or to the body being dismembered, or the severed member becoming another body, or one body being devoured and expelled by another, and so on. Rather, it is *words* which are most susceptible to such cannibalistic and scatological processes—words suffer loss, decay, and mutilation, and some of them are expelled and then given a strange new life. Comparative philology recovers the site of this primordial "accident," the moment in which the words go astray, and it retraces the vicissitudes of words in the general history of language.

•   •

But so far we have traced only one aspect of Max Müller's theory of mythology. The other aspect, in a sense, moves us out of his philological workshop, the world of ancient, fragmented, corrupt words.

Even though Müller understands the formation of individual myths to be such a catastrophic process fraught with loss and fortuity, once he places the phenomenon of myth formation itself within the larger context of the history of human thought, it immediately acquires the look of universal necessity. Despite his singular philological awareness of disjunctures and fortuity, in the last analysis Müller's overall perspective is shot through with a kind of naturalist impulse to see a continuum, conformity to hidden necessity or to some kind of law. In fact, he suggests, it would be all too repugnant a theory if we were to "admit in the gradual growth of the human mind, as in the formation of the earth, some violent revolutions, which broke the regularity of the early strata of thought, and convulsed the human mind, like volcanos and earthquakes arising from some unknown cause, below the surface of history."[46] Thus he accepts, and even extends, the well-received dictum of his day and proposes that not only nature, but history, too, makes no leaps. The dictum, however, directly contradicts everything he has to show philologically, regarding the vicissitudes of words.

At any rate, in this naturalizing manner the fantastic process of mythologizing, too, becomes but an ineluctable phase in the development of language. Thence comes the famous saying of his: "Mythology is inevitable, it is natural, it is an inherent necessity of language, if we recognize in language the outward form and manifestation of thought; it is, in fact, the dark shadow which language throws on thought, and which can never disappear till language becomes altogether commensurate with thought, which it never will."[47]

Few other passages in Müller are better remembered, more pregnant with suggestion, and more obscure. In effect, we are left in the dark, or rather, this convoluted statement thrusts into view that very darkness, the shadow, the palpable sign of the noncoincidence between language and thought, between the word and the concept, or, to refer to a more contemporary terminology, between the signifier and the signified. Naturally, we

69

would want to know the whence and wherefore of this shadowy gap, and moreover, how this "inevitable" and "natural" course of development comes to take on an expressly pathological character and becomes a myth proper in Müller's sense, "a disease of language." Or, are we to infer, after all, that "disease" is an entirely natural, inevitable process?

• •

Let me state summarily at the outset, and then discuss individually, those factors which he mentions here and there, which could be construed as accounting, in some way, for this non-coincidence, as well as for the ensuing pathological turn. The first of these factors is the *essential* metaphorical nature of language (every word is originally a metaphor); second, also constitutional to the structure of language is the superabundant confluence of words—that is, phenomena such as polynomy, homonymy, synonymy; third, the phonetic decay of words and the concomitant erosion of meaning; and finally, the loss of true etymological memory and the invention of a false origin, or so-called folk etymology.

70   To begin with, according to Müller, every word is at its origin a metaphor; metaphor is not a secondary and liberal use and abuse of language but rather its primary function. Having said this, it seems, he can hardly avoid the far-reaching implication that language as a whole, that is, as a system, could not have come into being except as a *system* of metaphors. At the same time, metaphor is "the transference of the meaning of one to other," as he states clearly enough.[48] And to say that the word is originally a movement from one place in the signifying network to another, that its very being is this transference, is tantamount to admitting— much as we might speak of "the original meaning" of a word which supposedly gets lost and subsequently ends up misrecognized—that in truth, the word has no "original site" which can fix its pristine denotation *apart from* the whole range of connotation.

But here we are somehow running ahead of Müller. What in fact he does say, nonetheless, is no less consequential. "Whenever any word, that was at first used metaphorically is used without a clear conception of the steps that led from its original to its metaphorical meaning, there is danger of mythology; whenever those steps are forgotten and artificial steps put in their places, we have mythology, or if I may say so, we have disease of language."[49] Here again, the forgetting of the *passage*—"the steps"— or obliteration of the traces of the metaphorical transference, is a crucial incentive for mythologizing. We shall return to this matter of "forgetting" shortly.

Also at this early stage in the history of language, Müller suggests, every word is a radix, that is, a word with no inflectional ending, and every radix signifies a certain characteristic.[50] An object is called by one or the other of its many characteristics; for example, fire might be severally called "bright," "warm," "burning." As any given object is likely to have more than one characteristic, and moreover, the same characteristic is almost always shared by more than one object, this gives rise to the phenomenon of polynomy (an object having many names), homonymy (different and unrelated objects having ostensibly the same name), as well as synonymy (words having similar meanings).[51] Under such conditions, a word can slide over and substitute for one another quite freely, and consequently the network of signification is marked by a particularly prodigious redundancy; or, to borrow a very apt term from psychoanalysis, every location in the signification network is heavily overdetermined.

This further adds to the heavy "unwieldiness" of words, which has been said to ensue from the fact that a word is originally a metaphor. For this reason, every word ever spoken evokes a whole network of transference; or as Müller puts it, words always end up saying "more than they ought to say, and hence," he continues, "much of the strangeness of mythological language."[52]

The two factors mentioned thus far—metaphoric transference and the overdetermination of the signification system—have to do with the essential, as it were, "prehistoric" nature of language. These factors account for the noncoincidence between words and concepts in terms of the incessant slippage of words over what they are supposed to denote, while this slippage itself is constitutional to the function of language. The third factor, phonetic decay, brings the issue to the domain of philology proper, that is, the domain of time and history.

Words decay and lose some of their sharp edges through long years of use, much as rocks do as they are washed by streams and waves. Though perchance originally a vibrant image full of poetry, once relegated to the service of everyday use a word becomes a mere instrument of mundane communication, shorn of all its unwieldiness which is its poetry. Its essential truth is compromised for the sake of, say, the facility of pronunciation. For instance, since "God be with you" is too wordy to pronounce at every parting, "good-bye" has become good enough.

This is how words lose their way. Not only are they cut, mutilated, and mangled, they are immediately given a false identity as well. For example, we fail to recognize "God" in "good-bye," not only because *good* no longer sounds like *God*, but also because this syllable *good* happens to be identical with the *good* of, say, "good luck," "good morning," and "good night"; hence the phrase "good-bye" joins a new set in which it finds itself readily at home, though originally alien.

The phonetic mangling of a word followed by the restructuring of its meaning in an entirely new context takes place not only when a word travels through time and is transformed, but also when it migrates from

71

one language to another. To cite a couple of examples from Müller's list: (1) the uncomprehending English made "beef-eater" out of the French *buffetier;* (2) a root vegetable of the sunflower family, called *girasole* in Italian—meaning "sunflower," rotating around *(gira-)* the sun *(sole)*—was transmogrified into *"Jerusalem* artichoke," and this further led to the creation of the culinary substance called "Palestine soup," verily marking the birth of the mythology of a nouvelle cuisine.

We have already touched upon the fourth factor, which is particularly pertinent to the issue of the mythologizing power of language. To wit, a word tends to "forget" its original site; this forgetting obliterates all traces of the transference of meaning—whether the transference in question is a metaphorical or historical one—and then, some "origin" or "history" has to be forged on the basis of its current location, as if it were its proper site *ab origine.*

Apparently, we have only so much tolerance for the word that does not communicate anything to us, the word that does not disclose an account of its origin, its true meaning. In such a case, the word is often changed further so that it does come to say something (for example, from *girasole* to Jerusalem) even if what it now says bears no relation to its previous sense. Or sometimes some dubious story is invented to account for the strange word even if the story told turns out to be positively more weird than the word it explains.

Just as the body is overtaken by a disease when it is weak, the mythogenic disease of language, too, is likely to seize the victim in a vulnerable, transitional period:

> Now there is in most languages, but more particularly in those which are losing their consciousness or their vitality, what, by a name borrowed from geology, may be called a *metamorphic process.* It consists chiefly in this, that words, as they cease to be properly understood, are slightly changed, generally with the object of imparting to them once more an intelligible meaning. This new meaning is the most mistaken one, yet it is not only readily accepted, but the word in its new dress and with its new character is frequently made to support facts or fictions which could be supported by no other evidence. Who does not believe that *sweetheart* has something to do with *heart?* Yet it was originally formed like *drunk-ard, dull-ard,* and *nigg-ard;* and poets, not grammarians, are responsible for the mischief it may have done under its plausible disguise.[53]

Thus once again the poets, who took the credit for the original, metaphoric vibrancy of language at the moment of its birth, are held responsible for its later mutations as well. Yet, in a sense, "the poets" are us. Or

72

else, we are "philologists" of sorts, too. As Müller puts it, there is in the human mind "a craving after etymology, a wish to find out, by fair means or foul, why such a thing should be called by such a name."[54] And when the fair means of scientific philology is not at hand, there is always paronomasia, or puns, with which to fabricate an imaginary history.

•   •

Yet just how much of this mythologizing process does Müller wish to say hangs on a pun? He concedes that probably no myth of a narratable size can be completely and exhaustively analyzed because there will always be what he calls, rather elusively, "historical factors," which are incidental and unrelated to language per se, and thus falling beyond the pale of philological analysis. However, this does not prevent him from suggesting that the crucial pivot of the mythologizing process is indeed a pun, a play on words, or some slightly faulty etymological construction, deliberate or otherwise—in short, a parapraxis of language. As such, mythology lurks everywhere;[55] for language casts its powerful shadow wherever it operates. "Depend upon it," he writes, "there is mythology now as there was in the time of Homer, only we do not perceive it, because we ourselves live in the very shadow of it."[56]

Now, we must take note here, one of the things that fall outside of philological analysis, according to Müller's own admission, is the question of the origin of roots, or radices.[57] This Müller dismisses as something belonging to psychology, not philology.[58] But this dismissal also puts an important limit on what philology can say about the *linguistic* origin of deities. For there will be a moment when the philologist is asked, Well, it is fine to know the true identities of some mangled words, but how did some of them get to be "deified" and become supernatural beings bearing these distorted words as their names? If Müller's *philological* side is strictly followed, there should be nothing to be said. At any rate it is not a properly philological way of posing the question. It is indeed a nature mythologist's question. There is no "deifying" for the philologist, because mythological "gods"—which, of course, are not to be confused with God the Infinite—are those beings that flicker in the passage of words; they are particular cases of the excess of signification. We can recognize that some of these monstrosities of words have become "deities" only when we recognize them as false gods, that is, as shadows of someone else's thought. But we, too, live amidst mythology because we live in language, only we do not recognize our shadows as "gods" because we are completely under their sway. "Depend on it."

Had Müller stayed strictly within the confines of his philology, this may have been the end of the path of inquiry, and nothing else forthcoming. But he did not.

73

• •

This finally leads us to the question, What does this ubiquitous figure of the shadow and signifying excesses have to do with the mythology of the sun? Insofar as can be surmised from the arguments offered in those essays covered up to now, very little indeed. For nothing but a gap opens before our eyes whenever Müller's discourse moves from his philological study to the subject of solar mythology, that is to say, from the domain of words traversing the field of signification to the domain of heavenly bodies traversing the azure. As a rule, the latter subject is introduced rather abruptly and unceremoniously, with a remark of the following sort: "Let us now return to mythology in the narrower sense of the word. One of the earliest objects that would strike and stir the mind of man, and for which a sign or a name would soon be wanted, is surely the Sun."[59]

Here, it is not language that calls forth (and fabricates) an object, but it is the other way around: an object (the sun) goes in search of words. It is therefore no longer a matter of language generating a mythical being; on the contrary, language takes a secondary, derivative position. A sign or a name merely follows and satisfies a psychological demand which precedes it. To avert one's attention from the power of language and to resort to a prelinguistic psychology of this sort—is this, after all, what it means to "return to mythology in the narrower sense"?

A certain reversal or reversion appears to have taken place in his train of thought here. While Müller the philologist acknowledges that signifiers are *essentially* polysemic and mobile owing to their (metaphoric) nature as well as to their historicity, Müller the demythographer in turn appears to be intent on stabilizing the signifiers and on restoring them to their (purportedly) original locus, that is, to the natural world, to the domain of the proper (*propre, eigentlich,* that is, literal). And the intent of his mythological study seems to be to demythologize "mythemes" by anchoring the signifier to a certain prelinguistic reality, so as to prevent it, presumably, from becoming a mere sound, or remaining a mere figure sliding across the network of signification. Is such a project not bound to repeat the very process of myth making, which the demythologizing analysis was supposed to reverse? Is Müller the demythographer not, like the myth makers themselves, forcing denotation upon words, and literalizing metaphors? Is this not, in other words, an unintended repetition of that "inevitable" passing and metamorphosis that is said to take place in the history of language, that is, passing from words to gods, from names to divine beings, or, as Müller puts it most famously, from *nomina* to *numina?*

Let us immediately note that this very passage, in Müller's own formulation, hinges on a pun. The turn of the phrase "*nomina* becomes *nu-*

mina," which emblematizes the turn of the argument from philology to mythology, at once points to the logically impassable gap *and* at the same time embodies the transgressive move crossing over the impassable, a move effected, moreover, by virtue of a certain excess—the play—of language.[60]

The idea that a myth narrates and by so doing dis-solves or rather glosses over a certain antinomy has been made familiar to us since Lévi-Strauss. According to this understanding of myth, the effect of a mythical narrative is that the antinomy, the vertigo of logical ambivalence, is *contained,* that is to say, held together without really being resolved. Seen in this light, Müller's passage of thought—from study of language to "mythology in the narrower sense"—amounts to mythologizing of his own philological discourse. But even at this critical juncture where philology is suddenly exchanged for psychology, words exchanged for things, it is precisely his *philological* thesis—that accidents of language, such as puns, propel our thought—that holds sway. Meanwhile the reader, witnessing such a strange passage, is left wondering all the more how seriously one could count on the power of this Latin pun, unsure, that is, as to whether this "play" ultimately has the effect of naming and legitimating the transgressive passage, or, on the contrary, of discrediting it. Playful and figurative, this punning phrase is the sign under which Müller lets himself succumb to the powerful shadow of language.

75

•   •

It appears that the shadow of language never lifted from his German workshop; in point of fact, it remained the most powerful figure. For Müller's quest for the literal/proper signification enthralled him all the more in the umbrage of the figurative and the mythic, as his own discursive practice demonstrates. Even as he speaks of the sun—"the being in nature" par excellence, whose essence he now postulates *before* language—he speaks only in figures. The quintessential power of the sun, in Müller's rhetorical configuration, is always heralded and represented by the image of the dawn. The dawn is the luminous young god who precipitously emerges at the rim of reality, who rolls away and vanquishes the dark of the night. Thus it happens that, every time, the ineluctable accompaniment and accomplice of the sun—the being of beings—turns out to be the figure of figures, the shadow.

Perhaps nothing short of the myth of the sun would have sufficed for the rumination of a philologist such as Max Müller. In the somber nave of his biblioworkshop—a veritable mausoleum of dead words—he continued to contemplate the possibility of pure, literal signification, free of figures, beyond all names, something like a primordial sign announcing its own origin, a perfect word of shadowless illumination.

History on a Mystic Writing Pad: Freud Refounds Time

Freud's Beginnings

76 TODAY, WHEN WE HEAR the opinion that the notion of origin, together with that of the unilinear organization of time, has become altogether problematic, no other name is more readily evoked than that of Sigmund Freud. Whether it is blame or credit that we ascribe to him for this recent intellectual disturbance, his deeds are well known: Freud, the discoverer of such strange phenomena as "diphasic onset" of sexuality and "deferred action" *[Nachträglichkeit]*; Freud, who rendered every *ur-* (primal) word— *Urszene, Urphantasie, Urverdrängung*[1]—constitutionally unstable. Let it be noted, incidentally, that he also tried to explain the origin of internal time consciousness, no less, by means of an analogy with a child's toy.[2]

Given this publicity in recent decades, it is all the more noteworthy that there exists another kind of indictment—this one somewhat older but unabated, and clearly accusatory—namely, that Freud in fact went after origins and got them outrageously wrong.

Arguably, the foremost among Freud's outrageous claims concerning origins is the famous story beginning with "once upon a time,"[3] the one about brothers killing and eating their father because of their desire to marry their mothers and sisters, the tale told in the last essay of *Totem and Taboo*. That, presumably, was to account for the origin not only of religion but of law, morality, kinship rules—in short, the origin of civilization itself.

Although this peculiar tale is not the whole story of *Totem and Taboo*, the critics were surely right in seeing in it the whole *point* of the story, a climactic moment in Freud's carefully crafted argument. Being the boldest among his explicit statements concerning the origin of religion, this astonishing parricidal episode set the tone for what was to be known as

"Freud's theory of religion." Whether or not Freud really had such a theory, there is nothing to indicate that he at any later time or in any way wished to retreat from what he said in this controversial text. On the contrary, he celebrated the principal argument of *Totem and Taboo* by mounting upon it an even more daring speculation when, in 1938, he published from his deathbed his last work on the subject of religion, *Moses and Monotheism*.

In the Beginning . . . the Ends of *Totem and Taboo*

Freud's beginnings are indeed many. To many of the conundrums he sought to resolve, he gave an answer in the form of an origin. This should come as no surprise if we take into account, for instance, the following popular rendition of what psychoanalysis is about: "Psychoanalysis is a science which is based upon narration, upon telling. Its principle of explanation consists in getting the story told—somehow, anyhow—in order to discover how it begins."[4] And Freud himself stated, "In my search for the pathogenic situations in which the repressions of sexuality had set in and in which the symptoms, as substitutes for what was repressed, had had their origin, I was carried further and further back into the patient's life and ended by reaching the first years of his childhood."[5]

That psychoanalysis attempts to lead back, even though in a sinuous way, to an origin thus appears to be a matter taken for granted. Whatever the ultimate goal of such backward paths may be, it has been suggested, *ana*lysis, by definition or at least by etymology, means a certain movement backward, "progress in regression, [going] back ever farther toward infancy, farther toward the beginning."[6] Or so it seems.

First of all, there are "beginnings" that are most immediately pertinent for Freud as a practicing analyst. If each individual illness of his psychoneurotic patients must be unraveled into a narratable, or almost narratable sequence of events, such a sequence, it would seem, has to have a beginning. At another level, for years Freud sought to classify various types of mental disorders in terms of their distinct etiology, that is, in terms of the structures of their origination. These probes at the diagnostic level further led Freud and psychoanalysis to speculate on the origin of sexuality itself—not only the derivation of adult sexuality from infantile sexuality, but more fundamentally, the origination of sexuality as such. As we shall see, this origination takes the form of a very specific sort of departure from the pregiven order of human organisms, that is, a deviation from instinct *[Instinkt]* proper.

But in the last analysis, among all these beginnings, none is more fundamental, more seminal, and for that reason more problematic, than the prehistoric murder of the primal father, upon whose dead body all the *ur*moments of the subsequent histories, collective or individual, finally seem to converge. It appears that the unresolved opacity of each beginning obscurely refers back to that origin of origins. This proto-origin, moreover, is depicted as an *event* rather than an atemporal state before all events. It is a matter of "one day," of "once upon a time," even though, to be sure, for us who live in the subsequent histories, this "one day" might as well be "the first day."

The extent of the shock effect caused by the narrative of parricide may be measured by the fact that, when it comes to the question of "Freud and religion," eyes are repeatedly averted from this glaringly obvious focal point in favor of some others. The result is that what receives more attention is not this scandalous story but Freud's later, more "humanistic"—if also more pessimistic—essays, *The Future of an Illusion* and *Civilization and Its Discontents*.[7] (This seems to be an especially prevalent phenomenon in the classroom when it comes to the most typical Freud reading assignments.) This shift in emphasis, however, goes generally against Freud's own appraisal of these texts. Admittedly, in the final days of writing *Totem and Taboo* also, Freud confessed that he was unhappy with the result; but his unhappiness was a matter of habitual doubt and discomfort that attended him at the completion of every major work—a factor which often caused delay in publication, sometimes for years. But once published, Freud always counted *Totem* among the most important of the works he had ever written, especially the fourth essay containing the parricidal episode he considered "his best-written work."[8] In contrast, he consistently derogated both *Future* and *Civilization,* branding them as "childish" and "banal."[9]

If the truths in these popular books are banal and even contrary to Freud's true professional views, whatever it is that constitutes the kernel of *Totem and Taboo*—a historical fact? a myth?—is, in a word, incredible. This evasive narrative of scarcely half a page in length is inserted with all the tentativeness and ambiguity of its fairy-tale inception, protected and qualified, moreover, by a lengthy footnote at the end. This brief narrative has been a stumbling block for generations of readers. On the other hand, as it is said from of old, a missed step in the ordinary course of thinking could be the beginning of philosophy; perhaps by the same token, this slight and seemingly unsurmountable hump in the Freudian text may be a moment of singular opportunity, perhaps a beginning of the long road to "understanding Freud." Although the present reading may carry us only so far, we may be certain of one thing: this bewildering crux of *Totem and Taboo* is inextricably tied to the gist of psychoanalytic theory. And it is just for this reason, Freud might say, that it is more prone to meet resistance and repression. As Freud states in many occasions, anything having to do *essentially* with psychoanalysis is hard to take in.

•   •

In that habitual averting of the eye from *Totem and Taboo*, one may in fact detect something resembling the mechanism of defense *[Abwehr]*, or more precisely, something indicative of "disavowal" *[Verleugnung]*. Shocked, rubbing one's eyes in disbelief, one goes on to act as if one saw nothing, or rather, one goes on to substitute something else in the place of what was seen, or what was missing from the scene. But the reader is nonetheless affected in some way; perhaps it has struck a chord *elsewhere*, somewhere other than where the reader thought Freud was pointing; but where is he pointing anyway?

The ambivalent, possibly duplicitous response to Freud's work was typical even of his earliest reviewers, especially when they dared to address themselves to *Totem and Taboo*, a text in which Freud's stakes were exceedingly high. For instance, consider the reaction of the young Alfred Kroeber, soon to be an eminent American anthropologist hailing from Berkeley, California. Written in 1920, Kroeber's review of *Totem and Taboo* seems on balance negative, if we take into account, that is, all eleven of his objections, any one of which appears rather damaging, if not to say fatal. Those objections are raised primarily from the ethnologist's point of view, the standpoint which by right he represents. But here is one among the exemplary sentences reflecting Kroeber's judgment: "This book is keen without orderliness, intricately rather than closely reasoned, and endowed with an unsubstantiated convincingness."[10]

Apparently, the reviewer distrusts the very compelling power of the text; he finds Freud's argument suspect, above all because he feels that Freud does not reveal his true objective until the very end; once this objective—which, for Kroeber, can be nothing other than the account of the murderous prehistory of the humankind—is identified, the critic is quick to declare the whole argument a failure. And yet, he goes on to say, "with all the essential failure of its finally avowed purpose, the book is an important and valuable contribution" [53]. And further, "However precipitate [Freud's] entry into anthropology and however flimsy some of his syntheses, he brings to bear keen insight, a fecund imagination, and above all a point of view which henceforth can never be ignored without stultification" [55]. In sum, Kroeber's judgment seems to run something like this: it is totally unfounded, but it is convincing; it seems extremely unlikely that the scene Freud visualized could have taken place, but for all that his "point of view" is so keen that one would be a fool ("stultified") not to acknowledge its "value." The rest is for us to wonder, How do we calculate such a prodigious value? What does Kroeber see Freud seeing, from the point of view that seems to see nothing but a false scene?

What is striking here first of all is this ambivalent response of disbelief and profound impression at the same time, this state of being taken in and taken aback by the argument which this reviewer calls "insidious," but which he also admits is capable of producing "convincing" results that are highly instructive without being true. What is exemplary about Kroeber's review, in other words, is this very propensity of Freud's *récit* to astonish and impress, just at the time its reality is being denied. This scene of Kroeber encountering Freud is emblematic, to be sure, because this is not the only place where Freud surprises his readers with an account of an incredible scene. This, however, is not merely to draw attention to the now widely accepted opinion concerning Freud, that he was a literary genius and master plotter who is given to orchestrating a high drama of suspense culminating in a breathtaking disclosure.[11] While it is certainly true that Freud's rhetorical gifts are considerable, something very much other than a sheer dramatic skill seems to be involved in producing this remarkable effect. And if this something concerns the nature of psychoanalysis in a fundamental way, before we can be trusted to ponder whether Freud got the origin of religion wrong or whether he made the whole business questionable, there is a certain task incumbent upon us. To wit, we must ascertain the status of *Totem and Taboo*, and especially the status of the amazing scene of the murder, without taking leave of the psychoanalytic theory, but on the contrary, by focusing our attention on the extent to which this scene participates in Freud's theory formation. For with all the unbelievable drama it contains, *Totem and Taboo* remains a singular and incomparably pivotal text linking psychoanalysis to the subject of religion.

· ·

Ultimately, it appears, what we should really like to know is the *status* of this momentous event. Did it happen, or did it not? Call it ontological or epistemological, this is the query in its most unadorned presentation. Over the years, critics have variously cast this question into more nuanced formulations in the hopes of overcoming the impasse and resolving the issue once and for all. Some of the more familiar formulations include: "Is it history, or is it a myth?" "Is it a fact, or a fiction?" "Is it an actual occurrence in time, or is it a structure in phantasy?" What is most remarkable about the situation is that Freud's own answer remains conspicuously inconclusive, notwithstanding the fact that he does offer, in a way, his last word: "without laying claim to any finality of judgement, I think that in the case before us it may safely be assumed that . . . ."

But before we get to that last word, let us note that this closing statement of *Totem and Taboo* is pronounced as a solution to a sticky situation ensuing from the basic premise of Freud's main argument developed in the book, namely, the analogy between primitives and neurotics. ("As with the neurotic, so with the primitive.") Psychoanalysis knows that neurotics, more often than not, suffer from an excessive and unruly sense of guilt not on account of some deed actually committed by them but one merely desired and fantasized. The question then arises, Did the prehistoric people, just as the neurotic ones are apt to do, take their desire or fantasy for a deed and suffer as a result all the consequences of the imagined action as if it had been committed in reality? Or, did they—as the unbridled savages that they were, living in the condition *before* there was any law—for once commit the act, thereby bringing about the lasting psychic effect on the subsequent humanity?

"Here we are faced by a decision," so Freud tells us, "which is indeed no easy one." It is here also, however, that he quickly moves to undercut the legs on which this difficult decision might stand: "First, however," says Freud, "it must be confessed that the decision, which may seem fundamental to other people, does not in our judgement affect the heart of the matter. If wishes and impulses have the full value of facts for primitive men, it is our business to give their attitude our understanding attention instead of correcting it in accordance with our own standards" [160].

"Our standards" are the standard of reality, or, as Freud puts it more precisely, of "material (or historical, or factual) reality," in contradistinction from "psychical reality." On the other hand, "the heart of the matter" is less clear, though what probably comes most readily to mind is the *practical* matter of analytic procedure. By advocating that "we" give more attention to the reality of the primitive-neurotic instead of denying or devaluing it in the face of "our" reality, Freud seems to assume the position of the concerned clinician, whose cardinal duty is to deal with this mental fact, whether it actually refers to a real (material) event or only to an imagined one. As an analyst tending symptoms (that is, psychic effects and reaction formations) that are eminently real, he suggests here as elsewhere,[12] the material reality-status of the deed in question is, ultimately, immaterial.

Yet, since this advocacy comes so late in the text, the reader may very well be surprised by Freud's sudden shift in posture here. Much as he is entitled to speak in the name of pseudoclinical concerns, this is not the position of the author who has carried out the argument up to this point in *Totem and Taboo*. This author, above all, has been pursuing the primordial catastrophe that explains in one fell swoop a vast, global history, and he has been persuading us that the shrouded mystery of the prehistoric time, whatever it might have been, is at the core of today's neurotics' fantasies, of those neurotics who are seldom found privy to the monstrous acts that they imagine as their own deeds.

Be that as it may, this is not where Freud finally rests his case anyway. Having reminded the reader of this point—that is, that it makes no differ-

81

ence "for us" psychoanalysts, one way or other—Freud goes on to reassess the primitive-neurotic analogy itself, which has been the driving force of his principal argument, and which, as he comments at this point, "led us into our present uncertainty." Freud's reevaluation of the analogy yields the following observations. First, "it is not accurate to say that obsessional neurotics, weighted down under the burden of an excessive morality, are defending themselves only against *psychical* reality and are punishing themselves for impulses which were merely *felt. Historical* reality has a share in the matter as well. In their childhood they had these evil impulses pure and simple, and turned them into acts so far as the impotence of childhood allowed. [160–61].

For Freud, the existence of such evil *impulses* and murderous *desires* is beyond doubt; he thought he saw them every day on his couch in distorted forms, as well as in the behavior of his own children and grandchildren "pure and simple," and those children, for all we know, were irreproachably "normal." The question is whether, or when, such an impulse could have been carried out into an actual—that is to say, "material"—deed. Regarding the particular deed that is at issue in *Totem and Taboo*—sons murdering the father—it is not merely a question of some anomalous occurrences, such as those we might find from time to time in the tabloids, but rather an act most fundamental and constitutional, such that all subsequent parricides, whenever they occur, are in some sense unconscious reenactments of this primal deed, and such that those tabloid murders are exceptional occurrences only in the sense that they reenact the common legacy of the species not only in "thought" but by "acting out."

In short, the passage just quoted reminds the reader that, although the memory that afflicts the adult neurotics is for the most part an "evil" committed only in fantasy, in our childhood, when we knew little inhibition, we are all likely to have acted out these impulses straight, and that the only thing that saved us from becoming actual murderers and cannibals was our fortunately inadequate ability to carry it out to its desired end.[13] This reflection leads Freud to conclude that "the analogy between primitive men and neurotics will therefore be far more fully established if we suppose that in the former instance, too, psychical reality—as to the form taken by which we are in no doubt—coincided at the beginning with factual reality: that primitive men actually *did* what all the evidence shows that they intended to do" [161].

Yet the very next paragraph—which happens to be the last of the book as well—moves to break up the analogy, although this ultimately leads to the same verdict: "Nor must we let ourselves be influenced too far in our judgement of primitive men by the analogy of neurotics. . . . neurotics are above all *inhibited* in their actions: with them the thought is a complete substitute for the deed. Primitive men, on the other hand, are *uninhibited:* thought passes directly into action. With them it is rather the deed that is a substitute for the thought" [162]. Either way—whether we let ourselves be carried very far by the analogy or stop short—we seem to come to the same conclusion. "And that is why, without laying claim to any finality of judgement, I think that in the case before us it may safely be assumed that 'in the beginning was the Deed' " [162]. So ends *Totem and Taboo.*

The circumspect ("without laying claim to any finality of judge-ment") yet firm ("it may be safely assumed") conclusion, however, seems to leave many readers confounded, who cannot but notice the strange transposition rapidly taking place here at the very last. To be sure, this is not exactly a telos anticipated by a scientific treatise, or a textbook case of Q.E.D. As it happens, this is a quotation from a literary author, the one to whom Freud is in the habit of referring simply as *the Poet [der Dichter],* Goethe. This recalls one of Freud's characteristic rhetorical moves, with which he takes leave of science in order to appeal reverently to the well-nigh divine authority of art, or *Dichtung* [poetry, creative literature]. On such occasions Freud implies something to this effect: when science drags its sure but prosaic foot, art prances ahead, announcing the truth that is only dreamt of by the poet, yet unassured. In other words, here, science bows to literature, and "facts" slip into a veritable realm of "fiction."

83

Moreover, this particular literary quotation contains an additional momentum for further twists and turns. We recall that the statement is from *Faust,* where, shortly before the appearance of Mephistopheles, Faust, the heroic seeker of knowledge, is grappling with a particularly dif-ficult theological problem. Unwilling to accede such preeminence to "Word" *[Wort],* the Doctor hazards an alternative "translation" of what was really "In the Beginning." The statement itself is therefore a torsion, a dangerous twist of the pristine words of the holiest of books. Here, it is given a double twist, first by Goethe-Faust who substitutes *Tat* [deed] for *Wort* [word], and then by Freud who chooses to tag this gravely modified biblical opener at the close of his text. Suspecting, no doubt, some illicit deals in this series of turnabouts, some of Freud's readers have been wary of the "conclusion," others simply incredulous.

The treacherous ease of transition from "science" to "literature" is but one indication of the complicity or communicability between the terms of opposition variously set up to resolve the cardinal question of *Totem and Taboo:* Did it happen, or did it not? The opposition of "myth" to "history" is notoriously difficult to maintain. Between "fact" and "fic-tion" lies a strange complicity. It might be noted that these contrasting terms lead back etymologically to "doing/making" *[factus, facere]* and "shaping/fashioning" *[fictus, fingere]* respectively, thus confounding our usual assumption that "facts" are found in reality whereas "fictions" are "made up."[14] Instead, their etymologies seem to suggest that someone's hand is in them both. Indeed, was it not *the Poet* himself who made a most eloquent case as to how "poetry" *[Dichtung]* will have to be commingled with "truth" *[Wahrheit]* in order for a life—his life, for instance—to be narratable?[15]

But of course, at this particular juncture in *Totem and Taboo,* more than narratability is at stake.

What, then, are we to make of Freud's "last word," this "deed," and the wayward path leading up to it? In the ensuing sections, we will be making a detour of sorts, dwelling in some neighboring texts, hoping to gain some illumination from the proximation and analogies. Yet, we shall expect to find our way back to this very question at the end of a round-about journey; for, as we shall see, no analogy in Freud would ever remain a matter of mere parallels; invariably, we will come upon a crossroads.

Application, Analogy, Archaeology

84

There is a warning in the author's preface to *Totem and Taboo:*

> The four essays collected in these pages aim at arousing the interest of a fairly wide circle of educated readers, but they cannot in fact be understood and appreciated except by those few who are no longer strangers to the essential nature of psycho-analysis. They seek to bridge the gap between students of such subjects as social anthropology, philology and folklore on the one hand, and psychoanalysis on the other. Yet they cannot offer to either side what each lacks. [xiii]

Today, there may be few who regard themselves as a total stranger to psychoanalysis, yet knowing its "essential nature" is perhaps another matter. What did Freud have in mind exactly, in 1913, at the time of this pronouncement? Whatever it was, the essence of psychoanalysis is not spelt out in these four essays, which are in fact more generous with the ethnographic information and citations—such as they were available at the time to amateurs like Freud—than with psychoanalytic exposition. It appears that the general readers are merely to have their interest aroused and must perforce renounce satisfaction so long as they are unaided by other sources in reading this book.

To take this caveat seriously, it seems, one would have to perform a kind of cross-reading between the two wings of the psychoanalytic publication, which might be respectively termed the work of "psychoanalysis proper" on the one hand and that of "application" on the other. Yet the task before us is something more than a mere balancing act between different wings of psychoanalysis. Nor is it a matter only of becoming better informed about the theoretical aspect of psychoanalysis in order to judge better the legitimacy of its application to subjects such as religion. As we shall see presently, the relation between psychoanalytic theory and the general study of culture and history is not what Freud's own rhetoric sometimes leads us to believe. One might assume that "applications" are secondary, derivative sort of activities which, as significant as they may be to humanistic interests, strictly speaking, the psychoanalytic theory could do without. But once the overall record of Freud's engagement with the theory and practice of psychoanalysis is viewed comprehensively, it is the notion of application itself—along with the notion of analogy—that comes to be too interesting to lay to rest in its conventional meaning.

• •

To return to Freud's rhetoric in the preface to *Totem and Taboo*, Freud appears to imply that entertaining the question of religion means for him something of an extraterritorial venture. It is construed as a task which moved him from the clinical context of psychoanalysis proper to a more general area of inquiry, to the realm of *Geist* overall. He calls this move an instance of *application [Anwendung]*, and such instances are to be kept distinct from the more technical and theoretical endeavors of psychoanalysis. Freud maintained and institutionalized this differentiation, first of all, by means of the two principal journals he established for the International Psychoanalytic Association:[16] on the one hand, *Internationale Zeitschrift für ärztliche Psychoanalyse*, whose title speaks for itself,[17] and on the other, a journal named after a certain novel, *Imago*, which also carried a subtitle *Zeitschrift für die Anwendung der Psychoanalyse auf die Geisteswissenschaften*.[18] As Freud commented sometime later, the latter publication was "designed exclusively for the application of psychoanalysis to the mental sciences" *[ausschließlich für die Anwendungen der Psychoanalyse auf die Geisteswissenschaften bestimmt]*.[19] Freud's phrasing here suggests that it was meant to accommodate the type of study in which the findings and hypotheses developed within psychoanalysis are brought to bear upon the sciences that are, strictly speaking, extrinsic to it. As is well known, Freud and his followers attempted a number of such "applications" not only in the realms of religion, mythology, and social psychology *[Völkerpsychologie]*, but also in the study of literature and of art.

85

The impression one is likely to get from a publication policy such as this is consonant with the widely accepted assumption that Freud's work on these cultural topics are extraneous to, farther afield from, and consequently less incontrovertible than, the rigorous science of the mind *[des Geistes]* that he founded.[20] But at the same time, there is much to suggest that "application" is also a natural extension of the domain of psycho-analysis itself, rather than an invasion or forcible annexation of distant foreign territories. In fact, the continuity and community of the fields traversed by Freud's "application" is evidenced by the common name that encompasses them all: *Geisteswissenschaften*. This term is nowadays usually translated as "human sciences" or "humanities," but whenever Freud mentions it the *Standard Edition* renders it more literally as "mental sciences," as if to adumbrate the legitimacy of the domestication of these "other fields" by the mental science in a more specific sense, that is, psychology.[21]

This is as much as to say that psychoanalysis from the beginning emerged as a practice comprising new entities and concepts, new rules, and new boundary formations of its own making; consequently, by its very nature psychoanalysis violates some of the most well-established demarcations of scientific "fields" and cultural "domains." Admittedly, Freud does recognize preestablished, institutionalized boundaries such as between "medical" and "lay" practices, divisions among the expertise of "physiology," "anatomy," "biology," "neurology," "psychology," and so on, and between truth-bound science *[Wissenschaft]* and creative literature *[Dichtung]*. But he does so just to the extent that these demarcations can be exploited in a new, fructifying way. His maintenance of these boundaries is tantamount to his strategy for negotiating footholds and carving out positions for his psychoanalytic practice. If we observe Freud's negotiations long enough, we may have an impression that such positions must be in some way expedient, because it is not a domain or territory circumscribed, secured and legitimized with respect to other fields or domains, but instead it is above all a stance, or a post, which could be occupied for specific strategic purposes; as such, it could be posted anywhere and, by the same token, it could be evacuated at any moment.

Whether this lack of a stable, permanent territorial settlement is a strategic advantage or, on the contrary, a lamentable condition of the nascent science facing an army of opposition—Freud complains in this latter mode frequently enough—we must recognize this fundamental mobility and interterritoriality of "psychoanalysis proper." With this in mind, let us note here, provisionally, that what is at play in the "application" of psychoanalysis to the question of religion is the full spectrum of what the term *Geist* covers: from the *mental* reality at one end to the *spiritual* one at the other, including the shady area of the go-betweens, or *ghosts*.

.   .

In this wide range of psychoanalytic application, the most powerfully operative devices are analogies or arguments based on parallels. The most prominent of the Freudian analogies exploits the presumed isomorphism between phylogenesis and ontogenesis, that is, the parallel between the prehistory of the human species and the forgotten primordium of the individual child. Of course, most of us today are well trained to be wary of any argument based on this particular analogy, which capitalizes on such figurative expressions as "infancy of human race," which doubtless smacks of some evolutionist scheme in its eighteenth- and nineteenth-century formulation. As if by reflex, the question immediately comes to the mind of the contemporary reader: Is there really such a correspondence between the species and the individual?

But the conceptual problem may run even deeper and older: What does an analogy prove? With Hume's skepticism in mind, one might bring the question to Aristotle's doorstep, the proprietor of *ratio,* and of all matters of *logos,* including *ana-logos,* argument based on proportion. Call it *ana*logy or *para*llelism, such an argument depends on a comparison taking place between here and elsewhere, between two different domains. With what power could one structure force itself upon another? Is it not something like a leap of faith that allows the argument to move between two parallel lines?

Whatever answer one may be inclined to give to such global questions, one thing that can be said about this particular analogy—phylogenesis corresponding to ontogenesis—is that it is far from being a straight argument running between two simple lines. Freud's argument comprises a complicated system of parallels, the full extent of which does not readily come into view when *Totem and Taboo* is read in isolation. To begin with, this analogy itself is a transfer from another field, namely from biology. As Freud attests, it is biology that first suggested that the development of the individual member of a species is in some significant way analogous to the development of the species as a whole.[22] Thus, by drawing parallels between biology and psychology, Freud goes on to assert that "the individual's mental development repeats the course of human development in an abbreviated form."[23]

These parallel lines, moreover, are not simply left juxtaposed. Aside form the "memory" of the parricide—an obvious point of convergence, to which we shall return later—throughout Freud's corpus, we repeatedly come across a common figure mediating between phylogenesis and ontogenesis, a locus of communion where the two sides of the analogy come to engage each other. This common locus in turn amounts to yet another analogy, another figure, another field. The field is archaeology,[24] a quintessentially chthonian endeavor. For, especially in the imagination of the

Victorian amateurs—as we have seen also in Max Müller—archaeology is an art of unearthing the dead, recovering the forgotten, and restoring them to the original world of signification; this science reconstructs the lost world long after the fact. Under the sway of this archaeological figure, each type of primordium—of the species and of the individual child— emerges as a domain of the past buried alive, as a necrotic underworld which continues to transmit nameless subterranean powers affecting the living present of the world above.

The idea is as old as psychoanalysis itself; it dates at least as far back as 1896, the year in which the name *psychoanalysis* appeared in print for the first time.[25] The following passage occurs at the point where Freud is illustrating his new clinical method, in contrast with the then-popular "anamnestic method." This latter method constructs a case history (or something like it) based only on the conscious material derived from interviews with the patient and his or her family. Freud delineates the difference in this figurative way:

88

> Imagine that an explorer arrives in a little-known region where his interest is aroused by an expanse of ruins, with remains of walls, fragments of columns, and tablets with half-effaced and unreadable inscriptions. He may content himself with inspecting what lies exposed to view, with questioning the inhabitants—perhaps semi-barbaric people—who live in the vicinity, about what tradition tells them of the history and meaning of these archaeological remains, and with noting down what they tell them—and he may then proceed on his journey. But he may act differently.

That is to say, he may act like a psychoanalyst instead, in which case,

> he may have brought picks, shovels and spades with him, and he may set the inhabitants to work with these implements. Together with them he may start upon the ruins, clear away the rubbish, and, beginning from the visible remains, uncover what is buried. If his work is crowned with success, the discoveries are self-explanatory: the ruined walls are part of the ramparts of a palace or a treasure-house; the fragments of columns can be filled out into a temple; the numerous inscriptions, which, by good luck, may be bilingual, reveal an alphabet and a language, and, when they have been deciphered and translated, yield undreamed-of information about the events of the remote past, to commemorate which the monuments were built. *Saxa loquuntur!* [Stones talk!][26]

According to this analogy, the consciousness of the neurotic patient is equivalent to the half-knowing contemporary inhabitants of the region in ruins—"perhaps semi-barbaric people"—and what the patient and his or her family members can relate to the physician concerning the origin of all this mess ("rubbish") is woefully limited. Unlike an incidental tourist satisfied with the superficial surveying of the landscape and with the inadequate communications from the contemporary inhabitants, the psychoanalyst instead digs into the ruin and induces not the inhabitants but the rocks and stones do the talking—that is, not the present consciousness of the patient but the dead inscriptions, or, the marks buried alive in him or her. Here, one would readily understand how psychoanalysis came to be popularly called "depth psychology," despite its characteristic attention to *surfaces,* despite its privileging of the seemingly insignificant details, or things that appear to be merely superficial. The "depth" of the psychoanalytic probes refers only to the metaphorical depth of the burial; it pertains to an analogical dimension *elsewhere,* located in the simile of ruins.

The alignment of the neurotic and the barbaric instructs us in another aspect of the archaeological analogy. These contemporary "barbarians" stand in a unique relation to the prehistoric people who are now lost, to those original bearers of the world now in ruins. The neurotic stands in an analogous relation to a past, the world of the child, now lost. What makes the neurotic (in comparison to "normal" adults) a specially instructive case is the same as what makes the contemporary semibarbarian (in comparison to civilized peoples) instructive: they both represent, in a particular way, the remnants of a past, for they are those who do not, cannot, get done with a past, and so they continue to preserve and embody a piece of archaic reality in a distorted *[entstellt]* manner; their past persists, often against their will or without their cognizance; they dwell upon the ruins.

89

Yet, here again, the analogy is not just a parallel. The past of the neurotic and the archaeological past begin to merge and mingle under Freud's speculative power. According to psychoanalysis, the most elemental psychic factors constituting the mind and the behaviors of the neurotic adults are an admixture not only of the legacy of the individual's experiences but also the inheritance of the race. At first glance, it seems a peculiar contention on the part of Freud that each of the principal remnants that analysis excavates from the ruinous past of the neurotic patient—the residue of reality that makes up so-called primal fantasies—belongs to both kinds of past, personal and historic. But he suggests this idea clearly enough, for instance, in this famous passage: "It seems to me quite possible that all the things that are told to us today in analysis as phantasy . . . were once real occurrences in the primaeval times of the human family, and that children in their phantasies are simply filling in the gaps in individual truth with prehistoric truth."27 So it seems that the "parallels" in fact cross here, in what is known as "complexes," the disquieting abode of primal fantasies.

When Freud reiterated his impression over forty years later, the great antiquity of the mind of the neurotic was pushed even further back, roughly by five hundred million years: "With neurotics it is as though we were in a prehistoric landscape—for instance, in the Jurassic. The great saurians are still running about; the horsetails grow as high as palms."[28]

This impression, among the last to be recorded by Freud, comprises elements of surprise, if not of shock, assuming that this is more than an idle play of fancy. After nearly half a century of psychoanalytic practice, why this image of monstrous proportion, this extravagant extension of the human psyche to a paleontological past? At the very least, one could say that even in his last days Freud was certainly not about to relinquish the line of thought he boldly put forward in 1920—in the notoriously celebrated *Beyond the Pleasure Principle*[29]—concerning the correlation between the biological, evolutionary development of species on the one hand and the successive states of human psyche at present on the other.

The element of surprise does not end here. In fact, shock and surprise—and the initial resistance to accept—is said to be endemic to the psychic excavation, regardless of what is thus being uncovered. Freud repeatedly observed in his clinical practice that the first reemergence of a remnant from the patient's past always takes the patient by surprise, eliciting a response typically of disbelief and dismay. He emphasizes that this reaction is not due to any particular content of the forgotten memory, but it is the return itself that is ghastly. In another well-known essay, "The Uncanny," he demonstrates how even the most familiar and friendly segment of one's past life can return, by the sheer fact of the return, as a peculiarly frightening apparition. If the past is necessarily the time lost and fraught with death, a fragment of the past forgotten and repressed acquires the status of the undead, or, as Freud puts it, a *revenant*, a specter.

For over four decades Freud came face to face with those apparitions—albeit mostly someone else's ghosts—on a daily basis; when he submitted himself to nine hours (sometimes as many as eleven) of analytic work, those were the hours spent observing the "ruins" spread across his couch. It was his task as an analyst to demystify these revenants for the sake of the patients, who carried those undetected aliens in their suffering body. True to his archaeological imagination, Freud on occasion called into his service the troop of his antique collection, as he explained his analytic theory to his patient:

> I then made some short observations upon *the psychological differences between the conscious and the unconscious,* and upon the fact that everything conscious was subject to a process of wearing away, while what was unconscious was relatively unchangeable; and I illustrated my remarks by pointing to the antiques standing about in my room. They were, in fact, I said, only objects found in a tomb,

and their burial had been their preservation: the destruction of Pompeii was only beginning now that it had been dug up.[30]

The analogy with archaeology and the resultant parallel between childhood and prehistory thus leads to further parallelisms, between analysis and excavation, between mental disorder and "an expanse of ruins." These figures—which are more than "mere" figures—are ever recurrent in Freud's writing from the earliest to the last. The ghost haunting the ruins, too, makes its appearance from early on; it is especially conspicuous in the essay with which Freud attempted, for the first time, an extensive application of his new science to *Geisteswissenschaften.*

Answering Calls from the Past

With "Delusions and Dreams in Jensen's *Gradiva*" (1906)[31] Freud inaugurated the psychoanalytic monograph series aptly entitled "Papers on Applied Psychology."[32] Jensen's *Gradiva,* the subject of Freud's paper, has attained certain fame—like some of Freud's patients—primarily by virtue of the fact that it was analyzed by the founding father of psychoanalysis. What made this otherwise unremarkable novella an immediately privileged object fit for analysis was, no doubt, the conspicuous presence of the archaeological figure. A veritable revenant is the principal allure of the story. The story offers these elements: an archaeologist hero; an anonymous antique fragment which cryptically points to an object of desire; mysterious signals from the underworld (dreams, apparitions) which turn out to be a call from the archaeologist's own childhood; and in the end, fortunate restoration of the undead past to the light of the living present, a process which resembles the successful completion of an analysis.

The reader attempting to plot exact psychoanalytic parallels in this novella will soon note, however, that the analogy is less than perfect, that the various positions of the analytic situation do not correspond point by point to those in the novella. To begin with, the protagonist, who suffers from delusions and dreams and, on that account, occupies the position of the patient (analysand), also plays the part of the analyst insofar as he is the one who initiates the excavation project and eventually disentangles his own past. Atypical, perhaps, but no more so than the singular status of Freud himself, who occupies the unimaginable position of the "analyst number one,"[33] the one who analyzed himself. Like Freud, this hero is fascinated by antiquity and is inexplicably drawn toward ancient cities in Italy whenever his spirits are disturbed. And this is where the story proper begins.

The archaeologist is devoted to his antiquarian science so much so that he is quite oblivious to the living present, especially to living women. In "a museum of antiquities" in Rome he comes across a certain bas-relief depicting a young woman with an "unusual and peculiarly charming gait," whose beauty he commemorates by naming her Gradiva. The hero, incidentally, also has a propensity to dream copious mantic dreams. Moved by an unnamed desire, he travels to Pompeii, where he believes the woman immortalized in the relief once lived and was buried alive on the day of the famous volcanic eruption in the year 79 C.E. At this point it is evident to all but the hero himself that his spurious scientific [wiss-enschaftliche] research travel is a thin disguise for his phantasmagoric pursuit of the dead woman, or more precisely, of her Geist. As if summoned by his frenetic call, the ancient beauty appears to him in broad daylight, in the noon hour, which in this southern region is known as "the hour of ghosts." Through a rather remarkable coincidence which another critic might have judged improbable but which served Freud all too well,[34] this archaeological remnant of a woman turns out to be the hero's long-forgotten beloved from his distant childhood, but of course not so distant as to be from the Roman antiquity, and closer to home than Pompeii, that is, from his own German town. To make it a happy ending, the two dead women, or the two women buried alive in the two kinds of past—one in historical antiquity, the other in the hero's childhood—are merged together and resurrected in a single living woman, who turns out to be the grown-up version of his childhood love. At that point, the archaeologist's scholarly training serves him well, for he manages to solve philologically the enigma of the names surrounding this double image of a woman: her name is Zoe, meaning "life" in Greek,[35] and she is also Miss Bright-Step, or Fräulein Bert(brecht)gang, alias Gradiva. The hero is thus cured by Miss Life and relieved of the delusions and necrophiliac obsession hidden behind his morbid and mortuary scientific occupation.

If the positions of the analyst and the analysand are somewhat intermixed or transposed, the story nevertheless depicts the scenario fundamental to psychoanalysis. So perfectly does the story embody the etiological plot of neurosis that, Freud admits, he developed really nothing new psychoanalytically in writing this essay; rather, he has found an unexpected confirmation of his theory in the novel by the Danish author who apparently was completely unacquainted with psychoanalysis.

In point of fact, Freud was not even the first to discover this novella for psychoanalysis, but it was one of his newly acquired followers, C. G. Jung, who drew Freud's attention to it. Jung reportedly told Ernest Jones something to the effect that Freud had written the essay "expressly to give him [Jung] pleasure."[36] The episode belongs to the earlier, felicitous days of Freud's friendship with Jung. It was also at this time that Freud published his first "incursion into the psychology of religion," an essay entitled "Obsessive Actions and Religious Practices." This paper was presented before the Vienna Psychoanalytical Society on 2 March 1907, at the "meeting at which Jung was present for the first time."[37]

·   ·

This is but an early episode in the chronicle of Freud's associations and dissociations with his disciples, a long and complicated history which adds another layer of parallelism, so to speak, to his venture into the domain of *Geisteswissenschaften*. From the start Freud's direct engagement with the question of *Geist*, and in particular with the question of religion, was precipitated, sustained, and further stimulated by his association with his colleagues, including those who were to be his future dissenters.

What these associations and dissociations produced were more than a vastly expanded range of application, more than the ramification and diversification of psychoanalysis. For it was through these struggles that Freud carried out the full articulation of what amounted to, and what he chose to call, "the essential nature of psychoanalysis." Through them, Freud made psychoanalysis truly his own.[38]

93

Jung and the so-called Zürich circle was the first major group of supporters and followers to come Freud's way from the Gentile medical profession.[39] In the half-dozen years in which this relation was happy, Freud produced three major case histories ("Little Hans," "Rat Man," and "Senatpräsident Schreber"), and was actually at work on the fourth ("Wolf-Man"),[40] all of which were to provide material for his future work on the *Geist*-related studies. By the time this fresh productive current reached the first watershed in 1913, however, the Freud-Jung alliance had thoroughly deteriorated. Thus the culminating work published that year, *Totem and Taboo*, was correctly viewed by its author as an instrument of dissolution, a catalyst for the relation already turned sour: "In the dispute with Zurich it [*Totem and Taboo*] comes at the right time to divide us as an acid does a salt."[41]

This falling out with Zürich, which, in Freud's mind, had the decisive effect of dissociating psychoanalysis from "all Aryan religiosity,"[42] did not by any means mark the end of Freud's application to the question of religion.[43] Nor did the archaeological figure lose its efficacy in this connection. What Freud affirmed with renewed rigor in the occasion of this controversy was the reality of the past buried alive, the subterranean survival of the debris of the infantile sexual drama, and the uncanny contemporaneity of the child in every adult. For Freud this presence is never a matter of innate disposition or permanent ideational constitution, but always a legacy of "once upon a time"; everything happened "one day."

Meanwhile, Jung moved the subject of religion from the sphere of temporal primordium to that of timeless universals, where certain "archetypes" can be mapped out and identified, so to speak, "phenomenologically." This move proffered to erase from religion the taint of infantile sexuality, which remains the indelible mark of everything Freudian.

Lessons of the Wolf-Man

The Judgment Day

With the publication of *Totem and Taboo,* Freud may have wished to close his case with Jung, but this apparently was not to be. In order to put the record straight in the wake of the latest disturbance, Freud quickly proceeded to write "On the History of the Psycho-Analytic Movement" (1914), the first of such histories to be recorded by the father of the movement. It has three chapters: the first recounts the ten years in which Freud was the only practitioner of the new science; the second chapter covers the next decade or so in which psychoanalysis grew and became a veritable "movement"; and the third, the time of controversies and defections. To mark the tumultuous occasion for its writing, and no doubt also to assure confidence in the future course of the movement, he prefaced the text with one of his fond phrases, this one from the coat of arms of the City of Paris, *"Fluctuat nec mergitur."*[44]

Despite its visibly contentious motives, this history attempts to strike the pose less of a polemic—in the sense of either inviting or responding to a hostile engagement—than of a forceful reassertion of authority over the psychoanalytic legacy. Freud's claim to the progenitor's prerogative is pronounced in the name of creativity and innovation: "For psychoanalysis is my creation; for ten years I was the only person who concerned himself with it, and all the dissatisfaction which the new phenomenon aroused in my contemporaries has been poured out in the form of criticism on my head. Although it is a long time now since I was the only psycho-analyst, I consider myself justified in maintaining that even today no one can know better than I do what psycho-analysis is. [*SE,* 14:7]

At the opening of the third chapter, where the account of the controversy actually begins, Freud again lets his paternal impatience show through with a particular literary flourish, as he quotes this scatological bit from his favorite author, Goethe:

> *Mach es kurz!*
> *Am Jüngsten Tag ist nur ein Furz!*
>
> [Make it short!
> On the Judgment Day it's only a fart!]

94

In its native context, in *Faust,* this cutting remark is pronounced by no less than God the Father, who of course is to preside over the *Jüngsten*— literally, "last," "youngest," "Jung-est"—Day.

In retrospect, few would doubt that precisely around the time of this altercation—roughly, the 1910s—the sire of psychoanalysis was at the height of his powers; but apparently Freud himself saw the situation then quite otherwise, and he repeatedly and publicly confessed to feeling old and weary. In point of fact, he relates in this book, it was largely for the anticipation of his own demise that the thought occurred to him in the first place to remove all the onerous responsibilities of spearheading psychoanalysis from his own person and from his home city, the deeply Catholic and incorrigibly backward Vienna, which continued to be hostile to the new science (and to its predominantly Jewish adherents); he wished to pass on this task to a more favorable clime, to "a place in the heart of Europe like Zürich," and to "a younger man, who would then as a matter of course take my place after my death" [14:42–43]. Who else, indeed, could have better fit the bill than Dr. Jung (Young) from Zürich, son of a Protestant minister, as it happens, and thereby free from any umbrageous eastern European descent?[45]   **95**

Yet no sooner had this plan for succession become public knowledge than this young man and his cohorts, as if to play out the prehistoric scenario of the parricidic overturn, began to act very much like the rebellious sons intent on defying the authority of the father of the movement. Not so coincidentally, the dissident followers contested the father over the issue of the Oedipus complex. In Freud's view, to deny the reality of this cardinal moment of infantile sexual history was tantamount to desexualizing the child and the family altogether. In fact, it would not be farfetched to suggest that this desexualizing revisionism was threatening to castrate psychoanalysis itself.

As Freud saw the matter, Jung's perfidious "modifications" of psychoanalysis amounted to something close to giving up the ghost; it was a capitulation/decapitation in the face of the complacent and censorious public of the day, who would have nothing to do with such monstrous ideas as the new science promoted, ideas about the murderous strife within the sacrosanct institution of the family, and about the sexuality of their innocent children. In this regard, Freud refers to a telling letter which he received from Jung in America, wherein the latter "boasts . . . that his modifications of psycho-analysis had overcome the resistances of many people who had hitherto refused to have anything to do with it" [58]. This alarming report of Jung's "success" indicated to Freud nothing but a sure course for regression. Therefore, despite Jung's "appeal . . . to the historic right of youth to throw off the fetters in which tyrannical age with its hidebound views seeks to bind it" [58], the father was forced to conclude, "his approach to the standpoint of the masses, his abandonment of an innovation which proved unwelcome, make it *a priori* improbable that Jung's corrected version of psycho-analysis can justly claim to be a youthful act of rebellion" [59]. In short, Jung's is a "retrograde movement" [58], since it *repudiates [verwerfen]*—in the strong, psychoanalytic sense of the term—everything really new about psychoanalysis. Thus it came to pass that Jung was denied even the honor of being banished as a rebellious son; he was declared to be no youth, no son at all.

Twice upon a Time . . .

Even after this definitive history, however, Freud is still not finished with the Jung affair. Later in the same year, he is again found writing another kind of history, very much with the same quarrel in mind. This is the celebrated case history of the Wolf-Man, officially entitled "From the History of an Infantile Neurosis." Although the intervening war delayed its publication for nearly four years, the author clearly notes the circumstance of its initial writing in a footnote at the beginning of the text: "At that time I was still freshly under the impression of the twisted re-interpretations which C. G. Jung and Alfred Adler were endeavouring to give to the findings of psychoanalysis" [*SE* 17:7].

At issue, again, was what was for Freud the very heart of psychoanalysis, the libido theory. In particular, he charged, these revisionists were undermining the reality of infantile sexuality, ascribing all erotic elements of early childhood memories to adult fantasies, and suggesting that those fantasies may not even originate in the neurotic patients themselves but rather in their analysts. The case history of the Wolf-Man was to be a positive vindication of the libido theory against all such allegations and retrograde "re-interpretations." For here is a case of an *infantile* neurosis; it demonstrates how early in childhood sexual effects show up in the form of dreams and neurotic symptoms, which are so many consequences of even earlier sexual experiences.

As we enter the text of this case history, the analysis rapidly comes to focus on one particular episode, or a scene. This scene, according to Freud, who himself analyzed the case,[46] represents the earliest point of the etiological course; it is the virtual point of inception for a protracted psychical process, which was to erupt sometime later, but still in childhood, as a neurotic disorder. This is, of course, the primal scene *[Urszene]*; its content was parental coitus, witnessed by the child (patient) at the age of one and a half. Thus the scene is primal in an overdetermined sense: not only is it situated (or posited) at the originating point of the history of the illness, this scene refers, representationally and by repetition, to the origin of the child himself, to the moment of his own conception.

Anyone who is not particularly well disposed to psychoanalysis may be incredulous as to the likelihood of the child before the age of puberty ever apprehending such matters as the connection between sexual activities and the production of babies. Here it is only to be remarked that psychoanalysis indeed was the first to show that such apprehension is not only possible, but it must be assumed to be a regular phase of the child's development. For the import of "infantile sexuality" is not only that children at a so-called tender age are already endowed with active sexuality— albeit structurally and perceptually different from adult sexuality—but they also have an active cognitive interest in all matters sexual: the origin of babies, the anatomical difference between the sexes, the real nature of coitus, childbirth, and so on. In fact, Freud observes that sexual curiosity is the earliest of children's inquiries, and that it spurs and sets the course for all future intellectual pursuits. Not that children always understand these matters correctly; typically, they take copulation to be an act of violence, childbirth is somehow confused with defecating, and perhaps most fatefully, they misunderstand the anatomical difference of the sexes.[47]

Moreover, Freud is not here making the case that the child at that very moment of observation acquired such an understanding; strictly speaking, it may not be even accurate to say that the child *experienced* this scene. For, experience/knowledge *[Erfahrung]* is not to be had in an instant, but, as its etymology (at least in German) shows, it involves traveling *[fahren]* a certain distance, and it is by way of covering this distance in time that one arrives at knowledge or at experience, properly speaking. At any rate, as far as this type of experience (that is, "witnessing" the primal scene) is concerned, this structure of delay and distance is a necessary component. The experience is not accomplished until some later moment. But more on this shortly.

•   •

An intimate connection between the Wolf-Man case and the "case" of *Totem and Taboo* can be variously rendered, not only because of their proximity in time of composition and the same express motive to argue against Jung and Adler. Above all their affinity lies in the shared structural difficulty concerning the moment of origination, the same indeterminable yet absolutely seminal status of the scene speculated or constructed in the analytic process, and, finally, the same astounding claim, pronounced by Freud, to the effect that, ultimately, it doesn't make any difference whether it *really* happened or not.

Here is a brief description of the now famous case of the Wolf-Man.

97

The patient, who was a wealthy Russian, came to Freud as a young man in early 1910, suffering for some years from an array of symptoms so incapacitating that he had to travel in the company of two attendants (a valet and a personal physician). But the case is not about this illness. It is rather about an earlier episode of neurosis (roughly, from age four to ten), which came to light in the course of the analysis. In his infancy he had been a good-natured child, but at about the age of three and a half, he became suddenly irritable and violent. The night before his fourth birthday (which is also the eve of Christmas in the Russian calendar), he has his eponymous dream—the wolf dream—and awakes in terror. This dream is remembered vividly; for some years thereafter, not only was he afraid of wolves (animals which he knew only through fairly tales and picture books), but some other animals on occasion also gave him sudden attacks of anxiety. When he was four and a half, his mother introduced him to Bible stories in the hopes of ameliorating his turbulent character. This caused him to become exceedingly pious, so much so that Freud had no difficulty in identifying the dramatically changed behavior of the child (no longer intractable but excessively conscientious) as a case of obsessional neurosis.[48] At the same time, his inordinate piety was crossed by what could only seem a totally incompatible attitude, that is, recurrent compulsive blasphemous thoughts, particularly having to do with feces and the anus. This phase of illness—although this was not recognized as such at the time—lasted till he was ten years of age. From then on he had some years of relatively "normal" childhood, until the onset of the later illness at the age of seventeen, which was precipitated by a gonorrheal infection.

This much seems to have been known fairly early on, if not at the outset of the analysis. There are other significant events that came to light in the course of analysis, which we know to have lasted more than four years. The primal scene, however, is distinct from all these other scenes in that (1) it is the earliest of the series that constitute the patient's psychical history, and as such, diagnostically and etiologically speaking, is situated as the virtual point of origination, and (2) this, unlike subsequent scenes, was not remembered spontaneously by the patient but was *constructed* by the analyst, and even at the completion of the analysis, the scene was not "reproduced as recollections," that is, the analyst's presentation of the construction was not followed by an actual remembering on the part of the patient.

But no matter, concludes Freud. In his opinion, it is not necessary that such a positive verification of the constructed scene should come in the form of a conscious recollection, because there is more than one way to remember.

> It seems to me absolutely equivalent to a recollection, if the memories are replaced (as in the present case) by dreams the analysis of

which invariably leads back to the same scene and which reproduce every portion of its content in an inexhaustible variety of new shapes. Indeed, dreaming is another kind of remembering, though one that is subject to the conditions that rule at night and to the laws of dream-formation. It is this recurrence in dreams that the patients themselves gradually acquire a profound conviction of the reality of these primal scenes, a conviction which is in no respect inferior to one based on recollection. [51]

Instead of a memory, the Wolf-Man produced dreams which confirmed, according to Freud, the reality of the primal scene. The wolf dream is naturally the most important because it happened during his childhood and because it thus constitutes part of the course of illness; but in addition, during the years of analysis the patient produced other dreams which, presumably, had the effect of indicating to Freud that his construction was correct.

Freud's analysis demonstrates that the primal scene, through a circuitous route via several fairy tales involving wolves, goats, and other figures, came to be represented [vorstellt], or rather "distorted" or (mis)represented [entstellt], in the wolf dream. The key to the primal scene, therefore, lies in this dream, which is here quoted in full:

99

"*I had dreamt that it was night and that I was lying in my bed. (My bed stood with its foot towards the window; in front of the window there was a row of old walnut trees. I know it was winter when I had the dream, and night-time.) Suddenly the window opened of its own accord, and I was terrified to see that some white wolves were sitting on the big walnut tree in front of the window. There were six or seven of them. The wolves were quite white, and looked more like foxes or sheep-dogs, for they had big tails like foxes and they had their ears pricked like dogs when they pay attention to something. In great terror, evidently of being eaten up by the wolves, I screamed* and woke up. My nurse hurried to my bed, to see what had happened to me. It took quite a long while before I was convinced that it had only been a dream; I had had such a clear and life-like picture of the window opening and the wolves sitting on the tree. At last I grew quieter, felt as though I had escaped from some danger, and went to sleep again.*" [29]

In this dream, it seems, nothing ever happens, nothing except the initial opening of the window ("of its own accord"), unless the fixed staring of the wolves can be said to be a "piece of action" in some sense. But the dreamer, during the analysis, volunteered the suggestion that this opening of the window at the beginning "must mean: 'My eyes suddenly opened.' I was asleep, therefore, and suddenly woke up, and as I woke I saw something" [34].[49] The thoughts and associations surrounding the wolves led to two fairy tales that were familiar to the dreamer at the time, one concerning the wolf and seven little goats, the other about an old wolf who lost his tail owing to the cunning of a tailor [*Schneider;* literally, cutter]. The preliminary analysis of these materials led to a familiar array of items: animals (wolves) serving as father surrogates, threat of castration, and so on.

What finally gave this dream away? Above all, the unusually vivid, persistent sense of reality that made a lasting impression upon the dreamer. As we know as a general rule of dream interpretation, not only the content of the dream, but also its framing devices, that is, the general impression reported (unusual clarity, or vagueness, "gaps," "something missing," and so on), as well as the words and statements used to report the dream, have to be interpreted as part of the meaning of the dream. Here "the lasting sense of reality" has an import of [assuring] us that . . . the dream relates to an occurrence that really took place and was not merely imagined." This is a significant indicator, especially in light of the fact that so

100   much of the dream was clothed in *fairy* tales, that is to say, in patent unreality.[50] Freud thus arrives at the assumption that "behind the content of the dream there lay some . . . unknown scene—one, that is, which had already been forgotten at the time of the dream" [33].

Once the elements of the manifest content of the dream are delineated and their associations laid upon the analytic table, the dream yields this much: *"A real occurrence—dating from a very early period—looking—immobility—sexual problems—castration—his father—something terrible"* [34]. Yet very soon after this Freud announces, "I have now reached the point at which I must abandon the support I have hitherto had from the course of the analysis. I am afraid it will also be the point at which the reader's belief will abandon me" [36].

Just at this juncture of ill boding, however, with aplomb that can only be described as rhetorical daring, Freud immediately proceeds to declare, in no uncertain terms, what this scene really was. "What sprang into activity that night out of the chaos of the dreamer's unconscious memory-traces was the picture of copulation between his parents, copulation in circumstances which were not entirely usual and were especially favorable for observation" [36], namely, "a coitus *a tergo* [from behind]" [37]. On circumstantial evidence, Freud further calculates that the scene must have occurred when the boy was one and a half years old; at the time, the child was suffering from diurnal attacks of malaria, which came around five o'clock every afternoon; he was sleeping in his cot in his parents' bedroom, when suddenly he woke and opened his eyes.

After all, Freud suggests, "there is nothing extraordinary" about such an occurrence, that young parents should ignore the presence of an infant child during their *siesta*. On the contrary, it is "entirely commonplace and *banal*" [38]. Moreover, what the child experienced and understood—and why what he saw should be so terrifying—is also something quite common and well known to psychoanalysts. The "understanding" in question concerns the possibility of castration.[51]

· ·

Somehow, then, the history—or perhaps *pre*history—of this "case" begins with the Wolf-Man in his cot, whence he was "able to see his mother's genitals as well as his father's organ; and he understood the process as well as its significance" [37]. The significance, above all, was the dreadful "reality" of castration. Specifically, the "knowledge" that follows from it: the cost of fulfilling one of his strongest desires—to identify with and to take the place of the mother and to have coitus with the father, in short, his homosexual desire for the father—is castration. For, apparently, this was the fate his mother had met. (Sometime before the wolf dream, the Wolf-Man recollects, he once was accompanying his mother as she was seeing off a physician who had come to examine her, and the boy overheard her lament over her weak physical condition, which he interpreted to be a dreaded consequence of castration.) **101**

But Freud hastens to qualify, albeit in a footnote, the nature of this "understanding" that dawned upon the boy. "I mean that he understood it at the time of the dream when he was four years old, not at the time of the observation" [37]. This signals one of the most pivotal principles of psychoanalysis: deferred action/effect, *Nachträglichkeit*. It refers to the notion, roughly, that it takes *at least two moments*, not one, to constitute an experience—at least an experience of the kind that is germane to sexuality and sexual trauma.

And now to the destination—or first destination?—of the primal scene: the Wolf-Man's nightmare. The understanding of castration came to him in a long line connecting the primal scene and the wolf dream. In other words, this *experience [Erfahrung]* was accomplished in the arc bridging the two points in time, separated by as many as two and a half years.[52]

What took place in the intervening years was not only the boy's overall development in sexual organization (or, to be precise, the emergence of genital organization), but also various episodes that left their mark. Particularly significant among the latter are: (1) the "seduction"—exposing and touching of genitals—by his sister, who was two years his senior and "very much his superior," when he was a little more than three; (2) various episodes involving his mother, his beloved nurse (Nanya), or a hated governess (including the episode with the mother just mentioned above), all of which are in themselves insignificant events but somehow suggestive, directly or indirectly, of the possibility of castration; and finally, (3) a memory that came to light only very late in the course of the analysis: a scene with a long-forgotten nursemaid by the name of Grusha. All these, together with the natural, physiological process of sexual development, prepared the way for a sudden, full comprehension of the primal scene; this "knowledge" occurred, no doubt fomented by some unnameable stirring during sleep, on the night before his fourth birthday.

This is not to say, however, that the "understanding" came about by way of a gradual, developmental course in time. For the arc that spans the distance of two and a half years, that is, the trajectory of this "experience" from start to finish, traversed something other than the exoteric time of history, something other than time, strictly speaking. Rather, it passed through that region which knows no time, the realm full of memory-traces from which nothing is ever lost, and yet is utterly timeless: the unconscious.

• •

102   Here we come up against a quandary that is not an altogether rare occurrence in reading Freud; this crossroads of doubt must be familiar even to casual readers of his texts. Here is the predicament: if the unconscious is that *other place* where such incredible—if not to say improbable—workings of some long-distance communication between times/minds separated by years, or where such telegraphic transmission of undecipherable "impressions" from one point of sexual development to another is indeed taking place, does it not mean that the unconscious, as well as the science loyal to its working, is always beguiling the ordinary course of time, thus distracting and deceiving consciousness? Where is the foothold of such a science? If the unconscious is tantamount to the alibi of psychoanalysis, where could one stand to articulate one's doubt concerning psychoanalysis's account of the unconscious's working, or concerning psychoanalysis's way of conducting commerce with the unconscious?

The skeptical would-be outsider to psychoanalysis finds herself in an untenable position, for it would be difficult for her to deny summarily the "reality" of the unconscious in the world as we know it, given the overwhelming infiltration of the psychoanalytically generated discourse into our everyday world—global, local, and domestic.[53] The difficulty is compounded when she realizes that one of the domains in which the standpoint of doubt is most rigorously and energetically incorporated, put to work, and made productive, is none other than psychoanalysis itself.

• •

Let us now focus on the doubt concerning the "reality" of the primal scene. Freud has already established that such an episode could have easily happened. "The content of the scene cannot therefore in itself be an argument against its credibility." Rather,

> doubts as to its probability will turn upon three other points: whether a child at the tender age of one and a half could be in a position to take in the perceptions of such a complicated process and to preserve them so accurately in his unconscious; secondly, whether it is possible at the age of four for a deferred revision of the impressions so received to penetrate the understanding; and finally, whether any procedure could succeed in bringing into consciousness coherently and convincingly the details of a scene of this kind which had been experienced and understood in such circumstances. [38]

All three "points of doubt" have to do, ultimately, with the nature of the unconscious. For this reason, it may be profitable for us to consider possible psychoanalytically informed responses to these doubts, even before we turn to Freud's own rebuttal.

The first doubt mentioned above raises the issue of the unconscious' ability to record and retain, with such accuracy, an occurrence so early in life. As we recall, the infant observer did not, there and then, come to an "understanding" of what was seen. Rather, in that moment of observation, the scene by-passed the conscious cognitive faculty and was directly registered in the unconscious. In point of fact, Freud comments, the separation—of consciousness as we know it from the general psychical body called the unconscious—could have hardly been accomplished at the time.

This issue touches fundamentally on the nature of the unconscious, as well as on the foundations of psychoanalysis. For much of psychoanalysis is constructed on the notion (derived from the interpretation of dreams and other paranormal occurrences) that memory is by its very nature unconscious, that memory traces which constitute the unconscious are not just durable but absolutely unerasable. Nothing is ever lost from the unconscious; what we call "forgetting" is a failure—for one complicated reason or another—for a memory trace to be retrieved and brought to consciousness at will.

In the present case, the verity of the memory is in its effects. And these effects enlisted by Freud are the wolf dream, above all, but also numerous other episodes, fantasies, and dreams. For all of these, he claims and demonstrates, the "primal scene" holds a definitive explanatory power.[54]

The second point of doubt has to do with the "bridging" of the two

103

points of experience, between the primal scene and the night of the dream. Is such a comprehension possible, even at the age of four? Here it is to be recalled that the question has less to do with the cognitive, conscious understanding in the adult sense than a certain "penetration," not how an impression received long ago may be elevated to the level of conscious knowledge governed by universal, socially shared modes of verbal representation.[55] Rather, the question is how this memory can enter the psychical complex of the child besieged by the crisis of the four-year-old at the threshold of the so-called genital sexual organization and produce certain effects.

Produce it did, and the result was the nightmare. It is evident that the "penetration" into "understanding" took place in the domain of the unconscious; and no sooner did it enter consciousness proper than this memory, this "knowledge," was thoroughly *entstellt* [distorted, misrepresented], having been turned into an improbable image of a pack of wolves up on a tree with fluffy tails like foxes. It was not until two decades later, and only under rigorous analytic interrogation, that this knowledge offered itself to consciousness in the strict sense.

The third point of doubt questions this very ability of psychoanalysis to produce such a knowledge and to bring it to its ultimate destination: the critical consciousness of science. If indeed the unconscious is the domain, hitherto unknown, of such extraordinary, undreamt-of mental processes, how is it that Freud could possibly retrieve from this primeval jungle of a memory bank (someone else's jungle at that) what was thrown into it and presumed lost from the earliest days of childhood?

Of the three, this last is the most serious, most fundamental doubt, and it should be by no means an easy one for Freud to answer. As regards the Wolf-Man case, however, he says summarily that, after years of hands-on analytic work with the patient,[56] he finally had an analytic breakthrough, and *he* is convinced.[57] And it is his hope that this case history will allow the reader to share in, even if to an incomparably reduced degree, something of this conviction. Yet Freud also expresses his doubt as to how convincing this could possibly be to the reader who has not done the analysis herself,[58] and here and there he begs the reader to grant him a *"provisional* belief in the reality" of what he describes so that he can get on with the rest of the case history.[59]

This difficulty probably also explains Freud's repeated appeal to "facts"[60] and to "observation" supposedly unaffected by his own person, and conversely, his periodic declaration that he is disinclined to theorize and to speculate. Of course, all of this has struck many of his readers as slightly disingenuous or else seems to them like an unwelcome residue of the positivist streak in Freud the author. For instance, we see a statement like this posted at the outset:

104

Readers may at all events rest assured that I myself am only reporting what I came upon as an independent experience, uninfluenced
by my expectation. So that there was nothing left for me but to remember the wise saying that there are more things in heaven and
earth than are dreamed of in our philosophy. Anyone who could
succeed in eliminating his pre-existing convictions even more thoroughly could no doubt discover even more such things. [12]

Our likely reaction to a pronouncement of this sort is, no doubt, consternation. Surely, such a flat-footed insistence on the so-called objectivity of
observation is thoroughly incongruous with the extraordinary subtlety of
a mind such as his, not to mention that it harmonizes rather badly with
what psychoanalysis itself has to say on the nature of observation: that
the act of observation is extremely *interested* and often anxiety ridden, by
its very nature and from the beginning.

It seems that Freud did not want the unconscious to be his alibi, whatever the cost. It is the task of psychoanalysis, a science he invented, to
make the unconscious offer up its truth; it cannot hold the unconscious
hostage for its own legitimation. What else is there to do, then, but to
appeal to the opposite realm: the public, the open, the plainly visible to
everyone—in short, consciousness at its most overt—and to whatever
forces that might gather under the (prepsychoanalytic) flag of "observation."

Yet this is but an appeal. Freud's own business is located elsewhere. In
the course of narrating this case history, he returns time and again to various "points of doubt," so that he may tap their analytic and theoretical
potentials. As it happens, one of these spots responded to his probing—
for an extraordinary result.

Question of Reality

In Freud's rhetoric, the voice of doubt is often contrived to issue from the
position of another. When the doubt in question concerns infantile sexuality, it usually comes from the direction of his former disciples or their
acolytes, Jung and Adler above all. Even though it might be said that, at
bottom, what Freud is really battling against is his own doubt, given the
polemicodramatic context of his writing, there is little surprise that his
narrative scheme should take this form: doubt must be vanquished and
the brave new theory championed. While Freud may have a high degree of
tolerance for pregnant obscurity, when it comes to the state of doubt, that
is another matter. Doubt often signals to him something suspect, and succumbing to it, a failure of nerve, which leads to a failure of analysis. For
one of the lessons he has learnt from countless analytic situations is that

105

doubt expressed by the patient is invariably a sign of resistance, especially prevalent among obsessional neurotics.[61] By the same token, however, such faltering hesitancy of thought, like the most obstinate of symptoms, can be highly instructive for a tenacious analyst who resolves "to behave as 'timelessly' as the unconscious itself" [17:10].

In the chapter following the daring disclosure of the primal scene—whose palpable support so far does not add up to much more than the child's memory of a nightmare—Freud interrupts the regular course of narration and pauses to address the anticipated incredulity of his readers. At the beginning of this polemical interlude entitled "A Few Discussions," he rehearses the three types of doubt, which have been quoted previously. As mentioned before, he bruskly dismisses the third doubt on the grounds that it is "purely one of fact. Anyone who will take the trouble of pursuing an analysis into these depths by means of the prescribed technique will convince himself that it is decidedly possible [for psychoanalysis to bring into consciousness the details of an unconscious scene]" [48]. He then proceeds to address the first two, which he characterizes as doubts stemming from "a low estimate of the importance of early infantile impressions" [49]. He prepares to face these doubts by way of entertaining an alternative view of the primal scene, a version different from the one he has hitherto promoted:

> The view, then, that we are putting up for discussion is as follows. It maintains that scenes from early infancy, such as are brought up by an exhaustive analysis of neuroses (as, for instance, in the present case), are not reproductions of real occurrences, to which it is possible to ascribe an influence over the course of the patient's later life and over the formation of his symptoms. It considers them rather as products of the imagination [Phantasiebildungen], which find their instigation in mature life, which are intended to serve as some kind of symbolic representation of real wishes and interests, and which owe their origin to a regressive tendency, to a turning-away from the tasks of the present. [49]

The question, then, concerns at the outset the process of "retrospective phantasying" [Zurückphantasieren],[62] and the extent to which such a retroaction contributes to the formation of a psychical history. If the adult neurotic, when reporting a supposed sexual trauma from early childhood, is merely projecting back more recent experiences and problems to a distant childhood event, real or imagined, and in the course of this backward projection sexualizes the episode, then there is no need, Freud's adversary could argue, to bring anything so novel and objectionable as "infantile sexuality," no need for any *real* primal scene with its sexual content and its sexual effects.

It is evident why the Wolf-Man case proffered a singular opportunity for Freud, in the face of these skeptics, to vindicate his theory of infantile sexuality in its most fundamental form. The child of four is hardly to be credited for being burdened by a task in his contemporary life from which he seeks flight into (even earlier) childhood fantasies. The relative paucity of life experience—from whose resources, after all, fantasies are largely generated—also makes it less likely that the child could have concocted the scene entirely out of his imagination.[63] All in all, "the enormous shortening of the interval between the outbreak of the neurosis and the date of the childhood experiences which are under discussion *reduces to the narrowest limits the regressive part of the causation, while it brings into full view the portion of it which operates in a forward direction*, the influence of earlier impressions. The present case history will, I hope, give a clear picture of this position of things" [55; emphasis added].

Here Freud underscores the movement *forward* in the psychical history, notwithstanding the fact that, as we have just learnt, the strange warping of time called deferred action *[Nachträglichkeit]* is an essential factor in the formation of such a history. The belatedness of the "supplementary effect" (another possible translation of the same term) is not the same as regressiveness or a "retroeffect"; the effect does not revert backward in time.[64] It seems that Jung and others are in error because they completely confound these two processes. Or, as Freud puts it, their arguments rely on the "principle of *pars pro toto*," that is, they take the local phenomenon of regressive fantasy and generalize it to the extent that it is made to account for the entire formation of the neurotic history. In this confusion, infantile sexuality itself becomes something of a retrogressive fantasy, something not real.

In contrast, in Freud's reconstruction of the case history, the crux of the matter remains very much lodged in the primal scene, in its strategic position as the hidden point of inception for a whole series of occurrences which, in sum, amount to an infantile neurosis. The wolf dream is the second point of inception; this latter point marks the manifest beginning of the neurosis, since it is confirmed both by the patient and by the tradition in his family that his wolf phobia began in the night of the dream. Between the first and the second points of inception, this important relation obtains: the primal scene accounts for the dream, or, conversely, the dream testifies to the "reality" of the primal scene.

Freud, the founder of the *original* psychoanalysis, also the defender of the truth of infantile sexuality, was here prepared to put his own professional credibility on the line. Whereupon, with an unusual terseness, he offers the following uncompromising proposition: "either the analysis based on the neurosis in his childhood is all a piece of nonsense from start to finish, or everything took place just as I have described it above" [56].

Here, then, is what seems to be Freud's ultimatum: either accept as cogent the primal scene and what follows from it, or else the whole story will fall apart into bits and pieces of accidental occurrences; if the latter, there would be no story to tell, no history to account for.

. .

Yet not so long after this statement we come across a long parenthetical addendum, which puts this hard-line position in a different light. This inserted text of about three-pages in length at first appears to be a "supplement" *[Nachtrag]* in a sense surprisingly close to the import of that quintessentially Freudian term, *Nachträglichkeit*. The square-bracketed text was added at the time of the publication, which is to say, nearly four years after the original composition of the case history. In the meantime, some other events had come to pass, including the publication of the *Introductory Lectures on Psychoanalysis* (1916–17). Freud describes the circumstance at the beginning of the added text:

108

> Originally I had no intention of pursuing the discussion of the reality of "primal scenes" any further in this place. Since, however, I have meanwhile had occasion in my *Introductory Lectures on Psycho-Analysis* to treat the subject on more general lines and with no controversial aim in view, it would be misleading if I omitted to apply the considerations which determined my other discussion of the matter to the case that is now before us. I therefore proceed as follows by way of completion and rectification *[ergänzend und berichtigend fortsetzen]*.—There remains the possibility of taking yet another view of the primal scene underlying the dream. [57/GW 12:86; trans. mod.]

Perhaps this tertiary possibility will mediate, or cut a middle way between, the stark opposition of the choices he offered above. At any rate, Freud suggests, this alternative avoids [*ablenkt,* deflects] much of the conclusion he arrived at originally, and together with it, a good deal of what he calls "our difficulties." On the other hand, he warns, this new option will offer no compromise to those who seek to reduce the infantile scene to "the level of regressive symbols" *[die Infantilszene zu regressiven Symbolen herabdrücken]*.

A casual reader of this rather uneven passage might first note that a possibility for a critical second look was already available when the temporal structure of the experience/knowledge *[Erfahrung]* of the primal scene was discussed. For here is a dream, which is clearly remembered as having occurred, which is supposedly the moment of "understanding" of an earlier occurrence; then there is that occurrence, constructed through analysis but never "remembered" in the usual (conscious) sense, the pri-

mal scene; in between are two and a half years of a highly obscure psychical passage called early childhood. In the strictly conscious sense, then,
we know only of the end point of this "experience," the other, originating
point is merely implied by the one thus known. The question arises from
this two-point structure of the pathogenic "experience." If the only part
of this "experience" that is *known* in the usual sense is the second moment, the dream, and if this dream is but a deferred effect of an unknown
event, why could it not be a deferred effect of some other event than the
one reconstructed by Freud? Such an event could be one closer in time to
the night of the dream, perhaps closer in content as well. And why not,
instead of one, two, or more such events of a much less shocking variety
than the observation of copulating parents, but events which somehow
came to be fused together, owing no doubt to the work of unconscious
displacement, condensation, and deferral, to produce a single, imaginary,
and unconscious scene, the so-called primal scene?

This is the gist of the alternative "view" which Freud pursues in his
parenthetical addendum. Why not, indeed? He proceeds to reassess the
structural configuration of the pathogenic "experience" as a whole. He
first itemizes the necessary components, things that have to be there in the
scene, virtual or real, in order for it to be able to produce not only the wolf
dream but much of the subsequent neurosis. And this case of illness, as we
learn from Freud, ran the full gamut before the Wolf-Man reached the age
of puberty—from anxiety hysteria, animal phobia, hysterical affection of
the intestinal tract, and finally, to obsessional neurosis, and even a hint of
psychosis.

To begin with, Freud rules, "we cannot dispense with the assumption
that the child observed a copulation, the sight of which gave him a conviction that castration might be more than an empty threat." This conviction is the content, so to speak, of the *experience* of the primal scene/wolf
dream. Moreover, in order for this "observation" to be optimal or even
possible, and also in order to account for many later pathological and
sexual proclivities of the Wolf-Man, "it must have been a *coitus a tergo,
more ferarum* [copulation from behind, in the manner of animals]" [57].

On the other hand, Freud suggests, it is not absolutely necessary
that this copulation should have taken place between his parents; rather,
*it is necessary only that somehow, a copulation observed elsewhere—
perhaps between animals—was displaced* [geschoben] *upon the parents,*
"as though he had inferred that his parents did things in the same way"
[57]. Admittedly, this transference *[Übertragung]* of copulating animals
onto his parents does not occur as an "inference" in the usual sense;
rather, it must have been effected by the little dreamer's primal wish,
searching out in his memory an actual scene in which he had seen his
parents together and which could be coalesced with the situation of the

animals' copulation. Here is the alternative scene, then, as again hypothetically constructed by Freud:

> All the details of the scene which were established in the analysis of the dream may have been accurately reproduced. It was really on a summer's afternoon while the child was suffering from malaria, the parents were both present, dressed in white, when the child woke up from his sleep, but—the scene was innocent. The rest had been added by the inquisitive child's subsequent wish, based on his experiences with the dogs, to witness his parents too in their lovemaking; and the scene which was thus imagined now produced all the effects that we catalogued, just as though it had been entirely real. [58]

It is apparent here that what is beyond dispute is the virtual necessity of the primal scene itself, its necessary existence in the unconscious, so to say, quite apart from the question whether the scene is a "true" copy of an actual occurrence, or a forgery assembled from several discrete impressions *á la montage*. The scene must exist, must be "real" psychically, regardless of the question of its historical authenticity, in order for the dream, and all the rest, to ensue. This is as much as to say that, for Freud, what is not negotiable in all this is the validity of his interpretation of the wolf dream; the primal scene, *just as he described it*, is the meaning of the dream, the scene is its truth. Freud puts his authority fully behind this interpretation, and, as we saw, this resolve is manifest in the starkness of the choice he presented at first ("either the primal scene, or utter nonsense").

As it happens, this case was not an armchair analysis. Unlike the position of the reader of a text, the position of the analyst of a patient is in actuality not something that can be evacuated or substituted at will. Given this circumstance, any bystander to this case, that is, anyone who is not Freud himself, would have a difficult time of contesting the analyst's version; one is generally left to express, as one chooses, an opinion or two—that it seems incredible, that it is farfetched, and so on[65]—points which, incidentally, Freud does not dispute. After all, when it comes to a clinical case, the analyst is uniquely situated, since it is only from his strategic position that one can cause the "unraveling" of the conundrum into a story, which amounts to "analysis."[66]

Despite this privilege, Freud is ready to concede that this alternative (more prudently skeptical) construction—that is, a fantasized primal scene instead of a historically genuine one—would "greatly reduce the demands on our credulity." To begin with, it does away with the situation where a pair of well-born parents copulate in front of a child, "a disagreeable idea for many of us." It also reduces the amount of time between the crucial impression (of copulating animals) and the eruption of its effect as a dream, although this impression still had to reach back to a very early memory (that is, the scene of the parents, but not copulating). In addition, it is known that the little boy, shortly before the dream, accompanied his father on several occasions to see the sheep in their estate, whereupon he would have had an ample opportunity to observe the goings-on among animals, most particularly, sheepdogs. In point of fact, the wolves described by the dreamer—also attested by the well-known drawing he made for Freud of the dream—those white animals with fluffy tails look more like sheepdogs than wolves. Besides, Freud adds, at the time of the dream, our little Wolf-Man was just at the stage of development which Freud elsewhere calls "return of totemism" (see *Totem and Taboo,* chap. 4), the period when the instances of some animals substituting for the father figure is especially rampant. If the boy displaced the fear of his father onto the animal, he could just as well have displaced the copulation of animals to his parents.

With all these factors to boost the credibility of the analysis, how could Freud not abandon the earlier claim and adopt the alternative view of the "primal scene"? Of course, Freud anticipated this question all along. "If these arguments in favour of such a view of the 'primal scene' were at my disposal, how could I possibly have taken it on myself to begin by advocating one which seemed so absurd? ["Absurd"?] Or have I made these new observations, which have obliged me to alter my original view, in the interval between the first draft of the case history and this addition, and am I for some reason or other unwilling to admit the fact?" [60].

What he does admit instead is now quite famous: "I will admit something else instead: I intend on this occasion to close the discussion of the reality of the primal scene with a *non liquet.* ['It is not clear'—a verdict where the evidence in a trial is inconclusive]."

⋅ ⋅

The peculiarity of this move—resolutely indecisive—is matched only by the remarkable reputation it has acquired in recent years among the readers of Freud. One of the best known and most concisely articulated of such accounts is Peter Brooks's *Reading for the Plot.* In the chapter with a telling title, "Fictions of the Wolf Man: Freud and Narrative Understanding," Brooks maintains that the ultimate point of Freud's theoretical audacity was the very fact that he championed "undecidability" itself, and that this is "one of the most daring moments of Freud's thought, and one of his most heroic gestures as a writer."

What is remarkable is that, having discovered his point of origin, that which made sense of the dream, the neurosis, and his own account of them, Freud then felt obliged to retrace the story, offering

111

another and much less evidential (and "eventimential") kind of origin, to tell another version of the plot, and then finally leave one juxtaposed to the other, indeed one superimposed on the other as a kind of palimpsest, a layered text that offers differing versions of the same story.

Moreover, Brooks goes on to suggest, Freud's *non liquet* marks the moment of "an apparent evacuation of the problem of origins," the total effect of which is that "a narrative explanation . . . doubles back on itself to question that origin and indeed to displace the whole question of origins, to suggest another kind of referentiality, in that all tales may lead back not so much to events as to other tales, to man as a structure of the fictions he tells about himself."[67]

This suggestion, we might say in turn, is a daring move on the part of the narratologist, Brooks. In a way, he, too, takes a leap here, "splits the scene," as they say, and evacuates the immediate context of Freud's text. Admittedly, the Wolf-Man has indeed become less of a person "in real life" than a text, and this is not least of all due to his posthumous survival in the treatises written about him and his fame accruing thereof. Indeed, his recalcitrant neurosis contributed so much to Freud's metapsychological theory formation that he is now virtually an aspect of psychoanalysis itself. His lifelong career—the one that he was most successful at—was to be "the Wolf Man, Freud's most famous case,"[68] and, as Brooks notes, even while he was still alive, he could be considered "a living part" of the Freud Archives [267]. He became "incarnated" as a body of texts, as an ongoing "history" *[Geschichte]*, which continues to be written beyond Freud, beyond his second analyst (Ruth Mack Brunswick), and so on to this day. It is therefore entirely befitting if—to further Brooks's suggestion—the father of psychoanalysis were to declare that the Wolf-Man's beginning, or at least his neurotic beginning, was to be sought not in a particular "event" but in the narrativity of his (case) history.

Yet we should be wary of going astray from Freud's text and wandering off to the all-too-familiar idea, namely, that the question of origin somehow disappears into the intertextuality of narration. This easy way out must be temporarily blocked, even if we are sure that the Wolf-Man narrative in fact "evacuates" the immediate context, and that what is left behind ends up referring to some other text. For in closer scrutiny—as it will be shown presently—the question of origin is not really *contained* in this *non liquet*. We might therefore anticipate that it is bound to come back, not so much because Freud's decision (or nondecision) is disingenuous, but because this question is about something else, somewhere else.

Let us remember that Freud's judgment of nondecision is pronounced not over the first stark dichotomy he presented, which ran: *either* the primal scene, *or* the impossibility of narration. Ultimately, the narrativity is not in question; he assumes it, and this assumption in turn leans upon his very specific understanding of the "reality" of the primal scene. The question he is willing to entertain, rather, is about the grounding of this "reality." Drawing upon Brooks's rendition above, we might say that it is the question of whether the event grounds the narrativity or the narrativity produces (retroactively and fictively) the event as its own point of origination. Freud's *non liquet* may be construed as either that he has resolved to hold them both in the affirmative (in which case he appears to be something of a dialectician), or, what seems truer to his words, that he is simply declining to raise the question of having to choose between them. What the parenthetical *Nachtrag* [supplement, afterthought] does is to step back from his initial formulation of the choices (primal scene or nonsense) and by that very move somehow disable the question of priority. The temporal origin is made inoperative *within the narrative structure* just at the same time that it is disengaged and expelled from the narratability of the case, and left marooned in the outer orbit of irrecoverable time, the time that cannot be redeemed for the (case) history or any *Geschichte*.

113

·   ·

To get back to that *Geschichte*, however, this may be an appropriate moment to recall that we are in the middle of Freud's text, which has been doubly interrupted—we are in the chapter of a polemical interlude (interjected with a certain incidental air, entitled "A Few Discussions"), and within it, a parenthetical addendum. And the *non liquet* is not Freud's last word, not even of this bracketed passage. The actual last two sentences—immediately following the *non liquet*—seem to adumbrate something else, although it does end up, once again, referring to another text. "This case history is not yet at an end; in its further course a factor will emerge which will shake the certainty [that the revised and mitigated view of the primal scene is correct] which we seem at present to enjoy. Nothing, I think, will then be left but to refer my readers to the passages in my *Introductory Lectures* in which I have treated the problem of primal phantasies or primal scenes" [60].

It is true that the analysis of the case has hardly begun. Before this chapter of polemical interruption, Freud had given us a preamble, a dream, a number of portentous but fragmentary details, and a dramatic disclosure of the supposed scene behind the dream, the primal scene. Everything about the analysis of the case is yet to be explained. This is in fact what is carried out in the next three chapters, the last of which is another set of "supplements" to the "primal period," with another dramatic disclosure; it is entitled *"Nachträge aus der Urzeit—Lösung"* ["Supplementary Material from the Primal Period—Solution"]. Let us here anticipate in the briefest dispatch what is to come in these ensuing chapters: that the Wolf-Man's trouble, precipitated by the primal scene/wolf dream experience, stemmed from the dread of castration, the reaction to which was extremely complex, but the preeminent feature and the deepest determining factor of this reaction is regression to anal erotism.

The parenthetically considered view on the primal scene—the notion that the primal scene was a composite picture fantasized—remains in brackets, never assimilated into the main text, nor does it result in any revision of the course of Freud's argument.[69] And perhaps for good reason. Once out of the brackets it will appear as though Freud had pursued this diverting line of inquiry essentially as a theoretical possibility, merely for the sake of "completeness," so that the discussion would be well rounded, as they say. In this context of generalized consideration "in principle," he makes the point that analysts must expect both possibilities; for the veridical primal scene and the fabricated primal scene are equally capable of producing an identical effect—the same wolf dream, for example. In either case, the analytic procedure remains exactly the same; it must begin with this *psychical* reality, putting aside the question of its historical verity.

In effect, it appears that Freud did not give up the "reality" of the primal scene in the least. He abides by the conviction that the scene must have existed and have been available in the unconscious of the dreamer. The question left undecided in the addendum does not concern this reality. And, as regards this other question, the one concerning the historical authenticity of the scene, Freud was ready to "throw it out of court" as undecidable, and subsequently to declare the difference immaterial, *gleichgültig*, all the same.

His admission that, all things being equal, the idea of the scene as fantasized rather than historically truthful would be more plausible is perhaps more beguiling than yielding. The grounds for this mitigated view of the primal scene are in the main quite weak; to wit, he seems to say something to the effect that this revised version is less taxing on the natural inclination of our belief and on our sense of bourgeois propriety. In the end, Freud did not believe any of this.

•   •

It was perhaps daring on Freud's part to shelve with his parenthetical *non liquet* the issue of "reality" of the primal scene with a gesture of dismissal. To be sure, this refusal to decide did not arrest the narratability of the case or stop the flow of meaning in any way. But it has suspended judgment over the question of the historical authenticity, or material reality, of the primal scene. The issue thus "thrown out of court," however, does come back, most strikingly in the penultimate chapter of the case history. The title of this chapter, "*Nachträge aus der Urzeit—Lösung*," carries the full weight of its belated, deferred, or supplementary effect *[Nachträge]*, referring back once again to the "primal period" *[aus der Urzeit]*. But it also announces a "solution" *[Lösung]*. Will the question left unanswered in the earlier chapter, at long last, get resolved?

This new material was indeed late in coming, according to Freud. But when it did, it came as a memory, spontaneously remembered by the Wolf-Man himself, without being urged by a construction on Freud's part, although the analyst did add a significant detail to this memory to make it complete. The circumstances suggested that the "event" dates back from sometime before the age of two and a half, which is to say, closer in time to the supposed witnessing of the parental copulation (one and a half) than to the wolf dream (four). This recovered memory turns out to be the earliest the patient could reproduce consciously, but, in accordance with the ways of such crucial memories, it was the last to emerge in the course of analysis. Freud emphasizes the characteristically wayward, deceptively self-effacing manner in which the weightiest of memories come about, always seeming somehow marginal, fragmentary, like a supplement, not "central" to the main problem: "it may be that on one occasion some unpretentious remark is thrown out in an indifferent tone of voice as though it were superfluous *[etwas überflüssiges]* . . . on another occasion, something further is added, which begins to make the physician prick his ears; and . . . at last he comes to recognize this despised fragment of a memory as the key to the weightiest secrets that the patient's neurosis has veiled" [89].

The roundabout way in which everything came to light, as a delicate chain of images so befitting of the tender years of childhood, is recounted early in the chapter: the butterfly, the yellow stripes, the pear "with a most delicious taste—a big pear with yellow stripes on its skin," and finally, the long-forgotten nursery maid whom he loved, whose name was "Grusha," meaning "pear" in Russian. The passage depicting the steps of this recovery testifies to the tentative and intermittent manner in which the unconscious offers up its well-kept secret, but it also demonstrates Freud's dexterity in pulling out this fragile chain of associations. The passage thus presents a stark contrast with the impression afforded by Freud's dramatic but nearly violent handling of the wolf dream/primal scene interpretation.

The memory in question is in fact another scene, "incomplete, but, so far as it was preserved, definite *[bestimmt]*. Grusha was kneeling on the floor, and beside her a pail and a short broom made of a bundle of twigs; he was also there, and she was teasing him or scolding him" [91]. This

115

was as much as the Wolf-Man's spontaneous memory could offer. The analyst "completed" the work of recollection, much like an archaeologist restoring a broken piece of a pottery work, by supplying material drawn from other associations and memories that the patient produced in a different context. Thus a page later we read a conclusion of this scene, as reconstructed by Freud: "When he saw the girl scrubbing the floor he had micturated in the room and she had rejoined, no doubt jokingly, with a threat of castration" [92]. Let us make a note here of a point to which we shall have an occasion to return: that it is precisely "castration" that was missing from the patient's consciously recovered memory, but supplemented, as if to fill the gap, by a number of oblique associations in and around the memory.

This scene serves, in more than one way, as a crucial hinge articulating Freud's interpretive schema. Above all, "it provides an important link between the primal scene and the later compulsive love [being sexually aroused instantly at the sight of a woman kneeling, doing some menial work like scrubbing the floor, washing] which came to be of such decisive significance in his subsequent career" [92]. But the ultimate source of this attraction, Freud argues, is to be found in the mother, or more specifically, in her posture at the *coitus a tergo* witnessed by the infant Wolf-Man. It thus appears that, with an intervention of this "new" material, we have come back, despite the *non liquet* pronouncement earlier, to the historically authentic version of the primal scene, and that the original time table is reasserted with the newly discovered scene added to it. The time of "sexual development" again runs forward: "The compulsion which proceeded from the primal scene was transferred on to this scene with Grusha and was carried forward by it" [93].

Thus multiple services are rendered by this Grusha scene for the support of the historically authentic primal scene and its sexual content. First, as we have just seen, Freud understands the Grusha scene as the earliest (but, as always, belated) manifestation of the impact of the primal scene. Assuming the "completed" version of the scene augmented by analytic construction, Freud determines that the incident was clearly of a *sexual* sort, albeit in the form that was proportional to the stage of sexual immaturity of the little boy. This interpretation, if correct, already indicates that infantile sexuality is certainly not a retrogressive invention of the postpubescent neurotic, and moreover, that it presupposes an even earlier *sexual* impression (that is, at the time of the primal scene), of which the later scene can be most naturally interpreted as a deferred outcome.[70]

The Grusha scene is situated as a relay station between the two points of time that mark the journey *[Fahren]* of the "experience" *[Erfahrung]*, accomplished in the form of the primal scene/wolf dream trajectory. But if so, the primal scene, whether virtual or real, has to be present and available in the realm of psychical reality prior to the age of two and a half, which is to say, much earlier than the time of the nightmare. Hence the hypothetical alternative construction mentioned earlier, the notion that the primal scene was synthetically produced by coalescence of an early but nonsexual impression of the parents and an observation of copulating animals shortly before the dream, becomes untenable.

If we continue to follow Freud's train of thought, the Grusha scene supports the historical reality of the primal scene in yet another way, namely, by providing a certain parallel case. We are told that when this memory of the scene came up, it was in part through a dream:

> "I had a dream," [the Wolf-Man] said, "of a man tearing off the wings of an *Espe.*" "*Espe?*" I asked; "what do you mean by that?" "You know; that insect with yellow stripes on its body, that stings." I could now put him right: "So what you mean is a *Wespe* [wasp]." "Is it called a *Wespe?* I really thought it was called an *Espe.*" (Like so many other people, he used his difficulties with a foreign language as a screen for symptomatic acts.) "But *Espe,* why, that's myself: S. P." (which were his initials). The *Espe* was of course a mutilated *Wespe.* The dream said clearly that he was avenging himself on Grusha for her threat of castration. [94]

117

Although this dream was neither a nightmare nor a dream dating from childhood, its reference to castration, as well as its relation to the Wolf-Man's childhood phobia of the butterfly with yellow stripes (which was concurrent with his wolf phobia) is obvious. In this connection, the Wolf-Man has kept the memory of an episode in which he as a child was seized by anxiety while chasing after just such a creature [89]. Hence one can reasonably draw a parallel between the series: the primal scene / wolf dream / wolf phobia, on the one hand, and the series: the Grusha scene / (W)espe dream / yellow-striped butterfly phobia, on the other.

An inference that could be drawn from this parallelism is that both series refer to the threat of castration, and that the relative explicitness of the Grusha series proffers to enhance the veracity of the interpretation Freud has given to the wolf series. The wasp dream more obviously refers to the matter of castration/mutilation, and, through a clever double inversion, the dream manages to express both the threat directed to the dreamer himself ([W]Espe, S. P. being torn apart) and the revenge or counterthreat directed against the one who first issued the ominous words to him (Grusha, the yellow-striped pear/wasp torn apart). Now, what amounts to a critical difference between the two series is that whereas the primal scene is a construction and was never reproduced as a memory, the Grusha scene was spontaneously remembered, and it dates back from almost equally early childhood. Notwithstanding this difference it is quite possible, Freud would want to argue, that just as behind the wasp dream and the butterfly phobia there was a real scene, behind the wolf dream and the wolf phobia there is a real—not just imagined—scene pertinent to it.

Moreover, though the Grusha scene is equally sexual in its import, according to Freud's estimation, as a historical occurrence it contains "nothing objectionable or improbable" in it; "on the contrary, it consisted entirely of commonplace details *[banale Einzelheiten]* which gave no grounds for scepticism. There was nothing in it which could lead one to attribute its origin to the child's imagination" [96]. Still worried about the shocking nature of the content of the primal scene, Freud is seeking support for the greater probability of the primal scene from its much more commonplace and socially acceptable parallel case. The scene of a little boy of two or so, wetting his pants in the presence of his nursery maid who happens to be scrubbing the floor—what is so improbable about that? But if this perfectly ordinary occurrence can produce the rest of the butterfly-wasp series, then the parallel phenomenon of the wolf series should be granted also a historical origin, a scene, namely, the one Freud constructed.

All these considered, then, it appears that the advocacy of the historically authentic primal scene is back in full force despite the earlier *non liquet* pronouncement which dismissed or suspended—indefinitely, we thought—the whole question. And yet.

As it happens, commencing the discussion of parallelism above, we have already entered into yet another bracketed addendum, a text contemporaneous with the bracketed passage examined earlier. Halfway into this second circumscribed supplementary text, Freud again takes up that question of whether this incident at the age of two and a half was intrinsically sexual, or, instead, subsequently and retroactively sexualized.

> The question now arises whether we are justified in regarding the fact that the boy micturated, while he stood looking at the girl on her knees scrubbing the floor, as a proof of sexual excitement on his part. If so, the excitement would be evidence of the influence of an earlier impression which might equally have been the actual occurrence of the primal scene or an observation made upon animals before the age of two and a half. Or are we to conclude that the situation as regards Grusha was entirely innocent, that the child's emptying his bladder was purely accidental, and that it was not until later that the whole scene became sexualized in his memory, after he had come to recognize the importance of similar situations? [96]

This delineation covers all the possibilities considered earlier: (1) historically authentic primal scene, (2) fantasized primal scene (though, with the occurrence of the Grusha scene, the fantasy must have been produced prior to age two and a half), or (3) the whole narrative of interpretation a "nonsense from start to finish." As before, Freud declines to issue any final decision over them, which is as much as to say that he dismisses the whole case. Yet just at the time he is denouncing the question as undecidable and, moreover, unimportant, he makes a curious move of (re)claiming the credit, precisely, for raising the question in the first place. "On these issues I can venture upon no decision. I must confess, however, that I regard it as greatly to the credit of psycho-analysis that it should even have reached the stage of *raising* such questions as these" [96].

But now comes the next turn, as he immediately adds that "nevertheless, I cannot deny that the scene with Grusha, the part it played in the analysis, and the effects that followed from it in the patient's life can be most naturally and completely explained if we consider that the primal scene, which may in other cases be a phantasy, was a reality in the present one. After all, there is nothing impossible," and so on and so forth.

Furthermore, to make this a perfect repetition of the equivocal moves made in the earlier bracketed passage, Freud does not fail to interject in the very next paragraph the following observation. "I should myself be glad to know whether the primal scene in my present patient's case was a phantasy or a real experience; but, taking other similar cases into account, I must admit that the answer to this question is not in fact a matter of very great importance" [97].

In resumé, it may be worthwhile here to make a point of "explaining," that is, forcing Freud's moves, full of twists and turns, into one flat plain, in order to see them for what they are when they are deprived of the narrative contours that give them credible shape. The result is easily recognized as a case of what might be called Freudian double-talk (or triple-talk, as the case may be), which, as Freud has taught us, is characteristic of the work of the unconscious.[71] It runs roughly like this: (1) a historically authentic primal scene or a fantasized primal scene—the issue is ultimately undecidable; (2) in this particular case,[72] however, the analysis shows that the historically authentic primal scene is much more likely, *even though* it is more "improbable" [103] and "absurd" [60]; and (3) either way, the decision is inconsequential, it does not "make any difference," it does not matter.

What, then, matters? Perhaps the following points cover the ground which Freud hopes to have gained. That it is not *all* fantasy. That the neurotic's memory storage and the pathological display of its partial content is not all a matter of retrospective fantasizing of the adult, or worse, of the analyst. That, although fantasy does reach back in time, the time that

119

passes through the unconscious, through the psychical realm of the "timeless," is not eternal or permanent; rather, it moves in fits and starts; it also drags behind—the total effect of which is not unlike a discordant rhythm of a song "out of sync" with its own progression. That this peculiar tempo, this sinuous "passage" through the unconscious, is what amounts to the "time" of sexuality. And, above all, what gives this temporality its texture, and what functions as the fundamental coordinate—or the zero point—of the psychosexual "progression," is that which is feared most—the threat of castration.

It is to this last subject that we must now prepare to turn. We shall have to call to account the point which we accepted without much ceremony or scrutiny early in the discussion of the Wolf-Man case. This is the assumption that the "meaning" of the "experience" that spanned from the primal scene to the wolf dream was the "reality" of castration. Throughout the course of narrating the case, this is the one point Freud has sustained most consistently and defended most assiduously, against all incursions of doubt. This is the umbilical cord that keeps his analysis alive until its completion. Without it, we have been warned, the "case" would fall apart, and turn to "a piece of nonsense from start to finish."

It may be provisionally stated here that according to Freud's understanding, the "reality" of castration, which was first given to the patient in the primal scene, at last came to be *represented, in* a dream, *as* a nightmare, although, owing to the nature of the dreamwork, this representation *[Vorstellung]* was of necessity a case of distortion *[Entstellung]*, or, to call upon Samuel Weber's useful neologism, a "depresentation." Yet, what is noteworthy above all is this: castration is more than a particular content of the experience that may be called primal; rather, castration determines the shape, or even establishes the very possibility, of representation/depresentation.

Castration Lost and Found

> To reproduce is what one thought one could do in the optimistic days of catharsis. One had the primal scene in reproduction as today one has pictures of the great masters for 9 francs 50. But what Freud showed when he made his next steps—and it did not take him long—was that nothing can be grasped, destroyed or burnt, except in a symbolic way, as one says, *in effigie, in absentia.*
> Jacques Lacan, *The Four Fundamental Concepts of Psycho-Analysis*

We shall now come to the substance of Freud's analysis, the two chapters flanked by the polemical interlude and the penultimate "solution."

As the Wolf-Man enters the analysis proper in Freud's text, he also enters a larger context of psychoanalytic knowledge. His person, his illness, might very well have been like no other, yet this singular configuration, the "crux" of his case, can be illumined only in the great hall of psychoanalytic science, where not only his but countless other cases of mental suffering, all unique in themselves and absurdly personal, come to rest in categories and theories.

Here, then, we find the Wolf-Man, the anal erotic.

•   •

Analysts claim, based upon their encounter with examples that they say are ubiquitous, that children arrive at the momentous "knowledge"— the conviction that certain people *are* castrated—from the observation of female genitals, most likely of their baby sisters or little playmates. Invariably, so we are told, small children do not perceive the female genitals as a distinct organ in its own right but rather as a lack of the (male) organ, that is, as a wound resulting from its removal. At first a typical (male) child's[73] response to this "perception" of absence is an energetic denial, or what Freud calls "disavowal *[Verleugnung]*."[74] Little boys initially "disavow the fact and believe that they *do* see a penis, all the same." There is a duplicity in this response, however, since "they gloss over the contradiction between observation and preconception by telling themselves that the penis is still small and will grow bigger presently." From the temporary protection of this self-deception, "they then slowly come to the emotionally significant conclusion that after all the penis had at least been there before and been taken away afterwards."[75] In the face of this last, grave realization, the child will be forced to renounce certain desires, for he has just witnessed the implications of their fulfillment.

Up until the time of this so-called Oedipal crisis, the average child is said to have multiple and multiply crossed libidinal desires with relation to the most primordial pair of love objects, his parents. First of all—as is better known from the popular rendition of "Oedipus complex"—the child has a desire to take the place of the father (that is, to identify with and at the same time displace him) and thereby to establish *genitally* a sexual liaison with the mother—perhaps in order in part to compensate, however distantly, for the loss of the mother's breast, which was withdrawn from him and which he was thus forced to renounce.

The desire of his emergent genital sexuality, however, soon comes under duress because, under circumstances that are not so veiled and are in fact quite commonplace, the child meets the threat of castration. He is repeatedly reprimanded for his indulgence in genital pleasures; any childish exercise in masturbation, or even a little display, is universally discouraged by the adults around him. A typical form of reproof—at least in

121

Freud's day—goes something like this: that if he keeps doing that (fondling his penis, for example), something terrible is going to happen to it, that it will rot, fall off. Alternatively, he is warned that his offending hand will suffer some similar fate. In any case, this figurative admonishment is taken rather literally and seriously by the child, says Freud, if not there and then, certainly by the time he learns from another source (that is, catching sight of female genitals) that the loss of his penis is a distinct possibility.

But the (male) child has yet another current of desire, which is converse of the one just mentioned. This is the desire to identify with the mother, and by taking her place, to receive sexual satisfaction from the father. (At an earlier stage, this sexual liaison is understood to be anal, since the child prior to the genital stage—or, in fact before the "discovery" of castration—does not recognize the vaginal orifice, and therefore the intercourse is believed to be through the cloaca. As we shall see presently, this pregenital sexuality has a portentous determination in the case of the Wolf-Man.) But this "passive-homosexual" desire, too, comes under check when the child arrives at the following ominous realization: to take the place of the mother—to be a woman—is to be without a penis. In effect, "castration" is a *precondition* for the fulfilment of this desire.

Whichever way his desire turns, therefore, the (male) child comes under the threat of castration, just at the time when his sexuality is being organized around the genitals, overriding the older, pregenital (oral and anal) organizations. In this moment of crisis, the child will, as a matter of course, resolve himself in favor of his narcissistic interest to preserve his bodily totality intact, to avoid the consequence *or* the precondition of the fulfillment of those desires, namely castration. This renunciation is a milestone in the child's sexual development.[76] This is the first clear instance in which the child's ego drive (nonsexual drive) triumphs over his libido (sexual drive); for the first time, a move toward an immediate gratification of his sexual desire is inhibited by an *internal agent*. This renunciation of the child's incestuous desires marks the so-called dissolution of the Oedipus complex, thereupon the child enters a long period of *latency*, and his sexuality is to remain apparently dormant until its second onset in puberty.[77]

At times, however, the "overcoming" of the Oedipus complex does not proceed according to the usual course. The reasons for such deviance are not easily determined, and the difficulty is evidenced by the great obscurity of the concepts surrounding the issue: "fixation," "primal repression," and so on. It is conceivable that a given child has a particularly strong attachment to a certain type of sexual pleasure to begin with because of some physiological predispositions (thus leading to certain "fixations") and that this state of affairs makes it exceptionally difficult for him to achieve the renunciation of the infantile desires in the usual fashion, this "usual course" being: disavowal, gradual recognition and acceptance of the "reality" of castration, and renunciation of desire. It is also possible, on the other hand, that some out-of-the-ordinary event or trauma is responsible for the aberration.

· ·

In the case of the Wolf-Man, both factors, congenital and accidental, may have been at work. If Freud's construction of the primal scene is correct, it appears that this child was met with the "reality" of castration in an extraordinary way;[78] for it was not a little girl but a mature woman, the most respected and the most adored of all women, his mother. (As a rule, the mother is the last woman to lose her phallus in the imagination of little boys. Since the "discovery" of the mother's castration is a particularly horrific event,[79] it often calls for a special compensation or belated indemnity, which leads to fetishism.)[80] It can be speculated that, in the face of such a violent confrontation with the woman's "castration,"[81] *and* so early in the stage of sexual development (well before the genital organization), the boy did not, or could not, *disavow* the "reality" of castration in the usual way. The "normal" disavowal is, as just described, at bottom an ambiguous, indecisive, provisional attitude of half refusing and half accepting. No doubt, such a half measure of self-deception— which is at once self-serving and pacifying ("hers is small, but it will grow"), which might have been quite serviceable had he observed a little sister, rival, or playmate—was not possible with respect to his own adored mother.

123

Instead of an already ambivalent disavowal, the infant Wolf-Man's first reaction must have been an even more energetic, radical denial, or what Freud calls "repudiation" [*Verwerfung;* literally, "throwing away"; *forclusion* in Lacan's translation, or "foreclosure"]. This refers to a wholesale rejection of "castration," such that it does "not as yet even raise the question of the reality of castration" [85]. What makes such a radical rejection possible?

We recall that children at the pregenital stage consider childbirth to be equivalent to passing a stool, they do not know of the vaginal orifice, and assume that coitus takes place via the anus. In this infantile "theory" of sexuality, therefore, sexual intercourse does not have to have anything to do with "the wound" (vagina), or with its supposed cause, castration. Accordingly, says Freud, the Wolf-Man "rejected castration, and held to his theory of intercourse by the anus. When I speak of his having rejected it, the first meaning of the phrase is that *he would have nothing to do with it,* in the sense of having repressed it.[82] This really involved no judgement upon the question of its existence, but it was the same as if it did not exist" [84; emphasis added].

Moreover, this "regression" to anal sexuality seems to have offered a further advantage of making possible an altogether different configuration of the castration-renunciation-pleasure/desire relation. Just as the withdrawing of the mother's breast distantly and retrospectively alludes to castration,[83] in the anal stage, "giving up" of the content of the bowel, offering up of what is inside the body (thus part of his own body) *at the behest of the child's loved ones* (usually mother or her surrogate), adumbrates castration:

> Since the column of faeces stimulates the erotogenic mucous membrane of the bowel, it plays the part of an active organ in regard to it; it behaves just as the penis does to the vaginal mucous membrane, and acts as it were as its forerunner during the cloacal epoch [during the "anal-sadistic phase"]. The handing over of faeces for the sake of (out of love for) some one else becomes a prototype of castration; it is the first occasion upon which an individual parts with a piece of his own body in order to gain the favour of some other person whom he loves. [84]

In the secret recess of anal erotism, then, the yield of pleasure (stimulation of the mucous membrane) and "castration" ("parting with a piece of one's own body") are *not* antagonistic (one desirable and another horrific) outcomes of the same incestuous wish, but rather, in this fecal sense, castration—that is to say, "pain" of parting, of loss—*is* also pleasure. In effect, the little Wolf-Man could have it both ways; this "giving up" is not equivalent to renouncing of desire/pleasure, but on the contrary, acceding to its demand. Furthermore, through this pleasurable act of "offering up," the child is also obeying the command of the loved one.[84]

With all these phantasmic advantages, it is little wonder that the Wolf-Man, perhaps with a strong anal erotic disposition to begin with, found a recourse regressively in anal erotism.[85] In the solicitous complementarity of pleasure/"giving up"/obedience, the articulation of his homosexual desire does not have to "have anything to do with" the loss of his penis; "castration" does not have to threaten desire; the issue could be rejected, simply refused.

Despite the fact that Freud's terminology is not always consistent, it is nonetheless the Wolf-Man's case history above all that testifies to his understanding of repudiation *[Verwerfung]* as a distinct mode of psychical defense, distinguishable, in other words, from repression proper. The future course of the radically foreclosed and repudiated *[verworfen]* drive differs from that of what is suppressed *[unterdrückt]* or what is merely repressed *[verdrängt]*. A suppressed drive may be eventually sublimated; the initial sexual desire may be transformed into some "higher" form of aspiration. What is merely (and ambiguously) repressed, and thus pushed into the unconscious, may return from within, in a prima facie unrecognizable form, that is to say, in some typically neurotic fashion. In contrast, what is repudiated—thrown out "before the question of its reality could be raised," and thus "foreclosed"—can return only from *without*, so to speak, only as a piece of (external) reality, or, in truth, as a *seeming* reality.[86] It does not reemerge as an irrepressible internal feeling, sensation, or thought, but rather as a hallucination.

What complicates the case of the Wolf-Man evidently is that this repudiation/foreclosure was by no means the only response that he produced toward the "reality" of castration.

Such an attitude [of repudiation] could not have been his final one, even at the time of his infantile neurosis. We find good subsequent evidence of his having recognized castration as a fact. . . . First he resisted and then he yielded; but the second reaction did not *do away with* the first. In the end there were to be found in him two contrary currents side by side, of which one abominated the idea of castration, while the other was prepared to accept it and console itself with feminity as a compensation. But beyond any doubt a third current, the oldest and deepest, which did not as yet even raise the question of the reality of castration, was still capable of coming into activity. [85]

125

This third, then, arises from the oldest stratum, from anal erotism, which has been overlaid, but not erased, by the more typical, wishfully indecisive response, that is, disavowal (first denial, then eventual yielding). The result was a compounding of the contradictions and greater disparity within his reaction, making altogether impossible anything like the usual, gradual "overcoming" of the complex. Thus it comes about that the Wolf-Man at once did *and* did not renounce his homosexual desire towards the father.

This contradiction, this impasse, is the true pathogenic source, to which Freud traces back the multitude of symptoms and peculiarities of the Wolf-Man's case. We might at this point summarily list the principal manifestations of his infantile neurosis: (1) the Wolf-Man's libidinal love toward the father/mother comes under the threat of castration, and is repressed *[verdrängt]*; yet, irrepressible, this "love" returns unrecognizably as *anxiety;* (2) the anxiety, through displacement *[Verschiebung]*, becomes attached to another object, and produces the animal *phobia;* (3) his homosexual love toward the father continues to hold sway in some other psychic region, despite the castration threat, thanks to the regression to anal erotism; a fantasized and disguised (that is, unconscious) fulfillment of this desire manifests itself through somatic symptoms, specifically through his hysterically affected intestinal tract *(conversion hysteria)*; (3a) as a corollary to this, the Wolf-Man continues to identify with (that is, to take the place of) the mother, despite her "castration"; in fact he also identifies with her "castration" itself, for example, by repeating her words of lament. In this way, he draws a clandestine equation between the "pain of castration" (loss of the penis suffered by the mother) and the anal pleasure of "castration" (giving up of stools); (4) "castration" repudiated *[verworfen]* remains a separate current from all this, and its return is hallucinatory, as it appears when the boy at the age of five "sees" his little finger accidentally cut off and "hanging by the skin" (incipient *psychosis?*); (5) through the intervention of religious instruction by the mother, much of his erotic love of the father which has been suppressed becomes *sublimated,* that is, transformed into a desire of a nonsexual kind, into a spiritual "love" of God the father; (5a) however, owing to other coexisting currents or attitudes, this sublimated love continues to be crossed and abused by certain irrepressible, revolting thoughts and images, the ideas that contract the God (Father) - Jesus (Son) relation with the functions of the anus, most notably, the thought contraction: "God - shit" *[Gott - Kot];* all this immediately betrays the originally sexual (specifically anal) nature of his religious love; (6) in order to protect the sublimated love of religion from these subterranean attacks by the return of the repressed, the Wolf-Man is (internally) compelled to devise various preventive measures and ceremonials *(obsessional neurosis);* as in other obsessional neurotics, his exaggerated piety is a reaction formation, an emphatic denial of his most irrepressible sexual trend, anal erotism.

The Wolf-Man's childhood thus comprehensively diagnosed, the reader of this case history is expected to be duly impressed by the enormity of the castration complex—and by the critical significance of the primal scene as the first moment of the Wolf-Man's encounter with the "reality" of castration. However, we have also learned that this encounter is not the kind of "event" that takes place at one fell stroke—one summer afternoon, for example—but more obscurely, this "experience" gets accomplished somewhere in the warp of time. As such, this scene was less a moment of true *coincidence* (falling together in one instance) than a series of missed appointments—someone, or something, arriving too early, too late, from which all sorts of further ill-timed or mistimed consequences and belated recompenses were to follow, all amounting to a mass of mutually contradictory aftereffects.[87]

This understanding of the general nature of child's "sexual experience" also puts the status of the primal scene in a somewhat different light. For if the primal scene is to be construed as an etiological origin at all, it is no longer in the sense of an origin that contains within it "in the beginning," in a germinal form, all future manifestations of the illness as potentiality. Instead, it is the whole web of those trajectories of deferred effects and diachronic associations that can be properly called the *ground* [*Ursache*] of the Wolf-Man's neurosis. Accordingly, what rises to the fore when the analysis evokes the primal scene is not so much a particular afternoon, an event, but indeed *a scene*—that is, a particular semantic or narrative unit,[88] so to speak, which holds the nexus of those intersecting trajectories. For this reason, the Wolf-Man's neurotic history cannot be mapped onto the organic time of maturation and fruition. Rather, strangely as it may sound, the time of this "origin and development" is figured in the simultaneity of the network of the trajectories. And it is in this web that the primal scene and a number of other scenes are "freely"—that is to say, in accordance with the determination of the unconscious[89]—and diachronically coalesced and interpenetrated.

The Return of the Repudiated

This still leaves us with one odd question, which we have managed to contain, or rather suspend, in the course of the preceding discussion by means of a certain ordinary typographical device: What is the "reality" of castration? And what does it mean to *repudiate* this "reality," to refuse "even to raise the question of its reality"?

To begin with what most readily comes to mind, we might say, taking the empiricist standpoint of the naive and the natural, that "castration" is no reality at all; for *we know* that women and girls are not castrated. Then there is no reality to repudiate; what is thus refused is, really, nothing. But then, can rejection of a nonreality produce a pathology? Surely, that would have to be a bogus sort of "illness," having no substance or import, no rhyme or reason, thus offering no hope of analysis.

On the other hand, we might determine that the "reality" of castration is above all a *psychical* reality, founded in part on its genuine possibility (that is, castration *could* happen, provided that one is endowed with a penis to begin with) as well as on the perceived absence of the penis in women and girls; as such, the "reality" of castration is in the effects of its (mis)perception. Yet, one of these effects or reactions poses a further problem. For how is it that a total repudiation of this reality (which, in this reckoning amounts to a total repelling of the effects) itself produces certain effects, decidedly pathological ones that are marked, precisely, by the appearance of "the real"?

Unlike the return of the repressed (which results in one or other of the subjective/internal reactions—anxiety, phobia, somatic symptoms, or obsessive thoughts), the return of the repudiated (foreclosed) is characterized by a startling aura of reality. As noted earlier, the repudiated comes back (as if) from without, (as if) from the realm of external reality; it returns, that is to say, in the form of hallucination. In the present case history, Freud reports one such instance:

> "When I was five years old [the Wolf-Man relates] I was playing in the garden near my nurse, and was carving with my pocket-knife in the bark of one of the walnut-trees that come into my [wolf] dream as well. Suddenly, to my unspeakable terror, I noticed that I had cut through the little finger of my (right or left?) hand, so that it was only hanging on by its skin. I felt no pain, but great fear. I did not venture to say anything to my nurse, who was only a few paces distant, but I sank down on the nearest seat and sat there incapable of casting another glance at my finger. At last I calmed down, took a look at the finger, and saw that it was entirely uninjured." [85]

Freud's comments on the phenomenon of hallucination—which is a psychotic symptom—remains regrettably laconic in this context; he merely adds a few remarks which supposedly confirm the ideas that we have already rehearsed: that this hallucinatory terror results from a reactivation of the fear of castration; that this psychotic reaction indeed stems from the "oldest and deepest" current, that is, from the *verwerfend* attitude of "refusing to consider" the "reality" of castration; that this repulsing reaction is made possible by the psychical regression to anal erotism.

At any rate, a further probe into the question of the "reality" of castration comes to grief over this strange phenomenon of repudiation and its return. For whichever way we may take, we will end up having to consider such improbable phenomena as grave effects of a nonexistent perception, or effects of nonexistent effects.

If we are to do better than finding ourselves adrift at this impasse and abandoning further query, if, that is to say, we are to begin our analysis with this very point of impasse, what opens before our eyes is certainly alien—some call it uncanny—terrain, a landscape which, however, is by no means unfamiliar to psychoanalysis, since it was psychoanalysis that discovered this domain for science. And here, psychoanalysis "knows," what is repudiated/foreclosed/"thrown out" will not disappear or dissipate but survive, though hidden. Should the opportunity knock at a particularly propitious moment, the exile is bound to come back; it will masquerade in the guise of the real, and assert itself as something other than a *mere* psychical reality.

· ·

At this juncture, what becomes increasingly inescapable is a suggestion of some opaque correspondence between the "reality" of castration and the "reality" of the primal scene. Let us qualify immediately, however, that this is not a matter of simple parallels. To begin with, there is a palpable difference which we feel about our own sense of certainty and uncertainty. Concerning the "reality" of castration, we feel quite certain that children are mistaken in their perception, or in their judgment; at bottom, this is a "reality" strictly within fantasy. As for the primal scene, on the other hand, we are less sure; what did or did not happen on one summer afternoon of the late nineteenth century in a haute bourgeois bedroom of a certain Russian estate?—that, we are inclined to say, is forever beyond our ken. Nor is this to suggest that one "reality" is necessarily contingent upon the other, or that there is an inference to be drawn immediately from the resonance between these two questionable "realities." The shape of this parallelism—if that is what this is—is too convoluted to warrant an automatic application of some analytic solution.

What remains conspicuous nonetheless is the two-point (or *diphasic*) structure of the "reality" involved in both instances. Inferring from this, then, it might be said that, like the "reality" of castration, the "reality" of the primal scene is, *structurally speaking,* a nonperception, nonexperience, and that it is only in its unexpected return that it (re)presents itself as real, that it founds the real on the basis of this never-has-been. For is it not true that the structure of the "reality" that comes and goes—or is it the other way around, "goes and comes," *"fort - da"?*—also obtains between the primal scene and the wolf dream? Recalling the two-phase structure of the latter experience *[Erfahrung],* could it not be said that the primal scene is that original *nothing* of an experience, which comes back as a oneiric spectacle?

The peculiar status of this reality—though ultimately obscure—bears a definitive resemblance to that of the ghost *[revenant].* For a specter, too, surely must be *nothing* real to begin with; its very "being"—but its temporality is very strange—is its returning; only on its second coming is it vividly, visibly, *spectacularly,* real. This, therefore, corresponds to the structure of another quintessentially Freudian notion: the uncanny *[unheimlich];* and this alliance would lead us further into the region of death and the undead.

• •

Having followed the polymorphous and polyvalent aftereffect of the Wolf-Man's "encounter" with the threat of castration, we now register the extent to which the problem of castration determines the lay of this "foreign" land, this psychical terrain proper, the unconscious.

As much as one can glean from the Wolf-Man's case, castration is not merely a particular content of a (mis)perception but first and foremost signifies a crisis of reality, of perception and judgment ("yes," "no," "there is," "there isn't"). This is what Samuel Weber has called a crisis of phenomenality. His exacting articulation of the place of castration in Freud's metapsychology—though spoken in connection to a different Freud text—is pertinent here:

> castration involves a structuring of experience that far transcends the realm of the individual psyche; and what it dislocates by its violent movement is the primacy of what Freud termed the "System Perception-Consciousness," which dominates both everyday experience and the tradition of western thought as a whole. For what the child "discovers"—that is, interprets—as "castration" is neither nothing nor simply something, at least in the sense in which the child expects and desires it to be: what is "discovered" is the absence of the maternal phallus, a kind of negative perception, whose object or referent—perceptum—is ultimately nothing but a difference, although no simple one, since it does not refer to anything, least of all to itself, but instead *refers itself indefinitely.*[90]

130   This highly condensed statement sheds much needed additional light upon the psychical crisis which we have come to recognize under the sign of castration. What is violently dislodged from the stable position of quiescent dominance is the offices of perceptual reality-judgment itself. But by the very act of this dislocation, what is thus displaced enters, or rather initiates, another order of "reality," or what Lacan calls the symbolic. For it is here that desire begins its skid; dislodged but not halted, it inaugurates an interminable and indeterminable series of substitutions, always pointing toward, referring to, something, or somewhere; but what is referred to is itself an absent "object" standing in for that first absence that brought upon the crisis. Thus it is here that significance and signification "proper" begins.

Furthermore, it is in this context that the vague resonances and parallels between the question of castration and the problem of "reality" in general, which have been hitherto merely hinted at, come to appear as a definite connection, even necessary ones. For what the present turn of analysis suggests is that it may be precisely the crisis brought on by the threat of castration that grounds, that is to say, breaks the ground for, *cognition* and *judgment* as we know it.

But if the threat of castration breaks the ground and initiates signification, it does so not in the moment of some simple beginning (at birth, for example) but rather in the middle of things; it "inaugurates" by erupting amidst what, from another perspective, was already in progress, that is, the ordinary time of "personal history."

Thus comes to the fore the peculiar nature of this crisis of castration as an originary event: not only is the "etiological origin" dispersed through several points in time, the time already in progress, there is also something peculiar about the organizing principle of this dispersal. What pulls these moments together—ultimately fictitiously, we "normal" adults are inclined to say—and produces this crisis, is to be located in, or rather transported to, an entirely different order of time, the time of pre-history of humankind. As such, this beginning belongs to the category of things that Freud calls primal fantasies. These refer to the structures of fantasy that can be called "typical," in the sense that they are common, in fact universal, in all humans living today. This is because, according to Freud, they are common inheritance of the species, or what he calls "phylogenetic" factors.

·   ·

We recall here one of Freud's memorable statements cited earlier: "It seems to me quite possible that all the things that are told to us today in analysis as phantasy . . . were once real occurrences in the primaeval times of the human family, and that children in their phantasies are simply filling in the gaps in individual truth with prehistoric truth." The passage, which is from the *Introductory Lectures on Psychoanalysis,* lecture 23, was the very text that Freud kept referring to whenever he came to the point of impasse concerning the "reality" of the primal scene. It so happens, then, that in those moments Freud was urging us to look into the prehistoric "reality," to turn attention in the general direction of *Totem and Taboo.*

For the time being, however, let us dwell upon the point made in the quotation concerning the common stock of fantasies which are said to be of a prehistoric origin. These are represented as *scenes,* as "experiences," that is, as meaningful units of what has transpired. Like dreams, they can be rendered in verbal-semantic forms. The list of such typical fantasies include: "I was once inside my mother's womb" / "I experienced coming out of my mother's womb" (fantasy of intrauterine experience); "I saw my parents in *coitus,* repeating the moment of conceiving me, originating me" (fantasy of the primal scene); "I was castrated" / "My father is going to castrate me" (fantasy of castration); "I was seduced by my father, or alternatively, by some other older member of the family" (fantasy of seduction). Freud the analyst, of course, regularly heard these reports of his patients' alleged "experiences," upon which his suspicion grew. Eventually he came to understand that the reports he was hearing were often coming from somewhere much older than the childhood of these patients.

If these scenes seem to "fill in gaps" of the individual's history, it is not only, or primarily, because they supply particular *contents* that are missing from it. The characteristic modes of operation are above all pulling together of disparate elements, merging, superimposition and trans-

131

position. The efficacy of the scenes lies in their power to coalesce what are scattered in time into a factitious bloc of meaning called "experience." In the Wolf-Man's case, for instance, even if his own infancy should have lacked the historical primal scene, fantasy would produce one by conjoining the "innocent" scene involving his parents and the sight of copulation between animals.

Far from erasing the infantile sexuality by banishing it into the realm of fantasy, this notion of primal fantasies emphasizes the enormity of the Oedipal desire and of the threat of castration that crosses that desire; it turns this whole complex into a transgenerational, phylogenetic affair. Moreover, the primal fantasy of castration is responsible for transposing the words of threat that may have come from his nursery maid or some other female attendant onto his father; for the psychical structure dictates that the dreaded castrator be his father. To draw upon the Wolf-Man's case again, his unconscious clearly identified his father as the castrator, as one who has the will and the power to carry out such an act, before which the poor child would be entirely defenseless.

132 Having followed this train of inquiry thus far, we have deviated somehow from our earlier understanding of the significance of castration. Only a little earlier it was becoming increasingly apparent that "the threat of castration" is not just one of the (actual or fantasized) episodes in the course of the Wolf-Man's illness but it is what grounded his neurosis as a whole; and, with the help of Weber's suggestive reading of Freud's essay on the uncanny, we have come to understand castration as a structure that radically grounds, in the rather unusual sense discussed above, what we so disarmingly call "experience." Yet, here in the course of examining the list of primal fantasies, castration once again seems to retreat to the position of "one of the several" items belonging to the same category of fantasies. At first glance castration does not even appear to be the most radical or most original of fantasies. It is not a fantasy about the earliest or most seminal event in the chronological sense. In fact, if the moment of Oedipal crisis under the threat of castration indicates any kind of beginning, it is only in the sense that it marks the end of the early, pregenital sexuality of the childhood, a point of no return.

Somewhere at this juncture the suggestion may rise that neither the parental coitus (primal scene) nor the castration threat—which are claimed to be the decisive factors in the Wolf-Man case—are scenes referring to the earliest or most originary moments of life; is it not rather the case that the most primordial of all is the fantasy pertaining to the very moment of birth? The fantasy of the intrauterine experience—understood as a fantasy precipitated and shaped by the yearning toward one's origin, and the concomitant desire to be reborn and to rejuvenate one's world entirely—is this not the most fundamental determination of the psychical structure, including the case of the Wolf-Man? As we know, it was by no means Jung and his partisans alone who found this suggestion irresistible. (Thus the enormous popularity of Jung among the so-called religionists, in contrast to their general disdain for Freud.) But this suggestion amounts to a rethinking of the entire itinerary of the infantile sexual development.

We have had an occasion earlier to note that, according to Freud, giving up of feces and the withdrawing of the mother's breast are in some way premonitory forms of castration. By the same line of reasoning, it can be construed that the moment of birth—the moment when one's own being is being given up, so to speak, and being separated from its locus of primordial unity with one's own source—is also a precursor, in fact, the oldest one, of castration. Here, it seems only a short step from this idea to the "revisionism" of Otto Rank, who took this sequence, transposed the course of derivation, and put it in reverse order. Instead of conceiving of the moment of birth, weaning, or defecating as anticipatory castration, Rank lets the causal determination run the other way around. In his formulation, in other words, it is the "experience" of the moment of birth, not castration, that determines and structures all future psychical crises. In this reformulation, the crisis of castration—which, in the case of the Wolf-Man, drags with it the scene of parental coitus—loses its preeminence as a moment in childhood development. For castration crisis merely repeats, in some distorted fashion—and with necessary emendations owing to the later phase of the organic maturity of the child—the trauma of birth. Although it was still several years before Rank put forward this position, which caused the eventual rift between him and the master, Jung had already suggested something similar. This issue of (re)birth fantasy—which, according to some of Freud's challengers, was to be given the most foundational status, thus relegating the whole Oedipal drama as a secondary, derivative phenomenon—was indeed the last combat Freud was to engage in at the close of the penultimate "solution" chapter of the Wolf-Man case.

133

• •

At the end of that chapter, we learn further about the Wolf-Man. He repeatedly lamented that the world was "hidden from him by a veil" and that it was only occasionally that this veil was removed, when, specifically, he received an enema (which he did as a regular remedy for his stubborn hysterical constipation). Then and only then and only for a short while, he claimed, he "saw the world clearly." Freud reports that he faced a considerable obstacle before he could shed light on this aspect of the patient's complaint: "The interpretation of this 'veil' progressed with as much difficulty as we met with in clearing up his fear of the butterfly. Nor did he keep to the veil. It became still more elusive, as a feeling of twilight, 'ténèbres,' and of other impalpable [ungreifbaren] things" [99 / GW, 12:133]. In the last analysis, however, all this evasiveness and allusion seem to have prepared Freud well, so that when the Wolf-Man finally produced another memory, Freud immediately recognized the connection. The memory in question is as follows: "he remembered having been told that he was born with a caul [Glückshaube]. He had for that reason always looked on himself as a special child of fortune whom no ill could befall. He did not lose that conviction until he was forced to realize that his gonorrhoeal infection constituted a serious injury to his body" [99].

This last episode of infection, we recall, occasioned the outbreak of the Wolf-Man's adult neurosis. As may be expected, Freud recognizes in this threat of "a serious injury to his body" the most primordial of such threats, castration. Thus he continues immediately: "The blow to his narcissism was too much for him and he went to pieces [vor dieser Kränkung seines Narzißmus brach er zusammen]. It may be said that in so doing he was repeating a mechanism that he had already brought into play once before. For his wolf phobia had broken out when he found himself faced by the fact that such a thing as castration was possible; and he clearly classed his gonorrhoea as castration" [99–100].

All the same, Freud does recognize the intrauterine and birth fantasies in the Wolf-Man's preoccupation with the veil/caul. In fact, he finds in this veil theme both the fantasy of return to the womb and that of rebirth or reemergence into the world, such that he is able to show how both of those wishful fantasies are expressed, in a typical fashion of the unconscious, simultaneously and unrecognizably in the patient's symptomatic complaint. On the one hand, "the caul was the veil which hid him from the world and hid the world from him. The complaint that he made was in reality a fulfilled wishful phantasy: it exhibited him as back once more in the womb, and was, in fact, a wishful phantasy of flight from the world" [100]. On the other hand, the patient's belief in the efficacy of enema brings up the other aspect: "If this birth-veil was torn, then he saw the world and was re-born. The stool was the child, as which he was born a second time, to a happier life" [100].

While Freud insists on the primacy of the castration complex, all this may appear at the same time to be playing into the hands of Jung, who did not stop at drawing attention to the rebirth fantasy. For Jung, of course, this fantasy had its source in a universal spiritual endowment of humankind and as such it was ultimately of a religious nature. As Freud puts it, Jung "assigned [to the rebirth fantasy] such a dominating position in the imaginative life [Wunschleben] of neurotics" [100]. In contrast, Freud's own interpretive strategy—which is already obvious from the passage quoted above where he aligns the tearing of the veil with the threat to narcissism—is to subsume this palpable fantasy of rebirth entirely under the law of Oedipus and its principle, castration:

> The necessary condition of his re-birth was that he should have an enema administered to him by a man. . . . This can only have meant that he had identified himself with his mother, that the man was acting as his father, and that the enema was repeating the act of copulation, as the fruit of which the excrement-baby (which was once again himself) would be born. The phantasy of re-birth was therefore bound up closely with the necessary condition of sexual satisfaction from a man. . . . Here, therefore, the phantasy of re-birth was simply a mutilated and censored version of the homosexual wishful phantasy. [100]

In effect, according to Freud's line of analysis,[91] rebirth fantasy, far from being a primordial (and ultimately pre- or nonsexual) stratum of the human psyche, is a repetition of the Oedipal drama, which was originally played out in the form of the primal scene and its belated actualization in the wolf dream. Moreover, Freud goes on to say,

> this instance, I think, throws light on the meaning and origin of the womb-phantasy as well as that of re-birth. The former, the womb-phantasy, is frequently derived (as it was in the present case) from an attachment to the father. There is a wish to be inside the mother's womb in order to replace her during intercourse—in order to take her place in regard to the father. The phantasy of re-birth, on the other hand, is in all probability regularly a softened substitute (a euphemism, one might say) for the phantasy of incestuous intercourse with the mother. . . . This is a wish to be back in a situation in which one was in the mother's genitals; and in this connection the man is identifying himself with his own penis and is using it to represent himself.

The overall effect of Freud's analysis here is astonishingly neat, perhaps to the point of making us incredulous. This almost excessive neatness is more than reminiscent of his famous account of the Oedipal tragedy by Sophocles, as well as of his interpretation of the two fundamental laws of totemism. (We recall that it is said that Oedipus fulfilled the two most primordial wishes of man, and suffered as a consequence the fate of blinding or loss of the eyes, which for Freud signifies a displaced castration. Exactly analogous to this, he argued that totemic laws prohibit these same desires, by decreeing not to kill the totemic animal, and not to marry women of one's own kin.) Here on the subject of the intrauterine cum rebirth fantasies, the two desires in question are interpreted as veiled manifestations of the original bisexual desires of the child directed toward its parents: "Thus the two phantasies are revealed as each other's counterparts: they give expression, according as the subject's attitude is feminine or masculine, to his wish for sexual intercourse with his father or with his mother. We cannot dismiss the possibility that in the complaint made by our present patient and in the necessary condition laid down for his recovery [enema] the two phantasies, that is to say, the two incestuous wishes, were united" [102].

Apparently, for Freud, what is unshakable is the universal rule of the Oedipus complex, understood in this "correct," comprehensive version, with the castration complex as its absolute determining force and organizing principle of all desire. It is only under the dictate of the sign of castration that the whole of the Wolf-Man case—and much else—is rendered in any way comprehensible. The crisis brought on by this all-powerful sign is not an event that can be located at a precise point in time; for it is literally a complex, which arises codependently. They arise *in* and *as* the traces of diachronic cross-reference, interpenetration, and superimposition of "events" dispersed in time. Thus we come back to Weber's statement that "castration" is really a structure, a "moment" that grounds phenomenality. And this structure, Freud would of course insist, is not given first as an analytic scheme (that is, as something extrinsic to the life lived by the patient) but it is the structure of the Wolf-Man's experience itself, it is the shape of his past.

The Oedipal drama and its coefficient, castration, is not something that happens in the beginning in any simple chronological sense; it comes into effect sometime in the course of the individual's life, and assumes the position of an origin, or *Ursache* [ground]. Since it does invariably come into effect, everything that came before and comes after will equally fall under its dictate, so that innocence from it is impossible. The only "freedom" conceivable is a fantasy of escape, or a degree of disentanglement through analysis. The latter is only partial, whereas the former is illusory. The sexual innocence of the child implied by Jung's reinterpretation is declared a fantasy, in this precisely psychoanalytic sense, whose formation is itself under the sway of the Oedipal desire and concomitant prohibitions.

•　　•

Thus what began as a broader notion of infantile sexuality, Freud eventually consolidated under the sign of castration/Oedipus complex. This psychoanalytic discovery has been under attack from the very beginning, and no one knew this better than Freud. The constancy of the opposing voices, their well-nigh universal protest and appeal to "reasonable" standards and human decency, can only be matched by the constancy of Freud's insistence on its truth. Indeed, the fact that he remained so utterly unmoved by these criticisms demands utmost attention on the part of his readers. Above all, it alerts us to the probability that the castration/Oedipus complex is underwriting all chronologies and histories that Freud ever writes. This is not to conclude that Freud is, as they say, "reading the Oedipus story into" all histories. Rather, it should call our attention to the curious fact that his histories do not start from a beginning but always in the midst, not even in an unambiguously and unequivocally locatable "one day." The Oedipus complex and the Oedipal crisis name this unspecifiable—or rather, *multiply specifiable*—point in time, which, nonetheless, is situated as a zero point of experience, as a point of total transvaluation. It is the point on which the entire "experience" turns.

It is now left for us to reexamine some of these other histories and chronologies constructed by Freud in light of the enormity of the threat of castration in structuring a narratable time, and at the same time, in light of the extremely problematic, or radically indeterminable nature of castration's "reality."

137

Metapsychology of Temporality

From the early days Freud used the term *metapsychology* to designate the most theoretical of the psychoanalytic concerns. The *meta* of metapsychology is analogous to that of metaphysics;[92] for metapsychology, too, is a deeply philosophical—and often speculative—endeavor. If it ventures "beyond" traditional psychology, it does so, above all, in the sense that it is no longer defined by, or confined within, the domain of consciousness. Understanding the mental apparatus as a comprehensive entity far more extensive than consciousness, of necessity, metapsychology calls for new concepts and principles for explanation.

As a paradigmatic moment of metapsychology, one would first list the seventh chapter of *The Interpretation of Dreams* (1900). This difficult text explicates the psychical apparatus in terms of two distinct "systems": Unconscious (abbreviated Ucs.) on the one hand, and Preconscious/Conscious (Pcs./Cs.) on the other. Corresponding to these are two types of mental functioning characteristic of each system: the primary process and the secondary process. The first is dictated by the pleasure principle, seeking immediate discharge or hallucinatory satisfaction; it is exemplified by the modes of representation typical of dreams, that is, by condensation and displacement; it is the working of the mobile psychic energy, or "unbound cathexis." The secondary process is tainted, or rather, "educated," by the reality principle to delay discharge in order to achieve an eventual but "real" satisfaction, albeit through a circuitous route; its essential function is inhibitive, the working of the quiescent energy, or "bound cathexis."[93] At that time, Freud conceived of the relation between the two systems mainly in terms of censorship and repression.

This is but one instance of Freud's metapsychology. As is well known today, there was an earlier, unofficial version dated 1895, a lengthy manuscript exhibiting a remarkable tendency toward neurophysiological explanation of psychical processes. For one reason or another, this text was not published until long after the author's death, and it has been known since as "Project for a Scientific Psychology."[94] Then there were several later versions of metapsychology, which in some ways refined but more often revised earlier delineations, and at times introduced something entirely novel. The customary list of Freud's metapsychological works includes *Three Essays on the Theory of Sexuality* (1905),[95] *Beyond the Pleasure Principle* (1920),[96] *Group Psychology and the Analysis of the Ego* (1921),[97] *The Ego and the Id* (1923),[98] and *Inhibition, Symptoms and Anxiety* (1926).[99]

138   What first brought the term *metapsychology* to prominence was, however, a series of essays of highly exploratory nature, now commonly known as the "Metapsychological Papers."[100] Written in 1915, in the unexpected hours of leisure brought by the war—this puts them roughly contemporaneous with *Totem and Taboo* and the Wolf-Man's case history—these pieces were at once the fruit and the casualties of the war. They were what was left of an aborted project, originally conceived as a book, rather tentatively titled "Zur Vorbereitung einer Metapsychologie" [Preliminary to a Metapsychology]. All twelve of its chapters reportedly had been completed, but only five among them eventually saw the light of day with Freud's blessing. These surviving chapters were published in the following years, individually entitled "Instincts and Their Vicissitudes," "Repression," "The Unconscious," "A Metapsychological Supplement to the Theory of Dreams," and "Mourning and Melancholia" [*SE*, vol. 14]. The rest were presumed lost, having been abandoned by the author.

It should be added, however, that nearly half a century after the author's death a draft of another chapter—which happens to have a particular relevance to the readers of *Totem and Taboo*—turned up. This document is now known to have been intended as the last chapter of the phantom book. The manuscript clearly bears the heading in Freud's own hand, "XII. Übersicht der Übertragungsneurosen" [Overview of the Transference Neuroses]. The recently published English translation of the document draws attention to its striking content and adds a judgment of sorts, as it calls itself *A Phylogenetic Fantasy*.[101] The psychoanalytic associate with whom Freud was most closely in touch in the course of writing these consequential treatises was Sándor Ferenczi (1873–1933), among whose papers the only surviving manuscript of this last chapter had been buried until 1983.

It is above all to this last document I wish to turn, in order to return to the crux, the impasse, the conundrum with which I began this reading of Freud, namely, the scene of the primal parricide. Insofar as this way home to *Totem and Taboo* means going through the consummation of metapsychology circa 1915 (that is, via *Phylogenetic Fantasy*), another detour appears necessary. This seemingly circuitous route, however, may very well turn out to be a shortcut, insofar as it cuts through what Freud summarily referred to, at the beginning of the *Totem and Taboo,* as "essential nature" of psychoanalysis.

Infantile Sexuality in the Extramoral Sense

As even a cursory review of the metapsychological works listed above makes evident, at the time of *Totem and Taboo,* much of metapsychology was still in the making. The theory of the psychical apparatus was somewhere between the first and the second versions. The notion of censorship had been worked over significantly, and it was at the point of yielding to a new notion, the ego ideal; but this latter in turn was to be subsumed and replaced by the super ego in another ten years. The theory of the drive was being rigorously elaborated. The binary opposition of the two fundamental types of drives—libido (sexual drives) on the one hand, and ego drives or self-preservation drives *[Ego- oder Selbsterhaltungstriebe]* on the other—was fully operative in Freud's thinking, although this, too, was soon to be replaced, or overlaid, by an entirely new set of binary opposites: eros [life drives] and thanatos [death drives].

139

In this critical period of theory formation, what was increasingly commanding attention was the ego, not only as an active agency but also as a passive object, of love, of hate, and of reproaches. Also coming to the forefront were the processes that are crucial to the formation of the ego and its future career in various libidinal relations; psychoanalysis calls these processes "introjection," "incorporation," and "identification." In addition, various psychical defense mechanisms—by means of which the precariously constituted ego protects itself against the unwelcome and disruptive surge of the drives from within—were being described with greater precision; these are the mechanisms of "repression," "projection," and "sublimation."

These newly introduced or newly elaborated concepts, moreover, were to lay the theoretical foundation for the classification of the pathological types, or what Freud calls "choice of neuroses" *[Neurosenwahl].* Over the years, he variously attempted to correlate the types of psychoneurotic disorders with the "stages" of sexual development, and eventually to classify them etiologically in relation to the types of fixation corresponding to these "stages." Yet even in the final form, these "stages" do not amount to a unilinear, "developmental course" in the usual sense. What emerges instead is but a highly ambiguous composite picture, which the reader would have to reconstruct, based on the multiple—and not always consistent—treatises Freud wrote over two decades.

. . .

The quality of overlayering is nowhere more visible than in the *Three Essays on the Theory of Sexuality*. The text went through six editions (1905–24) during Freud's lifetime, four of which added text and notes. The individual essays comprising the book—"The Sexual Aberrations," "Infantile Sexuality," "The Transformations of Puberty"—express Freud's fundamental concerns: to describe the extended and significantly displaced sense of sexuality, as it is pertinent to psychoanalysis.

140   A redescription of sexuality became necessary, above all, because of the new psychoanalytic postulate, infantile sexuality. So self-evident to the psychoanalyst and yet so controversial, Freud had an opportunity to look back upon the career of this novel idea twenty years after the first publication of the *Three Essays*. Thus he writes in a retrospective essay called *Selbstdarstellung* (literally, "self-representation"; translated as "An Autobiographical Study"), "Few of the findings of psycho-analysis have met with such universal contradiction or have aroused such an outburst of indignation as the assertion that *the sexual function starts at the beginning of life* and reveals its presence by important signs even in childhood. And yet no other findings of analysis can be demonstrated so easily and so completely" [*SE* 20:33; emphasis added].

Soon thereafter, a slight yet consequential qualification follows. "The sexual function, as I found, is in existence from the very beginning of the individual's life, *though at first it is attached to the other vital functions and does not become independent of them until later;* it has to pass through a long and complicated process of development before it becomes what we are familiar with as the normal sexual life of the adult" [20:35; emphasis added].

This innocuously descriptive statement contains three of the most fundamental tenets of psychoanalysis regarding sexual development. First, even though sexuality is there "from the beginning," it does not begin as an essential "function" in and of itself, but rather, it develops parasitically, "attached to" or "leaning upon" what Freud here calls "other vital functions." This refers to the issue of *anaclisis [Anlehnung]*, to which we shall turn presently.

Secondly, it is mentioned here that sexuality must "pass through a long and complicated process" before it attains its familiar adult form; what intervenes between the infantile and the adult (postpubescent) sexuality is a period of some half dozen years or more, known as the latency period, during which sexual development, or rather sexuality itself, is said to remain dormant. Here we recall that it was none other than the Oedipal crisis—read, the threat of castration—and the eventual dissolution of this crisis through renunciation of the infantile incestual desire that brings about the period of latency. And it is not until the time of puberty that sexuality is mobilized once again. This peculiar structure of interrupted development is what is known as the "diphasic onset" of sexuality.[102]

The third point is merely alluded to. Although one would only have to turn to the *Three Essays* to see the point mentioned plainly, here in the *Selbstdarstellung*, it is merely blandly noted that sexuality will eventually "become what we are familiar with as the normal sexual life of the adult." The point is, the second onset of sexuality in puberty is not only a matter of reactivation of what has been dormant; there is a new element, and this new element is the biological maturity of the reproductive organ.

It is perhaps in this last point that the difference between the psychoanalytic and the conventional views on sexuality most readily shows up. For psychoanalysis, the organic reproductive function is "a new aim" [*SE*, 7:207] emerging only at the time of puberty; it was not there at the beginning. Conversely put, sexuality itself is there from the beginning—or *almost* from the beginning—and only secondarily does it become attached to the reproductive function.

Nor can this "new aim" of the adult sexuality be considered the predestined telos of the infantile sexuality. Sexuality *turns* reproductive only at the later date, and only incompletely. Even though it is generally expected that at puberty sexuality becomes subsumed and subordinated by this new aim, this is ultimately a matter of statistics, as they say, and Freud leaves plenty of room to entertain the possibility of its social (rather than natural, biological) determination. At any rate, he clearly signals that the jubilantly polymorphous sexuality of the original kind is not altogether superseded or essentially transformed. As Freud shows in some detail in the *Three Essays*, infantile sexuality survives more or less in its original form precisely *by attaching itself to the biological reproductive function*.[103]

Yet what is even more radical and "unconventional" about the Freudian theory of sexuality—even more so than the notion of this nearly fortuitous dependency or attachment of (infantile) sexual drives on the reproductive instinct from puberty onward—is the first point mentioned above, namely, the notion that the original, infantile sexuality does not emerge as something on its own (as any instinct would), but it is essen-

141

tially and structurally dependent upon, and at the same time deviant from, certain fundamental biological functions. In sum—but it will be discussed further below—it can be said that the whole of sexuality is *perversion from the very beginning;* that there is no such thing as "sexuality proper."

Origin of Sexuality

This constitutionally perverse, parasitically dependent nature of sexuality—the radical lack of its own essence—likely explains why it is so difficult for us to get a clear picture of something like the "origin and development of sexuality according to Freud." Ultimately, Freud does not give such a picture. Yet this fact itself, far from being a failure or an oversight on his part, can be highly instructive.

Let us begin at a place where he *appears to be* giving such a picture:

> [Sexuality] begins by manifesting itself in the activity of a whole number of *component instincts [Partialtriebe].* These are dependent upon *erotogenic zones* in the body; some of them make their appearance in pairs of opposite impulses (such as sadism and masochism or the impulses to look and to be looked at); they operate independently of one another in search for pleasure, and they find their object for the most part in the subject's own body. Thus at first the sexual function is non-centralized and predominantly *auto-erotic.* [20:35]

As it appears here, the infantile form of sexuality is for the most part without an external object; its aim is multiple and polymorphous and is directed toward production of component-specific pleasure.[104] Infantile sexuality is neither mobilized by nor directed toward an object; rather, the drive achieves satisfaction within the locus of one's own body.

If sexuality at this stage is an assortment of "component drives," at least some of these components seem to be specific to particular anatomical regions; the diversity of the sexual aims corresponds to the diversity of these so-called erotogenic zones. Soon, the predominance of some of these anatomical regions begins to provide sexuality with some form of organization. "Later, syntheses begin to appear in it; a first stage of organization is reached under the dominance of the *oral* components, and the *anal-sadistic* stage follows, and it is only after the third stage has at last been reached that the primacy of the *genitals* is established and that the sexual function begins to serve the ends of reproduction" [20:35].

This suggests that we should be able to plot the course of "sexual development" in terms of the shifting erotogenic zones.[105]

Thus far, two vectors of "development" seem to have been introduced. The first vector is the emergence of object love out of the state of autoerotism. The second has to do with the change in sexual organization. (In the first edition of the *Three Essays*, this latter course of development was delineated simply as from pregenital to genital organization. In the *Selbstdarstellung* version quoted above, it is elaborated as oral, anal-sadistic, and genital organizations. However, when the later edition of the *Three Essays* as well as some other papers on the related subject are taken into account, the stage of genital organization is in fact split in two, such that the more detailed version would be: oral, anal, phallic, and genital stages.)

Rendered this way, it appears that sexuality "develops" somewhere along the line of gradual, progressive recognition of the external object, that this progression is therefore the process of discovering the other, such a process being the inevitable lessons of reality. The notion is familiar. It is tempting to read Freud as if he were suggesting that every infant begins its life in the state of solipsistic, undifferentiated, objectless *jouissance,* or so-called autoerotism. Strongly evocative of some versions of Hegelian soteriology, this image of the prelapsarian infancy is not unlike the mythic Edenic state before history, when all is void and yet full. Then, the story goes, with the ineluctable forces of reality impinging and intruding upon its solitary bliss, the infant gradually comes to construct a cognitive boundary between the self and other for the first time. One looks in vain for textual underpinnings that would support such a—romantic? Wordsworthian?—"origin of the subject-object separation" scenario in Freud.

Nevertheless, in Freud's version also, the construction of the self and other seems to be a fundamentally violent process, as this construction materializes just at those moments of boundary violation: in particular, taking in food, and expelling fecal and other abject matters. Thus it comes about that these bodily loci of primary material transactions become particularly—and anxiously—charged, and they remain highly vested and interested sites of commerce with "others." These, for Freud, are the original loci of love, or "erotogenic zones." Libido becomes perceptible here for the first time.

This process, moreover, is vital to the emergence of what psychoanalysis calls the ego. The ego is a singular sort of "object" that poses as "the subject." As many Freud readers nowadays remind us, the ego is not a primordially given entity but something that has to be developed. And for this developmental process what is essential is love, or more precisely, libido. For to love another is to offer up part of the available libidinal energy and to confer it upon (cathect, *besetzen*) this other. To a greater or lesser degree this entails an evacuation of the psychical energy, and in order for this outpouring not to destroy the one who loves, the ego must be of a certain fortitude; but to achieve this state of stability and strength, the ego itself must be already libidinally cathected. It is only on the basis of this formative and fortifying self-love that the effluent love of an object proper can be established.

The newborn infant obviously does not love in this way. It survives for a time despite the absence of a developed ego because, presumably, its psychical energy exists in a totally self-centered, as it were, autocephalous state of indeterminacy. Of course, this psychic autonomy is, from the standpoint of its biological being, completely illusory; the infant's physical being is almost entirely dependent on others for the obvious reason that its body is premature and most of its natural faculties are wholly inadequate to accomplish even the most rudimentary functions necessary for survival; it would not survive at all unless others attend to these functions. It therefore seems that the infant's survival is contingent precisely on this contradiction, this interstice between the psychical and physiological realities, between autonomy and dependency. And it is in this interstice that pleasure and pain first come to take upon the meaning of "love."

144

The care thus given to the infant—and the "love" that ineluctably comes with it—is therefore both invasive and nurturing at the same time. It occurs at the barely formed, extremely sketchy boundary of the infant's own sense of what we casually call "the self." What is decisive here is that these contacts and negotiations which the infant's body receives offer not only assistance in its strictly biological functions, but always something more, some extra sensation, pleasure, meaning.

When psychoanalysis mentions the two forms of object choice—narcissistic and anaclitic—they refer to the types of object love that become prominent later in life: whether the choice of the object is modeled after the love one originally endowed upon one's own ego or after the love that developed along the care the infant received from others. While the distinction may appear unambiguous—self-directed versus other-directed—they cannot be placed in any form of chronological or structural priority. This is so despite the fact that Freud added in 1911 a so-called narcissistic stage to the general picture of sexual development. The difficulty of aligning primary narcissism in relation to the notion from another register, autoerotism, is articulated clearly in the essay "On Narcissism": "The primary narcissism of children which we have assumed and which forms one of the postulates of our theories of the libido, is less easy to grasp by direct observation than to confirm by inference from elsewhere" [SE, 14:90]. What is plainly observable instead—and comically obvious to all but the parents—is the source of the (alleged) infantile narcissism and psychical omnipotence.[106] This is tantamount to saying that, while narcissism is a necessary element in the formation of the ego, primary narcissism as a particular stage of development[107] may be as much a fantasy of the doting parents projected as the psychical state of the child. Indeed it is difficult to determine the location of this love, whether it is in the mythical bliss of the autoerotic child, or in the reactivated narcissism of the parents transformed into, and thus disguised as, an object love.[108]

The problematic nature of the category of "narcissism" is made even more pronounced by the peculiarity of its counterpart, anaclisis [An-lehnung]. The term Anlehnung—meaning "leaning on" or "propping"— immediately reminds us of the dependency of an infant's biological being on other humans, despite the near total autonomy of its psychical life. But what Freud refers to as anaclisis is not really about "dependence" in this sense. It is not the dependency of the infant on the primary care-giver (the mother or her surrogate), but the dependency of sexual drives [Triebe] on the biological, instinctual functions.[109]

Here we come upon the most intriguing and most elusive point of Freud's vision of the "origin and development" of sexuality. It is also at this juncture that the impossibility of coalescing and consolidating the various vectors of "sexual development" into a unitary, coherent, and unilinear schema becomes apparent.

145

•   •

At the outset, we seem to have a puzzling situation. The oral mode of "love" and its attendant fantasy of devouring and incorporation must, in a way, presuppose an object, even if the "consummation" of this love inevitably entails the destruction of that object qua external object. On the other hand, the earliest "stage" of sexuality is also called "autoerotic."[110] Does sexuality in these early days, then, have an object? An answer to this question comes by way of a curious example, which turns out to be the prototype of the sexual act.

The first *distinctly sexual* activity, that is, the pleasure-deriving activity in the oral stage—the very activity that confirmed for Freud the reality of the sensual pleasure in the oral region—does not seem to be really object directed or goal oriented. Rather, this activity is something quite empty: thumb sucking. It is to be assumed that this familiar activity, observed universally in children, is entirely derivative, that it is a substitutive act for something not so empty. In other words, we understand that this is an ultimately futile attempt to call forth something unavailable, that is, an attempt on the part of the child temporarily bereft of what it *really* wants: the mother's breast, the milk it gives, and the accompanying sensation of warmth and comfort. Accordingly, it seems, even though in itself quite objectless and aimless, the activity of thumb sucking is nonetheless oriented toward *an absent object* or an unavailable aim. It is significant that it is just this derivative, substitutive practice that psychoanalysis recognizes as the first sexual act "properly" speaking. It marks the originary moment of sexuality.

If this prototype of sexual practice harks back to another practice (feeding at the breast of the mother) and to another form of satisfaction (satiating hunger), it is because this other, nonsexual practice of nursing *already* yields to the child not only what it *really* needs but also something else: sheer pleasure. And it is this excess yield of pleasure that is reproduced in the "substitute" act of thumb sucking, without the presence of the provider, without the external object (milk, breast, or mother). It is thus as though sexuality arose at the moment of a loss—loss of the object; by losing sight of what the biological organism *really needs,* by deviating from the purposive, self-preservative, instinctual behavior, sexuality is born, perverting the secondary yield of pleasure into an end in itself. This complicated process is described in disarmingly easy prose by Freud:

> To begin with, sexual activity attaches itself to functions serving the purpose of self-preservation and does not become independent of them until later. No one who has seen a baby sinking back satiated from the breast and falling asleep with flushed cheeks and a blissful smile can escape the reflection that this picture persists as a prototype of the expression of sexual satisfaction in later life. The need for repeating the sexual satisfaction now becomes detached from the need for taking nourishment—a separation which becomes inevitable when the teeth appear and food is no longer taken in only by sucking, but is also chewed up. The child does not make use of an extraneous body for his sucking, but prefers a part of his own skin because it is more convenient, because it makes him independent of the external world, which he is not yet able to control, and because in that way he provides himself, as it were, with a second erotogenic zone, though one of an inferior kind. [7:182]

The libidinal investment in an object other than oneself, love conferred upon a person other than oneself, is modeled after the love that emerges "leaning upon" or "propping against" *[anlehnen]* not so much another object or person, but another kind of need, activities other than the sexual ones. Hence, the "origin" of allosexuality is in the obscurity of this other: instinctive, biologically conditioned, natural activities.

We may now pose the question afresh: In the beginning, does the infant's sexual love have an object? The answer may play out in this way: it has an object, but it is an *absent* object; or, conversely, it does not have an object *because it has already lost it;* or, still more strangely, it *never could* have had an object because that original, "real," absent object is always a wrong object, an object meant for something else.

•   •

Somewhere around here, those vectors of "sexual development" begin to unravel.

At some point earlier, it seemed that we could expect to find, ultimately, some biological basis for sexual-psychical development in anatomical regions, and that its elusive chronology could be mapped onto those various bodily parts. But this course immediately becomes entangled with the multiplicity of objects and the metaphoric proliferation of aims. As we recall, the oral stage is characterized expressly as "cannibalistic" and the anal stage as "sadistic." Freud seems to be conjoining the stages of pregenital organization with particular *aims [Ziele]*, which in turn call for particular modes of "loving" the object. Thus the goal of the oral mode of "love" is to take into one's body, to consume, thus to annihilate, and at the same time to incorporate and assimilate, the object. The prototype of the object here is food, but to the extent that this is a form of "love" and not a biological function of taking nourishment, the oral drive begins to reach out to anything that could be introduced into the oral cavity, either in reality or in fantasy. In point of fact, the fantasy of "taking into oneself" easily extends beyond this particular bodily region and becomes associated with other orifices and with other activities: breathing, seeing, and so on.[111] Similarly, the anal "love" is in fact more generally muscular than narrowly sphincteral, having to do with the expulsion (and destruction) as well as the retention (and control) of the object. The quintessential "object" here is the fecal matter, but this, too, immediately begins to acquire other symbolic values.[112] When we add to this situation Karl Abraham's refinement of the schema, the list of relevant body parts proliferate even further. For instance, Abraham proposed an intermediary stage between the oral-cannibalistic and the anal-sadistic stages, which he called "oral-sadistic," where the appearance of teeth and the act of biting is said to predominate.[113]

To be sure, the notion of "component instincts" Freud introduced in 1905 may appear to mediate between the anatomical regions and the developmental stages, but in fact it does more. The result is more unsettling than stabilizing as regards Freud's developmental schema. For with the notion of component instincts, Freud also postulates that there are certain aspects of sexual drives that are independent of those designated as "erotogenic zones":

It must, however, be admitted that infantile sexual life, in spite of the preponderating dominance of erotogenic zones, exhibits components which from the very first involve other people as sexual objects. Such are the instincts of scopophilia, exhibitionism, and cruelty, which appear in a sense independently of erotogenic zones;

147

these instincts do not enter into intimate relations with genital life until later, but are already to be observed in childhood as independent impulses, distinct in the first instance from erotogenic sexual activity. [7:191–92].

However that might be, Freud insists that the shifting dominance of the anatomical region will eventually settle, at about the age of four or five, on the genital primacy. But this primacy and ultimacy of the genitals—what may appear to be the *norm* of infantile sexual development—is radically divided. For one thing, this "genital organization" becomes, so to speak, the very site of interruption and latency. We have heard previously that the child before the age of five does not recognize the two distinct genitals, male and female, but only the presence and absence of one kind of genitals, the penis. Thus the sexual significance of the genital zone for the child is not limited to the "real" organ but, much more importantly, it becomes something whose significance is monstrously disproportionate and fantastic, the phallus. As such, the phallus is ultimately a sign; it is another name for, or obverse face of, castration.

To mark this difference between the infantile significance of the genital zone (qua phallus) and the later, postpubescent significance (qua genitals proper), Freud refined the schema in the 1924 edition of the *Three Essays* by introducing the *phallic stage,* which refers to the final, culminating point of infantile sexuality, whereas the term *genital organization* is now reserved for the second (adult) phase of sexuality. Thus in the revised version, the genital organization proper does not set in until the actual biological maturity of the reproductive organ. What happens in the meantime, under the lingering sign of the phallus cum castration, is nothing less than wondrous. For what happens in the interim is no less than the process of civilization itself. "The sexual impulses which have shown such liveliness are overcome by repression, and a *period of latency* follows, which lasts until puberty and during which the *reaction-formations* of morality, shame, and disgust are built up" [20:37].

Totem and Taboo Re-covered

The uncanny is the name Freud gave to the singular effect of a peculiar moment of survival, "something repressed which *recurs.*" As it is said in the celebrated essay of that name, the uncanny is "nothing new or alien, but something which is familiar and old-established in the mind and which has become alienated from it only through the process of repression."[114] Seemingly a localized, particular aesthetic effect, the uncanny thus turns out to be that familiar form of protracted "experience," the structure of signification that comes into effect for the first time only in its second visit. As such, this effect is a structural analog of the sexual trauma which we have come to recognize under the name of *Nachträglichkeit*.

There are several texts by Freud whose own histories seem to mimic the structure of the delayed signification, including "The 'Uncanny'" itself, which is something of an underpass connecting two of Freud's milestones: *Totem and Taboo* (1913) and *Beyond the Pleasure Principle* (1920). The actual origin of this essay remains obscure, as Freud relegates it to "an old paper . . . found in his drawer."[115] If such a beginning is suggestive of a kind of fortuity befitting another sort of tale—the "once upon a time" variety—we can be sure that this discovery was anything but a happenstance.[116] Yet, perhaps no other text by Freud enacts the structure of the uncanny return more vividly than the twelfth chapter of the phantom book project on metapsychology. Like a message in a bottle, its precarious survival and unexpected discovery after sixty-eight years seems fortuitous beyond belief, and at the same time, singularly intended.

The language of the discoverer, Ilse Grubrich-Simitis, in describing the circumstances of her encounter with this document, is reminiscent of the opening of so many tales of adventure: "Last year in London . . . I was looking through an old trunk of papers and other documents. . . . I came upon a manuscript in Freud's handwriting which from its title and content I could not connect with any of his published works. With the help of a brief letter Freud had written on the back of the last page, I soon realized what the manuscript was: the draft of the lost twelfth metapsychological paper."[117]

But what the note on the back dictated for the document was an extremely ambiguous future. It reads: "You [Ferenczi] can throw it away or keep it. The fair copy *[Reinschrift]* follows it sentence for sentence, deviating from it only slightly."[118] But the "fair copy"—meaning here, I presume, final draft—of course, did not survive, for reasons that must be seriously studied but ultimately can be only speculated, while this almost pure writing was to remain dormant in a trunk, whose own destiny was far from assured.[119] In short, the status of this consequential draft is equivalent to a dead letter, whose dictionary definition runs, "something that has lost its force or authority without being formally abolished." For this reason, while the exact identity of the document is unmistakable, it is difficult to say whether its survival and transmission to posterity was authorized or unauthorized.

The draft consists of two easily distinguishable sections, the demarcation of which can be discerned not only from the apparent content of each, but from the difference in style and the mode of argumentation. The first part consists of rather sketchy, abbreviated notations concerning the psychoanalytic nosography of neuroses. It appears to be meant as a summary of all of the preceding chapters; hence this part is most faithful to the title Freud gave the manuscript at the outset, "Overview of Transference Neuroses." (Hereafter, therefore, I will refer to this entire manuscript as "Overview.") The second section, in contrast, is rendered in much more finished prose, with far less use of abbreviations and telegraphic notations. It is this latter half that is foregrounded in the English edition, which is entitled "A Phylogenetic Fantasy." This editorial decision by the American publisher, which relegated to Freud's (and the German edition's) title the secondary status of a subtitle, is perhaps not without justification. For if the first part is a mere summary, this daring second half is where the nosographical categories of psychoneuroses are collated in relation to the particular "stages" [Stufe] of the history of the human species, or more properly, prehistory [Urgeschichte].

In this ultimate fantasy section culminates the entire metapsychological investigation of 1915, and it is here that what *Totem and Taboo* rendered as one catastrophic episode—though perhaps recurring over and over—is now extended and delineated as a series of successive stages, and at the same time these prehistoric "stages" are correlated with the so-called developmental history of the individual, which Freud had been elaborating in several editions of the *Three Essays*. Whatever the reasons for not publishing this apparent crown jewel of metapsychology, what was thus suppressed by the author, but what eventually came to light with all the ambiguities such an "unintended" return would necessarily entail, was an account of the most comprehensive temporality of human *cultural* history.[120] In brief, what this unauthorized document attempts is a construction of phylogenetic temporality mapped onto the nosographic classification of mental disorders as formulated by psychoanalysis.[121] (See figure 1.)[122] The result therefore is a version of the psychoanalytic picture of prehistory [Urgeschichte]. It can be delineated as follows.

•   •

As in all *Geschichte*, this, too, has to have an "onset," and Freud locates it in the beginning of the last Ice Age, the beginning of the hard times for humans and other living things, which thrusted them all into the general state of scarcity and want. The time before this beginning, in contrast, is said to have been a period of abundance. The paradisiac, perhaps semitropical clime—this could only be a phylogenetic equivalent of the fantasized intrauterine existence, or "mythic" state of eternal saturation and immediate satisfaction, where there is no desire because there is no want. "Dr. [Fritz] Wittels first expressed the idea that the primal human animal passed its existence in thoroughly rich milieu that satisfied all needs, echoes of which we have retained in the myth of the primeval paradise. There it may have overcome the periodicity of the libido, which is still connected with mammals."[123] The last sentence is an important

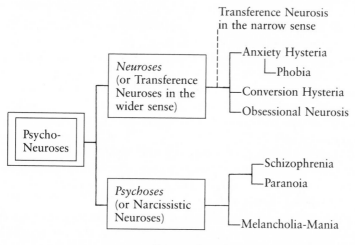

FIGURE 1

psychoanalytic addition. One notices that the beginning of sexuality as   151
drives *(Triebe)* divorced from biological instinct *(Instinkt)*—sexuality as
pure pleasure-seeking energy—is recognized already at this Edenic pre-
prehistory. The separation of the libido from the strictly biological function of procreation sets sexuality in motion, and the latter begins its own
deviant, "perverse" course.

At the onset of the Ice Age, Freud speculates, the general psychical
state produced by material scarcity was anxiety. In order to see how this
stage might correspond to anxiety hysteria, it is useful to review the clinical explanation of anxiety.

Let us recall that what Freud calls "wish" (or "desire," *Wunsch*) is an
"idea" ("representation," *Vorstellung*)[124] charged with ("cathected," *be-
setzt*) certain urgent, extremely volatile psychic energy, or what is called
"quota of affect" *[Affektbetrag]*. As a desire, that is, as something pro-
pelled by a pleasure-seeking drive *[Trieb]*, its energy is always libidinal,
that is, "sexual" in the radically revised, psychoanalytic sense.

Now, neurosis ensues when such a wish/desire is frustrated by some
internal (that is, psychical) reason and yet cannot be simply suppressed
[unterdrückt] or sublimated (its initially sexual aim transformed into a
nonsexual aim). It may happen that the very thought of the desire—let
alone its satisfaction—is inadmissible to consciousness, often on account
of some dire threat, actual or imagined. (We need only to remember the
formidably complex psychical situation in which the hapless little Wolf-
Man found himself.) In this manner, the desire comes to be *repressed [ver-
drängt]*. A neurosis is a partial failure of repression, in that, while the idea
of the desire is kept in the unconscious, its quota of affect escapes suppres-

sion and comes to be manifest psychically or somatically. To put it in a simplified fashion, the different types of neuroses are determined by the different structures of this failure.

Anxiety is an unpleasurable release of energy; it has no clearly determinable object; it is a sheer affect without an object. The quota of affect liberated from the original wish is transformed into a state of unaccountable fearful agitation, while the ideational content of the wish *(Vorstellung)* is withheld from consciousness.[125] This is the condition of anxiety hysteria.

Under the condition of want, thus Freud's speculation in the "Overview" goes, early humankind partially "abandoned the object-cathexis, retained the libido in the ego, and thus transformed into realistic anxiety what had previously been object-libido" [14].

Prehistoric humankind further confronted the necessity of curbing reproduction, whereupon libidinal satisfaction had to be sought elsewhere, in something other than heterosexual coitus, and in "perverse satisfactions" that do not lead to further propagation. Thus the "normal" sexual acts were substituted by, or converted to some other bodily practice. Here Freud suggests "the whole situation obviously corresponds to the conditions of conversion hysteria" [15].

In the case of conversion hysteria, the ideational content of the desire is entirely withdrawn from consciousness, but the repressed idea finds its expression in disguise, so to speak, in a particular segment of the body. The psychic energy is *converted* to a physiological one, and it induces an "innervation" (either over excitation or paralyzing inhibition) of the organ particularly associated with the repressed idea.[126]

There is an additional suggestion in the "Overview" that this condition affected women in particular because their sexual satisfaction (which, according to Freud, also serves their procreative desire) ran up against the problem of limiting propagation in a particularly exigent manner.

At this point, the first of Freud's bewilderingly light-footed yet enormously consequential moves occurs. He commences by saying "the subsequent evolution is easy to construct. It primarily affected the male":

After he had learned to economize on his libido and by means of regression to degrade his sexual activity to an earlier phase, activating his intelligence became paramount for him. He learned how to investigate, how to understand the hostile world somewhat, and how by means of inventions to secure his first mastery over it. He developed himself under the sign of energy *[unter dem Zeichen der Energie]*, formed the beginning of language, and had to assign great significance to the new acquisitions. Language was magic to him, his thoughts seemed omnipotent to him, he understood the world according to his ego. [15]

Therefore, while women continue to seek "perverse" satisfaction (which as a rule is not felt as pleasure) in hysteria by converting sexual pleasure into another *physical* excitation, men learn to sublimate it into a mental activity, thus learning to *control* the external, physical reality, even if to a very limited degree. Above all, the "energy" is associated with, or translated as, the sign,[127] and somehow this leads to the far-reaching cultural innovation: language, or speech *[Sprache]*. Thus it was that this tremendous "progress," the invention of speech—which must be assumed to have caused a definitive alteration in the makeup of human life[128]—is in fact a result of *regression,* specifically of the male libido turning back on itself. For this is also the period of the formation of the primal horde, the emergence of "a strong and wise brutal man" who controls all women, and prohibits access to them to all other males of the horde.

Freud sees this stage corresponding to obsessional neurosis in positive as well as in negative ways. Briefly, obsessional neurosis is characterized by overestimation of the power of words, either spoken or merely thought. In *Totem and Taboo* Freud discussed this type of neurosis with exceptional attentiveness, and he drew an analogy between the obsessional neurotic's behavior and the "magical" practices of primitive peoples and their "animistic" habits of thought. To be sure, obsessional neurosis *[Zwangsneurose;* literally, compulsion neurosis] is a contemporary mental ailment that is as much a reaction to the milieu of this prehistoric stage as it is a repetition of it. Therefore, "the overemphasis on thinking, the enormous energy that returns in the compulsion, the omnipotence of thoughts, the inclination to inviolable laws" manifest unchanged in obsessional neurosis, whereas other typical symptoms are the signs of "the struggle against this return" of the brutal impulses of the primal father [16].[129]

If obsessional neurosis corresponds to the psychical outlook of the primal father, the subsequent three "stages" are that of the sons. Here, then, is a radical shift, a decisive fault line in prehistory, and this chasm corresponds to the division between transference neuroses (neuroses proper, including anxiety hysteria, conversion hysteria, obsessional neurosis) and narcissistic neuroses (or psychoses, including schizophrenia, paranoia, melancholia-mania).

There had been a broad-stroke demarcation between neuroses and psychoses prior to psychoanalysis, but Freud offered new, etiological grounds for the distinction. Between the two categories there are several differences. First, the difference in the degree to which the etiological mo-

153

ment goes back in infancy.[130] There is an inversely parallel relation between the course of psychical formation and the time of the manifestation of illness.[131] The earlier, or more "primitive" its etiological moment, the later the actual onset (or manifestation) of the illness. Secondly, there is the difference in the severity of illness; psychosis is more impervious to treatment compared to obsessional neurosis, and hysteria more tractable than the latter.

Although obsessional neurosis involves a certain degree of regression, the transference neuroses as a whole are characterized by basic retention of the object relation; the desire, once spurned, maintains the outwardly, object-oriented structure, and the fantasy of its fulfillment either manifests itself in an apparently unrecognizable form—as indeterminate anxiety (anxiety hysteria) or as a somatic symptom (conversion hysteria)—or calls for an obsessive compensatory action (obsessional neurosis). One might say that in transference neuroses, under the pressure of an irrepressible desire and its equally indomitable counterforce, the psychical process may regress, but not to the point of reverting to the structure prior to the formation of the ego and, concomitantly, the discovery of an external object.

In psychosis, on the other hand, this is precisely what happens— regression to the homoerotic form of object love. Here, libido freed from the frustrated wish is not transferred or attached in fantasy to another object other than oneself, but rather it is turned towards one's own self.[132]

To return the "love" originally meant for another onto oneself, thus to "love oneself" instead of another, it is true, is not a total abandonment of the "object." For the ego, too, is an object, albeit an internalized one. At the same time, this object, which is a precipitate formed within what we are accustomed to calling one's "self," involves a differently structured object relation, such that it leads to different pathological preconditions as well.

Dementia praecox, the category of illness which loosely corresponds to what is today known as schizophrenia, is characterized by the withdrawal of libido from the external world generally, and by the deterioration of sublimation. It involves a regression to autoerotism, often resulting in infantile, "silly" behavior, or hebephrenia.[133]

In the phylogenetic schema of the "Overview," schizophrenia represents the condition of the sons castrated by the father, or else banished under the threat of castration, at the age of puberty. Deprived of all external love objects and their genital sexuality denied altogether, the sons, like the schizophrenic, had no other recourse but to regress to the state of autoerotism.[134]

Paranoia,[135] according to psychoanalysis, always has as its patho-

154

genic condition an exceptionally strong yet vigorously repressed homosexual desire. The libido withdrawn from the external world (that is, from the homosexual object) is narcissistically invested in one's own ego. This economic description makes intelligible the two principal features of this mental disorder: megalomania and the end-of-the-world delirium. For the general sense that the world outside is in fact diminishing, and that it is coming to an end, is a necessary counterpart of the increasing libidinal inflation of the ego.[136]

Paranoia, because of its underlying homosexuality, is thus an analog to the condition of the sons who have fled from the brutal primal father to escape castration, and who ally with one another through homosexual bonds. This is the fraternity in exile: "The social feelings that originate here, sublimated from homosexuality, became mankind's lasting possession, however, and the basis for every later society" [18]. Again, paranoia is a negative representation of this stage of prehistory, since its main symptoms—rather than being indulgence in, or repetition of, the prehistoric homosexuality—amount to a vigorous defense against the return of overt homosexuality.

Finally, with melancholia-mania, we come to the stage of the totemic festival: "If one looks at the characteristic alternation of depression and elation, it is difficult not to recall the very similar succession of triumph and mourning that forms a regular component of religious festivities: mourning over the death of the god, triumphal joy over his resurrection" [18].[137]

Melancholia-mania touches the earliest and the most primitive stratum of the "object relation"; it has to do with the very formation of the ego. As explicated in one of the surviving metapsychological papers, "Mourning and Melancholia," melancholia involves a hidden mourning. The libido is withdrawn into the ego, and in that very process the ego is identified with the abandoned object.[138] The mechanism stems from the most preliminary stage of object choice, the oral-cannibalistic phase; the object of love is a (symbolically) devoured object, an incorporated "other" that is identified with, and kept within, by the ego, without, however, being assimilated into it. The ambivalence originally felt in relation to an external object, now abandoned or lost, comes to be played out in relation to the internalized object; since the latter is identified with the ego, this ambivalence comes to manifest most visibly as a painful self-reproach.[139]

Yet this mournful state often slips into what seems to be its extreme opposite, the state of extroverted elation, namely, mania. But this is only an easy reversal, so Freud tells us, entirely characteristic of the fundamental ambivalence involved in melancholia. Mania represents the moment of triumph of the ego over the hidden object; the exuberance is but a mo-

155

mentary release of the pent-up libido. Although markedly different in their outlook, in melancholia and in mania the content is the same—the same object, the same complex. This elaboration on melancholia-mania makes it all but apparent that the object relation pathologically at work here is modeled after so-called primary narcissism, wherein both "love toward X" and "identification with X" form a mirroring mechanism and an extremely vertiginous structure.

The rest of this analogy is familiar: "This religious ceremony . . . only recapitulates in reverse the attitude of the members of the brother clan after they have overpowered and killed the primal father: triumph over his death, then mourning over the fact that they all still revered him as a model" [18]. The oscillating disposition of melancholia-mania stems from "this great event of human history, which made an end of the primal horde and replaced it with the victorious organization of brothers. . . . The mourning about the primal father proceeds from identification with him, and such identification we have established as the prerequisite for the melancholic mechanism" [18–19].

156   Summarizing this collation of the psychoanalytic nosography and the narrative of prehistory, Freud states:

> If the dispositions to the three transference neuroses [anxiety hysteria, conversion hysteria, obsessional neurosis] were acquired in the struggle with the exigencies of the Ice Age, then the fixations that underlie the narcissistic neuroses [dementia praecox (schizophrenia), paranoia, melancholia-mania] originate from the oppression by the father, who after the end of the Ice Age assumes, continues its role, as it were, against the second generation. As the first struggle leads to the patriarchal stage of civilization, the second [leads] to the social; but from both come the fixations which in their return after millennia become the disposition of the two groups of neuroses. Also in this sense neurosis is therefore a cultural acquisition. [19]

•   •

Thus, through this circuitous route via a dead letter of a manuscript—or, thanks to the message that was virtually dead on arrival—we finally find our way back to the scene of *Totem and Taboo*, to that blinding moment of the murder which left generations of readers stunned and confounded. By so doing, I am not about to claim to be other than blinded myself. In retrospect, Kroeber's review was at once discerning and courageous: stunned, yet still seriously attempting to come to terms both with the almost unaccountable compelling power of the text and "stultifying" chasm that opens up between the collectively and institutionally sanctioned history (that is, ordinary history) and Freud's version of—whatever it is—a tale, story, *Geschichte*. What I have done here is to attempt to take this moment of blinding *metapsychologically* seriously. In order to do so, I deflected my quest from the impasse into which *Totem and Taboo* finally thrusts the reader, and to study in some detail analogous moments in Freud's clinical-analytic work, where he seems more willing to elaborate on this difficulty, on the topic of the crisis of perception and *experience* generally. And, in order to return to the prehistoric moment, instead of going over the body of *Totem and Taboo*, I have chosen to find the same terrain elsewhere, even if this elsewhere is but an abandoned manuscript, thus an incontestably more uncertain ground.

No sooner has the bold speculation on the prehistory of the humankind been presented than is Freud on a retreat course. He hastens to add toward the end of the "Overview" that "the parallel that has been sketched here may be no more than a playful comparison *[spielerische Vergleichung]*. The extent to which it may throw light on the still unsolved riddles of the neuroses should properly be left to further investigation, and illumination through new experience"; and, as a way of closing the manuscript, he appends a few more pages, where he attempts to meet some of the anticipated objections, "which caution us not to overestimate the reconstructions we have arrived at" [19]. But then, he further concedes, these rebuttals presented in advance, too, "have basically done no more than save our scientific fantasies from being criticized as absurd" [20].

Enveloping all the uncertainties expressed in the "Overview" is the question of the uncertain status of this manuscript itself. Had it not been, after all, abandoned? Yet a simple answer to this, the answer, for instance, that decides the issue by appealing to Freud's authorization, is not exactly forthcoming. For at the moment of the discovery of this manuscript, the 1980s, the Freudian corpus is already uncontained by the boundary drawn by Freud's permission to publish. In addition to the fully authorized publications, the Freudian legacy has already drawn into itself not only the manuscripts left behind with seeming indifference but also some documents which the author actively sought to obliterate. The most significant of this latter, of course, are the drafts posthumously published as "A Project for a Scientific Psychology" [*SE*, vol. 1]. The publication of this manuscript in 1950 has permanently altered the way we view such significant but problematic texts as *Beyond the Pleasure Principle*—in many ways an unassimilable segment of the Freudian legacy. It also changed the way we understand the import of metapsychology. Above all, as Laplanche's work most effectively demonstrates, it has made it theoretically untenable to place Freud's writing in a simple chronology and to judge on that basis either that earlier works were superseded by later "improvements" or, conversely, that earlier insight was compromised by later "revisionisms." Freud's chronology refuses to support this kind of explanation and interpretation. In fact, despite Ernest Jones's effort, no other among the modern "great masters" has made it more difficult, more metapsychologically loaded a task to construct a chronology of his life and work than Freud. For with Freud, even the temporality of his "life and work" becomes something other than the time we can mark with days, years, and decades.

With this in mind we might renew our inquiry and pose the question afresh: what sort of temporality is represented in this bold speculative schema, which was adumbrated in *Totem and Taboo* but was never made fully public by the author?

It is, to begin with, a broad-stroke temporality mapped onto geophysical reality (the last Ice Age, and thereafter). Yet this is not a natural time of evolution, or an organic time of "development." Rather, this temporality comprises a series of catastrophes, a succession of scenes, each of which had to be in a sense *erased and obliterated*—rather than added onto—before the next stage could set in. There is not a single protagonist, even a collective one, that lives through these stages. This is a temporality in two acts and six scenes assembled as a history, *Geschichte*. What takes place in the transition from one scene to another is not merely a change in the landscape but rather a change in narrative loci.

Yet somewhere, imperceptibly, accumulation is taking place. We remember that Freud tells us that the ancient prehistorical endowments acquired at the different stages/scenes are *in toto* a collective heritage of us all, and that we inherit this entire past not only as potentially pathogenic dispositions, but in the very shape of our society, in the form of prohibitions, abominations, laws. In this way, all of us are at once hysterical mothers, obsessional fathers, and psychotic sons all at the same time.

This character assembly, perhaps, is something vaguely familiar. In Freud's prehistoric drama, it is true, these characters are entirely flat, two-dimensional; for as yet they have no unconscious; they could not help this because they are the inhabitants of the psychical universe before there was repression proper, *Nachdrängung* ("after-pressure"). Here a regular "historicist" might suspect that these characters are in fact protagonists of a drama of another sort, a witty but at bottom stolid Victorian family drama, be it comedy or tragedy, all taking place within the institution of the bourgeois drawing room. These figures that make up the six scenes of prehistory—are they *merely* endopsychic prototypes inhabiting the Habsburgian gentleman's mind, projected not only outwardly but onto the mythic time of historical beginning?

•　　•

The question is real enough, but the answer is difficult to establish, whichever side one decides to take. But to stop here with this question is to stop short of Freud's own deliberations. To be sure, there is an abrupt shift in the perspectives, a change in the location of the viewing point, from one scene to another. Between the position of the primal father and the position of the exiled or castrated sons, there is no natural continuity, but a sudden dislocation. Moreover, it would be absurd to suggest that the psychical disposition of the castrated or homosexual sons literally passed on from generation to generation, because, as Freud was quick to point out, those sons must of necessity exist outside of the chain of procreation and generation.

This is in fact the principal problem upon which Freud deliberates at the end of the manuscript. In the end, he finds a moment of escape from this predicament in the figure of the youngest son. The condition imagined by Freud is this: when the youngest son approaches sexual maturity, the father of the primal horde is already old, his power to rule over both his sons and his women is weakened by age; the mother's narcissistic love of her young may no longer be overruled by the father's brutal decree. Thus the youngest son survives, whole and intact, and he is poised most favorably to overtake finally the primal father. Freud had already pointed out in *Totem and Taboo* that, even though the privilege of the youngest son was to be eradicated eventually by the next stage of (pre)history (that is, by the triumph of fraternity), many a myth and fairy tale preserves this legacy of the youngest son as their favorite theme. And it is the exceptional position of the youngest that saves the day for Freud's speculation as well:

159

> The difficulty basically coincides with one that has been posed earlier, namely, how the brutal father of the Ice Age . . . reproduced himself. Again there appears the younger son, who later becomes a father—who, to be sure, is not castrated himself, but knows the fate of his older brothers and fears it for himself; he must have been tempted, like the more fortunate of them, to flee and to renounce women. *So next to those men who fall by the wayside as infertile, there may remain a chain of others, who in their person go through the vicissitudes of the male sex and can propagate them as dispositions.* [20; emphasis added]

Thus a surprising new insight enters. As the last sentence here incontrovertibly testifies, *there are not one but two lines of generation that make up the history of this psychical formation.* The temporality of the six stages is a narrative sequence which plots the sequence of "events" against the background of a geophysical modification. But this "lineage" cannot on its own transmit its own acquisition to posterity. Rather, the line of transmission is an alternate chain—almost an invisible one—here shouldered upon the figure of the youngest son.

Of course, it is a singular aspect of Freud's theory that the psychical transmission is carried out almost exclusively by the patrilineal relation, and that a possible alternate route through mothers is not considered in the least, except, possibly, as a vestige of the archaic hysterical disposition. If, on the other hand, we dwell on the position occupied by the youngest sons—our true fathers—it becomes evident that the transmission of the psychical dispositions, already at that prehistoric time, had to be saturated with fantasy. Fantasy is the only medium through which the youngest sons could pass onto us what may have been in reality the personal legacy of their older brothers.

And who, exactly, are we? We are told by psychoanalysis that our psychical inheritance comes from all of those changing protagonists of the prehistoric drama—brutal fathers, castrated sons, banished sons, homosexual sons, murderous sons—yet our own being is not a direct issue of those cultural heroes, for they did not propagate themselves. Instead, we are the descendants of this alternate, hitherto not widely mentioned line of "others," for those were the only ones with the ability to propagate. Those "others," moreover, did not partake of the monumental "events" marking each of the stages in reality; by and large, they were the deeds of their brothers. It is only in the climactic last moment of parricide that, presumably, the exiled brothers rejoin the lineage of generational transmission.

• •

It appears that this prehistory is indeed a note written on a certain tablet of wonder, or "mystic writing pad" [Wunderblock]. As Freud demonstrated in the wondrous little essay of that name, our "mind" lives through and records what passes as "one's life" by a delicate coordination of two distinct functions. On the one hand, the unconscious registers impact after impact infinitely; it retains absolutely everything, forgets nothing, for it is utterly without time. On the other hand, consciousness/preconscious works to register the impact temporarily, and at the same time to buffer the impact; it, too, has no sense of time because it forgets everything. The working of the mind is like the child's toy by that name, a "mystic writing block," comprised of a dark wax slab, upon which lies a translucent film, and a hardier clear sheet over the film; when the surface of this device is scratched with a sharp implement, the trace becomes visible on the translucent film, owing to its contact with the wax slab underneath. The surface of the film will be saturated with writing unless, of course, it is lifted from the wax slab ever so often and the visible marks on the sheet thus nullified. And it is this kind of periodic erasure of saturated images from the conscious/preconscious system, Freud suggests, that is the basis of our sense of time.

Thus "(pre)history" is written in two registers, or rather, the history is written/unwritten in a delicate coordination of two hands, one hand committed to continuity frenetically keeps writing, while the other introduces abrupt change, breaks, catastrophe, and erasure into this history. Here what we always thought as one thing—the line of descent and the narrative memory of history—turns out to be two essentially incompatible registers, two systems that seem to be contradictory and yet coordinated in such a way that the periodic interruption of one by the other, and the movement together in spurts, makes possible for us, for the first time, something like temporality.

FIVE

Dreams Adrift

162   IN 1973, TWO WORKS concerning the native peoples of Australia were
published to inaugurate a new monograph series entitled "Symbol,
Myth, and Ritual." The series editor, the late Victor Turner, celebrated
the occasion by noting the recently rekindled interest in "the role of symbols . . . in social and cultural processes,"[1] which called for the creation
of a new forum such as his series. The first volume was *Walbiri Iconography* by Nancy Munn, the anthropologist. This contribution is, in the
words of the editor, "an excellent example of William Blake's dictum that
'General Forms have their vitality in Minute Particulars'."[2] It is a detailed
ethnographic study of a central Australian people, the Walbiri, with a
special emphasis on their systems of graphic representation.

The other volume, according to the same editor, "presents a striking
contrast in perspective, method, and data, for it is phenomenological,
comparative, and based on written sources. It provides an example of the
approach to religious systems that has been developed by the burgeoning
discipline known as history of religions, and indeed its author is that discipline's most distinguished exponent."[3]

The author in question, Mircea Eliade, needs no introduction.[4] The
title of his book is at once sweeping and modest: *Australian Religions: An
Introduction.* This volume is, in effect, a textual study that takes issues
with—but also relies upon—the century-old cumulation of written
sources concerning the Australian aborigines. With these sources, the author does what many others before him have done with the same: he
showcases the latest approach to the phenomenon of religion, and further
deepens "Western man's" understanding of religion in general, and of religions of these most "primitive" peoples especially.

The contrast between Eliade's and Munn's volumes, however, runs deeper and is more interesting than what the conventional dichotomy of generalist versus particularist, or phenomenology versus anthropology, can signal. In more than a superficial sense, both works have to do with that category which is emblematically attached to the autochthonous Australian peoples in the imagination of "Western man," the dreamtime.

Eliade's rendition of this cardinal notion should come as no surprise to the reader of any of his previous books. The term promptly makes its appearance on the opening page of the first chapter of *Australian Religions:*

> The coming into being of man and the actual world took place in the Dream Time—the *alchera* or *alcheringa* time, to use the Aranda[5] terms for this primordial and fabulous epoch. The physical landscape was changed, and man became what he is today as the result of a series of deeds by Supernatural Beings. . . . The "Dream Time" came to an end when the Supernatural Being left the surface of the earth. But the mythical past was not lost forever; on the contrary, it is periodically recovered through the tribal rituals. [1–2]

This linking of mythic time and rituals also explains, for Eliade, why rituals are needed at all, what efficacies they have: "All of the ceremonies are only reiterations of these paradigmatic acts. The ritual reactualization of the mythical history reactivates communication with the Dream Time, regenerates life, and assures its continuation" [61]. It is this fundamental structure of mythic recreation that enables Eliade to understand the two preeminent types of rituals: so-called rite of increase and initiation rites. The first type reenacts the dreamtime for the purpose of regenerating the vitality of the season, vegetation, and animals; it is the prototype of what is known as "fertility cult." The second type of ritual causes the adolescent boy to "die to the profane world of childhood" [88], only to be reborn afresh, but this time, into the world of "spiritual" existence, or what counts as such, that is, properly male adulthood. This ordeal of symbolic death and rebirth therefore has the effect of partially canceling out his initial birth, that is, the merely natural, biological birth from the mother— the birth that took place, after all, not at the mythic time of beginning but in the middle of profane history. Following the scenario of this "death" and the "second birth," the initiation ceremony first separates the boy from the merely natural, postnatal existence still tied to the mother, and then reaffiliates him directly with the patrilineal ancestral beings—the dreamtime beings. The ceremony is officiated by his older male kinsmen exclusively.

This ritual structure is further made to account for some other prominent features of the Australian societies. First, despite the bisexuality of

some of the ancestral beings and despite the presence of specifically female beings of the dreamtime, and, moreover, despite the obvious birth-
ing images (especially having to do with blood) prominently associated
with the events of the dreamtime, guarding and transmitting of this
mythic knowledge, as well as the ritual reenactment of the ancestral
events are said to be exclusively the responsibility of the initiated males.
Here, "originating from a woman" is construed as the profane origination par excellence, diametrically opposed to the unitary, singular, and
"spiritual" origination directly in line and in communion with the "fabulous time" of cosmic beginning.[6] In this manner, "woman" becomes the
epitome of the profane, thus her exclusion from the religious practice except in the most marginal roles. This generally tallies with the widely held
assumption that women's practices, insofar as they relate to or resemble
(male) religious practices, are either subsidiary to the male rituals (as in
the cases where women are permitted to assist in the preparation or performance of a ceremony in some subordinate capacity),[7] or are derivative
and imitative of them. Whenever women perform a secret ceremony on
their own, it is further believed, it has less to do either with the ancestral
beings or with societal concern in general, but more particularly to do
with some personal aim, always involving matters of sexuality and fertility.[8]

Moreover, the exclusively patrilineal structure of Australian religions
is seen in direct relation to the aborigines' patriarchal responsibility and
exercise of power over geographical localities of their habitat. As is well
known, the native Australians traditionally do not reside in a permanent
dwelling but they migrate according to routes largely determined by their
complex kinship relations. Land rights are therefore not a matter of territorial demarcation and possession as we know it; the habitat is marked
not by boundaries and borders but by certain tracks or routes, and, very
importantly, by certain ritual rights and obligations associated with particular localities. These localities, of course, are directly tied to the
"mythic" events of the dreamtime. Or, as Eliade puts it, "what seems to
be peculiar to the Australians is the mysterious connection between *their*
land (i.e., mythical geography), the mythical history of that land (i.e., the
deeds of the Ancestors), and man's responsibility for keeping the land 'living' and fertile" [50].

"Peculiar," perhaps, but this should cause no surprise since the natural geographical "markers"—such as water holes, rock holes, hills, and
many other conspicuous geological formations—are believed to be the
traces left by the ancestral beings' wanderings. Those sacred localities are
either their footprints or other physical indentations, or else they are the
spots where some parts of their body, bodily excretions, or some implements belonging to them, were deposited. Particularly important are

those places where the ancestral beings are believed to have emerged from or entered into the ground ("disappeared," or "died"), since they are for that reason the most direct links to the fabulous epoch. In the society where there is relatively little in the way of material possessions, exchange associated with marriage and kinship and these ritual/myth-associated land rights are two of the modes in which power is claimed and circulated. Thus the patrilineal ritual rights also translate into the principle of patriarchal dominance over the land.[9]

The basic paradigm of the dreamtime proves enormously resourceful for Eliade, especially in view of the fact that the particular historicity of the Australian religions notwithstanding, this paradigm is not only the key to understanding the Australian cases but also "all other 'primitive' religions"; for, the dreamtime is but an Australian version of the mythic beginning *in illo tempore.*[10] Therein lies the "meaning" of all of these religious phenomena, which in the end can be put quite simply, as he does at the beginning of the chapter "Initiation Rites and Secret Cults":

> Ultimately, all Australian religious activities can be considered as so many different but homologous means of re-establishing contact with the Supernatural Beings and of immersing oneself in the sacred time of the "Dreaming." Every religious act—a ritual, the recital of a myth, a secret chant, the making of a sacred instrument, and so on—is only the *repetition* of an event that took place in the beginning of time, in short, an imitation of models revealed to the tribe by Supernatural Beings. [84]

Although this passage occurs less than half way into the book, it effectively summarizes the pith of what Eliade would want us to learn about Australian religions. Let us recollect, then, the difference that his study is to make, supposedly, in contrast with the types of analyses preceding his.

•   •

Eliade parts company both with his "evolutionist" and "romantic-decadentist" predecessors. Both orientations, according to him, made certain "ideological presuppositions" concerning the "primitive world": "Notwithstanding their radical differences, these ideologies have two things in common: (1) their obsession with the *origin* and the *beginnings* of religions; (2) their taking for granted that the beginning was something 'simple and pure'" [xiv]. It is therefore these ideologues' obsession with pure origins that makes them interested in the Australian aborigines, who were reputed to be the prime example, among the still living peoples, of those closest to, if not identical with, that pristine point of beginning. Whether the depiction of these "people without history" was positive or negative is of secondary importance, according to Eliade: "For the evolutionists, 'simple' meant *elementary,* that is, something very near animal behavior. For the romantic-decadentists, the primitive simplicity was either a form of spiritual plenitude and perfection . . . or the naive simplicity of the Noble Savage before his corruption and degeneration brought on by civilization" [xiv–xv]. Although both these perspectives delineate the "development/degeneration" of religion in linear terms, "such interpretations implied a *naturalistic* or a *theological* approach, not a *historical* one" [xv]. What is called for instead, in his words, is "a creative hermeneutics" [xxi].

In brief, what Eliade advocates is an authentically historical, yet not just historical but also "hermeneutical," approach to the subject. As such, "history of religions" would expunge the age-old reputation of the Australian aborigines as "a *Naturvolk* living somehow outside history," and demonstrate instead that their culture is far from "static and 'monolithic'"; rather, it will show that those native Australians are, "like all other cultures, 'primitive' or highly developed, the result of a historical process" [190]. Moreover, Eliade maintains, in order to understand the primitives as an irrefragably historic people, it is not enough to know that they are normal human beings, but one must know the modality of their "creativity." "We must always keep in mind the religious creativity of archaic man.[11] The fact that so many primitives have not only survived but prospered and developed until direct and massive contact with the Europeans, proves their *spiritual creativity*. And at that level of culture spiritual is tantamount to *religious*. Moreover, religious creativity is independent of technological progress" [xvi].[12]

Eliade is of the opinion that strictly sociological or anthropological studies—or social scientific studies generally—are inadequate for the task of comprehending the "genius" of archaic peoples, because those studies usually do not take into account this essential element of "spiritual creativity."[13] He leaves no doubt as to what he considers to be an especial task for "historians of religions," in contradistinction from those in other disciplines: to illuminate the "religious creativity" of "archaic man" by means of historical analysis.[14] This is more than a question of a different "method" or "approach"; he accords to "history of religions" a unique aptitude for understanding the real worth of those primitive peoples.

First, Eliade emphasizes that societies such as the Australians must be

judged on the bases of these [spiritual] *oeuvres,* and not on the basis of their family structures, social organization, or superstitions. Exactly . . . as French culture must be approached and judged on its masterpieces—the cathedral of Chartres, the works of Racine, Pascal, and all other great works of the mind—and not, for example, on the study of village versus urban economy, or fluctuations of the birthrate, or the rise of anticlericalism in the nineteenth century, or the growth of the yellow novel, or many other problems of the same type. The latter are certainly part of French social and cultural history, but are neither representative nor illustrative of French genius. [xviii–xix]

More than twenty years after this was originally written,[15] this inventory now likely gives us more than pause. Be that as it may, what makes this "hermeneutical" situation particularly intriguing is this question: What exactly is the nature of "religious creativity," when "creativity," as opposed to stagnation, means development and change in some sense, and at the same time "religion" is said to be a matter of staunchly resisting the flow of profane time that runs away from the origin, a matter of forever reenacting the permanent endowment of the mythic dreamtime? What is the "creativity" of "archaic man," in other words, if his essential characteristic is defined by his singular—"monolithic"?—preoccupation with the *arche?*

167

Eliade's advocacy of a *historical* study of the "so-called primitives" thus faces an immediate challenge, which he seeks to resolve in this manner: "the distinctive characteristic of Australians and other primitive peoples is not their lack of history but their specific interpretation of human historicity. They too live in history and are shaped by historical events; but they do not have a historical awareness comparable, say, to that of Westerners; and, because they do not need it, they also lack a historiographical consciousness" [190–91].

This leads to an inevitable conclusion. "The reconstruction of the cultural history of the Australians has a great importance for Western scholarship and ultimately for the Western understanding of 'primitive' peoples—but it is irrelevant for the aborigines themselves. This means also that the eventual reconstruction of Australian religious history will not necessarily disclose the meaning of the various aboriginal religious creations" [191]. At this final turn, Eliade shows a remarkable ambivalence in his own attitude toward the question of the historicity of "archaic" people, the very historicity upon which he insisted at the beginning of the book, objecting to almost all of his predecessors just on this ground.

Ultimately, it now appears, there is a considerable, if not to say unbridgeable, gap between the two activities assigned to the "historian of religion": the reconstruction of history on the one hand, and "hermeneutics" on the other. But the gap is as wide as the distance between "Western

man" and "archaic man" as construed by Eliade himself. What is today's
"*history* of religion" supposed to make of this peculiar "historicity" of
the archaic?

To be sure, Eliade is prepared to defend the significance of a historical
reconstruction even though it has no relevance to the archaic people who
are described as "historical"; thus he adds shortly that "this certainly
does not mean that the historical reconstruction is a vain endeavor. . . . it
was of the utmost importance in proving that circumcision, for example,
was introduced rather late into Australia" [192].

"The utmost importance"? Perhaps.[16] But how is this knowledge to
contribute to the ultimate purpose of "history of religions," that is, to
"creative hermeneutics"?

We are beginning to see what is compacted in phrases such as "religious creativity of archaic man": an extraordinary convolution, and
hardly acknowledged contradiction, of "time," "history," and "consciousness." The historicity of "archaic man" consists in the very refusal
of his own history; he creates history unconsciously, it seems to follow,
because he is said to "lack historiographical consciousness." Are we to
infer, then, that this unconscious historicity of the archaic, because it is
said to be "creative," is endowed with the same laudable quality and efficacy that is attributed to "Western" historical consciousness, the freedom
to liberate oneself from natural and material determination and to create
one's destiny—or freedom, at least, to fulfill one's destiny, to realize one's
own "genius"? But the genius of "archaic man" is supposed to be stub-
bornly fixated on the *arche*, the beginning; he is "spiritually creative" to
the extent that his mythic time devours and obliterates everything that
happens in those latter days; however much his history may "prosper and
develop," the ultimate "meaning" of his history is, according to Eliade's
own formulation, firmly lodged *in illo tempore*. Thus "archaic man's"
history will have to be written somewhere else, from some other place
than his own historical unconscious. And by whom but "Western man"?

But the problem repeats itself. "Western man," in turn, faces a di-
lemma here. The subject, "archaic man," is historical and creative without really knowing it; but the "meaning" of his creativity, its *telos*, is
anchored in the place outside of history. In the end, Eliade gives a gloss
over the gaping problem with an appeal to the well-weathered notion of
"meaning revealed in history." The aim of the history of religions, says the
author in the very last paragraph, is to understand "the innumerable
forms and aspect of *religious creativity,* such as they appear in the flowing
of time, in history" [200]. The task of the historian of religion does not
stop with "[pointing] out that there exist a certain number of types or
patterns of religious behavior, with their specific symbologies and theo-
logies, but rather, *to understand their meanings*"; for "such meanings are

not *given* once and for all, are not 'petrified' in the irrespective religious patterns, but rather are 'open,' in the sense that they change, grow, and enrich themselves in a creative way in the process of history (even if 'history' is not apprehended in the Judeo-Christian or modern Western sense). Ultimately, the historian of religion cannot renounce hermeneutics" [200].

At least for the time being, however, this knowledge of change, growth, and enrichment is a revelation only to "Western man," and it must necessarily remain "irrelevant" to those very people who are the protagonists of this history, until, of course, they, too, come to share in this "revelation in history."

How historical could such a revelation be? Even if the revelation takes place *in* time and *in* history, what is revealed in it is always what is not history, what is above history. In the last analysis, the true object of Eliade's "hermeneutics" seems to be something that has been lying in wait *from the beginning*. This is made explicit in another text, where he says that

> The hierophanies—i.e., the manifestations of the sacred expressed in symbols, myths, supernatural beings, etc.—. . . constitute a prereflective language that requires a special hermeneutics . . . . By means of a competent hermeneutics, history of religions ceases to be a museum of fossils, ruins, and obsolete *mirabilia* and becomes what it should have been from the beginning for any investigator: a series of "messages" waiting to be deciphered and understood.[17]

Here it is not "Western man's" "history" that swallows up the dreamtime of "archaic man"; on the contrary, "history" disappears into the timeless "message" of revelation; and there will be no trace of "historian" left.

As his last word in his *Australian Religions,* Eliade urged that "history of religion" not renounce hermeneutics. It did not. As a matter of fact, it appears that hermeneutics completely consumed the "burgeoning discipline," and together with it, hermeneutics devoured "history" whole. Meanwhile and elsewhere, there goes the other history of shifting sand.

• •

Nancy Munn's work is not a "historical" work in Eliade's revelatory sense, or any other ordinary sense of the term. There is one kind of temporality or "historical specificity" in this text, and that is the time of her stay among the Walbiri people. Munn briefly chronicles the progress of her fieldwork in the preface: what she was allowed to see early in her stay, where and with whom she spent her time initially, what circumstances forced her to change her dwelling, and what she was able to observe even-

169

tually. This story of her progress is roughly parallel to the book's own progress, without, however, her chronology being its organizing principle.

The immediate object of Munn's research is something at once tangible and elusive: the graphic "designs"—the signs that are not just "pictures" but not exactly "writing" either—which are used by the Walbiri in several distinct contexts, which thus have distinct functions. Some are ephemeral figures drawn on the sand, which last as long as the time it takes to tell a story, or rather, a scene of the story. Some are painted on the human body or constructed as regalia for some ceremonial occasion. Some are more or less permanently inscribed on ritual objects that are passed down from generation to generation. Yet many of the basic elements of these designs are common to all of these divergent contexts.

The dreamtime makes its appearance early in her text also, and the polyvalent meaning of the Walbiri term is described with surprising ease and in very plain words:

170

> Walbiri ancestors are usually personified aspects of the environment such as rain, honey ant, fire, wild orange, yam, and so on. Other ancestors are wholly human in form, and referred to by proper names. . . . Walbiri use the term *djugurba,* which also means "dream" and "story," to denote these ancestral inhabitants of the country and the times in which they traveled around creating the world in which present-day Walbiri now live.[18]

Thus the "mythic" dreamtime is not marked by any specific point in time, except that it is in some way *outside* the living present of everyday; it is "the pure world of predecessors," as Munn calls it, borrowing Alfred Schutz's felicitous phrase [24]; it is the time/world not overlapping either with the present or with the memory of the now living. The term opposite *djugurba* refers precisely to this "present": "The term *yidjaru* . . . denotes the world of the living, the ongoing present, or event within the memory of the living; the same term also means real or true, and waking experience in contrast to dreaming" [24]. Accordingly, in contradistinction from the ancestral beings [*djugurba*], human beings are called "people of *yidjaru,*" or *yaba yidjaru.*

Initially, having been denied access to men's society and their secret ceremonies, Munn encountered the dreamtime among women, in the occasion of their daily storytelling. With some surprise, the reader of classical Australian ethnography here learns that it is not exactly accurate to say that these stories *tell about,* or *reenact* the dreamtime; rather, it *is* the dreamtime. For *djugurba* also means just that: a story told on the sand. Such a story is narrated with a particular intonation resembling singing,[19] accompanied by a series of sand drawings made with certain stylized movements of the hand, and these designs are periodically erased and drawn afresh as the story progresses. Not only the story but those markings on the ground are also called by the same name, *djugurba* [61]. Thus the dreamtime in this context takes place right on the ground,[20] amidst the daily activities of a women's camp, not in any ritually restricted space marked by prohibition. Although any Walbiri may on some occasion casually use some graphic notations drawn on the sand to assist her or his verbal narration, only adult women are said to engage in this more or less formalized—though not restricted—way of telling stories.

> The social context of storytelling is the casual, informal life of the camp, unhedged by secrecy or ritual sanctions. . . . The women's camps are a common location. An average group at one of the camps might consist of three to ten women with their small children and numerous camp dogs. Even in the hottest weather the women tend to sit close together; without changing her position or making any special announcement, a woman may begin to tell a story. Occasionally an older woman can be seen wordlessly intoning a story to herself as she gestures and marks the sand, but ordinarily a few individuals in the group will cluster around the narrator, leaving whenever they wish regardless of whether the story is finished or not. At any time the narrator herself may break off the story and go to perform some chore, or even go to sleep in the process of narration. [61–63]

171

Thus the story commences without ceremony, except for a little clearing of space: "A space of about one to two feet in diameter is smoothed in the sand; the stubble is removed and small stones plucked out" [59]. This action "serves as a kind of 'curtain raiser'; children sometimes respond to this preparation by exclaiming, *'djugurba!'*—that is to say, 'Look, a story!'" [69].

This gesture of clearing and erasure recurs periodically through the course of the story, for it is one of the principal factors in marking and creating the temporality of the story, in structuring the narrative. The construction of time in the sand story narration is effected by an intricate play of multiple media, which Munn describes succinctly. "As the story is recounted, successive graphic elements appear on the sand, their sequence bound directly to the flow of narrative action. But while the sequence of elements reflects the temporal order of the narrative, the arrangement of elements on the sand reflects the spatial positions of actors and object. The spatial assemblage constitutes a graphic scene; division between scenes is marked by *erasure,* and a graphic story develops through the continuous cycling of scenes in the manner of a movie" [69].

What contributes to the rhythm of narration—with intermittence

that produces the sense of temporal passage and continuity—is not only
the erasure, but rather, Munn observes, it is those graphs themselves that
function as "a kind of visual punctuation of the total narrative meaning"
[69]. Yet the "totality" is never given as such, because the narration
evolves only in this punctuated, evanescent currents of voices, gestures
and signs, and the "story as a whole" can be only recollected as something that has already taken place, as something remembered but now
riddled with uncertainty. "Since the sand graphs disappear as the scene is
changed, the visual, extrasomatic channel [a medium existing outside the
narrator's body, such as graphs on the sand] is no more time binding than
the verbal and gestural ones; all are characterized by 'rapid fading.' A
particular story can never be looked at as a unitary whole, and no retell-
ing is likely to reproduce the exact arrangements and scene cycles again"
[72–73].

What, then, is a sand story about? Since there are no ritual restric-
tions or demarcations of this category of narration, it would be difficult to
demarcate definitively this modality of the dreamtime. *Djugurba* qua
sand story could refer not only to events ascribed to the ancestral time but
also to events of a more incidental nature. The same technique elaborated
in the story referring to ancestral beings may be used to convey personal
experiences or current gossip [61]. Moreover, we also learn that, even
when the protagonists of the story are said to be ancestral beings, they are
"anonymous persons . . . who lived in those times, rather than identifi-
able ancestors. Stories are not associated with any particular totemic species or ancestors, and they are not localized in geographical space" [77].

In effect, the stories told by women in this fashion cannot be anchored
by means of their specific referents, cannot be brought into definite relation either to specific localities fraught with ancestral power, or to the
world of the living, the real world, "now," *yidjaru*. When the narrator is
asked where the events of her story took place, her answer was, predictably enough, "*Djugurba*." Apparently, to Munn, the import of this answer was unmistakable; thus she translates this answer as: "No place—
djugurba" [77].

Yet it is also in this context of women's storytelling that *djugurba* begins to spill over into "here," "now," "everyday." To begin with, the narration itself takes place right on the ground, amidst the "everyday" life of
the camp, without being ritually marked off from the mundane except by
a casual sweep of the hand. Moreover, it *is* the life of the everyday, according to Munn, that really makes up the content of a sand story, even though
these events are typically ascribed to anonymous ancestors; these latter,
she adds, are not so much specific individuals but "characters" as
"types." "While these stories are regarded as traditional accounts of ancestral activities, it is obvious that we have here a narrative projection of

172

the cyclical day-after-day experience of daily routine and a recounting of the sorts of incidents and behavior also possible for the most part in the ongoing present of Walbiri daily life. It is, in effect, this repetitive daily existence that is going under the label *djugurba*, ancestral way of life" [78].

Thus, as regards its relation to the waking reality of the ongoing present *(yidjaru)*, the dreamtime of the sand story stands in a curious dual relation.[21] Ultimately, Munn speculates that this peculiarity is due to the structure of representation itself, rather than to some particular content [115–16]. In fact, this representational structure accounts for the peculiarly "distal" character of the dreamtime in all of its modalities. Munn renders Walbiri understanding of the matter thus: "wherever event sequences are cut off from the world of everyday life so that they seem to constitute a closed totality of their own and can be 'talked about' but not 'lived through' in the day-to-day involvement of social life, then such events are *djugurba*—stories, dreams, the ancestral past" [117].

• •

In addition to sand storytelling, women have another, more formally ceremonial—though not exactly "religious" in the normative sense— engagement with the dreamtime. The women's ritual called *yawalyu* ceremony, and the designs used for the occasion (always painted on the body), are considered distinct from men's ancestral designs *(guruwari)*, despite the fact that *yawalyu* designs, too, refer to specific totemic ancestors. They differ from men's designs in at least two respects: the way they are revealed and the way they are transmitted. The mode of revelation and transmission specific to *yawalyu*, moreover, introduces the second of what Munn calls "the three primary referents for *djugurba*" [115], dream.[22]

It is in *djugurba*/dreams that ancestral designs are said to be revealed to Walbiri people, men or women. In the case of the *yawalyu* designs, they are almost always dreamt by women, not by ancestral women but contemporary, living persons; hence the designs are believed to be "new" [37].

We are further told that the dreamer has an obligation to share the revealed design with her conjugal cohorts, that is, her husband as well as the cowife, if there is one. While the opinion is sometimes expressed that the woman should pass on her design to her daughter, Munn observes, this dictum does not appear to be followed with diligence, and the sharing among the cohabitants seems to be of much greater significance. The reason is in the logic of dreaming/*djugurba*. Married people—either a husband and a wife, or a husband and two cowives—share a camp, and are said to "share one sleep" [37]. Those who share one sleep must, at least in principle, share a dream as well. Thus the dream of a woman also belongs, in the honorary sense, to her conjugal mate(s). There is a further obligation incurring upon the dreamer: to reenact, or to "sing" the design revealed to her by performing a *yawalyu* ceremony. The participants and assistants in the performance are also the women related to her either through blood or marriage ties.

The conjugal context of the *yawalyu* revelation, sharing of the "dream" among those who "share one sleep," brings to the foreground the strongly sexual connotation of the dreamtime as well. In fact, it is believed that the agent of the dream revelation is an ancestral proxy, a little creature who is also responsible, on another occasion, for causing pregnancy [89–91]. Dreaming a design is therefore somehow analogous with being struck by a little missile thrown by the ancestral representative and becoming pregnant as a result. Furthermore, the uses of the *yawalyu* designs are also matters of sexuality, fertility, and growth. During the ceremony, the design is painted on the body of a woman or a child in order to enhance health and bodily growth, or to encourage pregnancy.

This network of sharing, or collateral transmission of women's ancestral designs, or *yawalyu,* is in marked contrast with that of men's designs, *guruwari,* which are passed on strictly patrilineally, from generation to generation. It is for the latter reason that the men's designs are considered ancient, or as themselves ancestral, even when they are dreamt by contemporary, living men. And it is largely on this account also that many writers, including Munn, consider the male ancestral cult to be cosmological (thus properly religious), whereas women's cult is local, immediate, and personal.

Once we enter the chapters describing men's designs and men's rituals, we encounter everything that we always have heard about "Australian religions" ever since the nineteenth century. There are the ancestral totemic designs that consist prominently of animal footprints and meandering lines representing ancestral tracks, together with concentric circles representing some specific localities (water holes, for example); the narrative is spread across the lay of the land, which thus constitutes a sacred geography. There are highly venerated ritual objects of wood or stone bearing the sacred totemic designs, which are inherited patrilineally. There are initiation ceremonies in which young men are ritually and physically separated from their maternal living quarters and these highly guarded ancestral designs are revealed to them in accordance with a strict patrilineal descent. There are totemic rituals purported to assure the abundance of plant and animal species as well as rain. And the ancestral designs are drawn on the ground and danced upon, painted on the body of the initiate, or recreated as an important part of the regalia for the officiant. The participation or even observation of these rituals by women and the uninitiated is scrupulously restricted.

Because of their elaborateness as well as the severity of sanction and, quite generally, the air of high seriousness that surrounds these male objects and events, we have been instructed for decades to recognize in these the epitome of *religious* practice, call it totemic or ancestral. And it is here and only here in these contexts, we have also learnt, that the dreamtime is properly what it is. It is here, in other words, that the mythic time of beginning is a treasure house of inexhaustible paradigms and prototypes, the only fixed point of history which is for that very reason outside of history, whereas history itself, as a domain of the profane, is but shifting sand.

It is as though Nancy Munn saw the whole structure of the Walbiri society backwards, or, hierarchically speaking, from the bottom up. Although, according to her own account, this was not entirely by design or by choice—she began her observation where she could—the result turned a priceless bounty: an account of the dreamtime that cannot be contained in one paradigm. To be sure, once the highest order of rites, those recognized as the most important religious practices, are observed and understood, it is possible for someone—or even for Munn—to turn the analysis inside out, so to speak, and to recast the entire data in light of the supposed prototypes, and to come away with a highly consistent, hierarchically correct organization of something like "the Walbiri religion and its ramifications." And one would likely find support in the Walbiri's opinions themselves for such a transfigured interpretation. After all, they do say, be they men or women, that *yawalyu* (women's ancestral designs) are "little" or "unimportant" in comparison to *guruwari*, the men's designs [34], and that the designs of the sand story are even less important [89–90]. Or, on a rare occasion when a man dreams what is believed to be a *yawalyu* design, he would reveal this to his wife or wives and she or they would ritually "sing" this gift; whereas under no circumstances, it is said, would a woman dream men's design, nor would what she reveals to her husband ever be incorporated into men's rituals.[23] Thus it might be possible to infer from this that the ancestral time that is guarded and reenacted by those "properly" religious practices is the anchoring point of all that is believed to be truly real and meaningful in the Walbiri life, and that, given the overwhelming power of the archetypal time of origins, the notion of dreamtime is ramified into every aspect of their life; as a result— one might continue—the Walbiri understanding of ordinary phenomena such as dreams is thoroughly dictated by this category, such that they cannot but see dreams as yet another, if lesser, recurrence of the ancestral time; and the same holds true in the case of "mundane" activities such as storytelling. According to this line of reasoning, the category of "the dreamtime," as if by power of contagion, affects everything it touches, so that dreams and stories that originally had little to do with ancestral past, or even the little markings on the sand associated with these stories, come to be called by the same name.

To her credit, and luckily for us, that is not Munn's book. Although she does not challenge the natives' own hierarchical thinking, neither does she commit the fateful act of translating the hierarchy into a generative, pseudochronological order of derivation. Here I might suggest that she was helped both by her sagacious choice of focus ("iconography") and by her keen structuralist frame of analysis.[24] Her focal point was "graphic representations," which she of course understood as a sign system, and, as we know, the last thing a structuralist would expect from a sign system would be to anchor reality. For, it was linguistics and structuralism that taught us that the very working of the signs is to refer to one another rather than to correspond to any "things"; as such, the system "works" by its polyvalence, its multiple modes of shifting, translating.

Thus it is that Munn, unperturbed by the rapid combination, recombination, transmutation of signifying elements, manages to show the workings of the Walbiri graphic signification in almost quiescent clarity. In the meantime, the dreamtime, that archimedean point of analysis for all religious hermeneutics, no longer seems the primordial point of anchorage and plenitude, either for the observer or for the observed. For the dreamtime, too, now begins to look like a measure of shifting, and of making difference.

• •

The dreamtime that appears and disappears with a stroke of a hand; the intermittence that forges the sense of time—these might be but a few emblems of a postfoundationalist "historical consciousness" that finally liberates itself from hermeneutics.[25]

CONCLUSION

IT IS TIME TO ARRIVE finally at our *post-*. Time to gather our chips or, perhaps, time to recollect the movement of the hand that has just finished something.

What, then, are my results? Although I do want to claim that each reading brings into relief an aspect of Durkheim's, Müller's, or Freud's legacy that has been hitherto neglected or perhaps unsuspected, I do not envisage that the aspect thus "recovered" in my reading would somehow "fill a gap" in the existing scholarship and thus contribute toward its greater perfection—as if one should be expecting such a providential moment of completion sometime in the future. Nor is it my expectation that the "recovery" would occasion a wholesale transformation of the established intellectual legacy in such a way that it would be reorganized in accordance with a new pivot, new principle. I resist both these plot trajectories on account of their totalizing assumptions, be they completionist or transformationist. And I resist them because the nature of the recovery resulting from these readings is palpably incongruous with any such teleological scenarios. Least of all do I claim to have unearthed from these old texts some newfangled "tools" ready for immediate use by other research scholars in the field. I reject this utilitarian script because of its blatant positivism. What underlies such a script is a powerful, profoundly delusionary image of who we are as a student of religion, or rather, we as "Western man"; it deludes us to think as if so-called theory and methods were but a useful if also dangerous set of instruments mediating "the researcher/subject" on the one hand, and "the object" on the other, while remaining extrinsic to both; as if, by suspending and canceling this third thing, we could hope to deliver both "the subject" and "the object" in their virginal innocence. No matter how familiar and how compelling this picture may be, I should reiterate: this project begins precisely at the point of turning around and interrogating this compulsive image-idea itself, so as to render visible this very compelling power, which—according to some hermeneut's reckoning—has been propelling the "Western man's" will to knowledge ever further toward its world-historical destiny.

In brief, it is this image of "Western man" confronting "history" and "the world"—and not the "tools" allegedly in the hands of this imagined subject—that needs to be displaced if we are to arrive finally at our present, however belatedly, and to reconfigure the grounds where we stand. It is just this displacement, or a gradual disintegration of this image, that may be called the end result of this reading. Admittedly, the three authors

I examine here did not address frontally issues such as the subject-object configuration operative in comparative religions or history of religions. *Nonetheless, a cumulative, and apparently unintended effect of their peculiar handling of time amounted to a quiet erosion of the fundament of this configuration.* Their individual quest for the origin of religion did not only result in discrediting itself, as later scholars like Eliade are eager to pronounce, but, far more radically, what they did in their quest gnawed at and steadily ate away the very backbone of our easy sense of history and time.

Historicity and temporality have been taken for granted for as long as we "moderns" can remember. Assuming all along the constancy, uniformity and utter objectivity of natural time, we qua "Western man" could feel assured that "history" as a truth narrative mapped onto such a steady flow of time must be more real, more tangible and reliable than, say, speculations about a tenuous point of origination that those metaphysical questers went after. Moreover, the modern historian's time is not only empirical, uniform, and measurable, but time can be cut up into "periods," "eras," and "ages." Thus the two-fold function of time in our "historical sense," as Johannes Fabian suggested in *Time and The Other,* has allowed us to play some remarkable conceptual tricks. That is to say, on account of this double structure of time, certain of our contemporaries can be classified as, in some strange way, noncontemporaries, that is, as "archaic," "premodern," "primitive," or, lately, "preliterate," "primal." This deliberate *ana*chronism has been a vital function in much of the modern historical discourse, and it has been too pervasive and too powerful for us to pretend that we had done away with it when we denounced some versions of evolutionism. (It must surely be significant that those various efforts to substitute new terms—such as *preliterate* and *primal*—for the purpose of avoiding the older ones that are now considered derogatory did not abolish the temporal sense inherent in those designations; and we continue to hear the anachronistic sense of "the originary" and "the anterior" in the newly chosen terms.)

Finally, the modern historicist crowning of its own age has moved us (qua "Western man") a step further, and most probably this was by far the most significant step. For now at this juncture, it is historical *consciousness* itself—or its alleged presence or absence—that has become the most powerful mark of difference between peoples, between the historically conscious subject ("Western man") and the historically unconscious or preconscious object (archaic, primitive, premodern), as we ascribe to one, and withhold from the other, a privileged relation to temporality.

All this, I now submit, is coming undone somewhere in the umbrageous folds of the textual legacy of these three figures. Above all, in their handling of time, temporality/historicity becomes something less than constant, it becomes *intermittent,* so to speak. This strangeness of time appears sometimes on the textual surface (that is, at the level of the progression of an argument), sometimes more explicitly as a theoretical articulation. At times this strange, antihistoricist sense of time shows up as a pure negativity of difference which interrupts, and at the same time sustains, a logical progression of the argument in search of the origin of religion, and, surprisingly, this pure negativity is directly equated with the very aim of the search, the essence/origin of religion (Durkheim). In another case, it shows up as a strongly antiteleological, nonorganic notion of history that cannot be contained and controlled by speech and thought; rather, human language itself turns out to be at once the culprit and the victim of the casuistic processes that masquerade as an organic history (Müller). Thirdly and most radically, positivity of time disappears altogether, while at the same time emerges a new, essentially negative sense of time—temporality as an effect of erasure, of forgetting (Freud).

It may seem paradoxical, if not to say perverse, that we should have to go back to those dusty old texts and to their exceedingly bizarre medita- **179** tions on temporality in order for us to arrive at our own present. Although I would not insist that it *had* to be this way, the reward of this outrageous detour, perhaps, is that when we thus finally arrive at our time, we no longer seem to be standing at our post qua "Western man." Somehow, we are estranged from that picture, from the image of him standing, confronting the panorama of global history before his eyes, as if he alone were riding on the neck of Chronos. Perhaps we begin to imagine a new picture, just at the moment when we feel our own ground giving way, drifting irrevocably to time and to history.

NOTES

Introduction

1. The designation is Mircea Eliade's, although by no means his alone. The matter will be discussed in the first chapter.

2. The overwhelming emphasis on "the living," "experience," and the "organic wholeness of religion" is a tendency particularly notable in post–World War II pedagogy. This was in part, I presume, intended as a corrective to the erstwhile predominance of philology and the disproportionate emphasis on the textual traditions up to that time, and it indicates a shift in focus, supposedly, from the elitist realm of "dead" letters to the world of everyday practice and practitioners of religion. This intent is reflected in the titles of some of the most widely used introductory textbooks of so-called world religions still in print today, such as R. C. Zaehner's *The Concise Encyclopedia of Living Faiths* (originally published in 1959), Ninian Smart's *The Religious Experience of Mankind* (first edition published in 1969), and the series of textbooks published in the 1970s entitled "The Religious Life of Man" (series editor Frederick Streng).

3. For a sustained articulation of this criticism based on shrewd interpretive alternatives, one can point to a number of works by Jonathan Z. Smith, for example. As one of the most concise examples of this criticism, see his "A Pearl of Great Price and a Cargo of Yams: A Study in Situational Incongruity," *Imagining Religion: From Babylon to Jonestown* (Chicago: University of Chicago Press, 1982), pp. 90–101.

4. To examine fully various operations of the origin-logic in the current field of religious studies would require another book, another kind of book. For, above all, such a book would call for a comprehensive documentary analysis of various contemporary scholarly and pedagogical practices, and that is not the focus of the present volume. Here I merely acknowledge the vast implications of, for instance, Michel Foucault's dislodging of "history" to "archaeology," Jacques Derrida's sustained critique of "sciences of man"—at the basis of which lies a thoroughgoing critique of the repressed metaphysical investments in such familiar implements of our thought as "man," "subject," "genius," "culture," "influence," "development," all of which presuppose the (ultimately unitary) point of origin and origination. This logic of origination will be further discussed in the first chapter.

5. We will have occasion to discuss the nature of the "failure of recognition." After Freud and after post-structuralism generally, such a failure can no longer be contained by "oversight," "limitations," or any other device that evokes *mere* contingency as opposed to, say, the necessity of the idea itself. Here, in the realm best sketched by psychoanalysis, contingency and necessity do not play themselves out in the way conventionally assumed.

6. By this gesture I do not intend to dismiss formalism itself as something intrinsically undesirable. That is not my opinion. However, when the opponents of post-structuralism equate it with formalism, it is always intended to be a negative comparison. See, for instance, Rosalind Krauss's rebuttal against this characterization in "Poststructuralism and the Paraliterary," in *The Originality of the Avant-Garde and Other Modernist Myths* (Cambridge, Mass.: MIT Press, 1985), pp. 291–95.

7. Walter Benjamin, in describing what *l'art pour l'art* stands for, "Surrealism: The Last Snapshot of the European Intelligentsia," in *Reflections: Essays, Aphorisms, Autobiographical Writings,* ed. Peter Demetz (New York: Harcourt Brace Jovanovich, 1978), p. 183.

8. That Freud made the notion of representation highly problematic and philosophically interesting has been extensively discussed in the last few decades. In brief, the status of representation is no longer to be assessed in terms of accuracy, resemblance to the original, and so on, as if representation were a matter of transferring the selfsame "reality" from one context to another, but that it is by nature a kind of transformative act; a change of place *(Stelle)* involved in representation *(Darstellung)* is necessarily a distortion *(Entstellung)* to some extent. Among the most lucid and didactic discussions on this point about Freudian representation are Edward Said, *Beginnings: Intention and Method* (Baltimore: Johns Hopkins University Press, 1975), pp. 158–88, and Samuel Weber, "The Blindness of the Seeing Eye: Psychoanalysis, Hermeneutics, *Entstellung" Institution and Interpretation* (Minneapolis: University of Minnesota Press, 1987), pp. 73–84.

182

Chapter One

1. *Reading after Freud: Essays on Goethe, Hölderlin, Habermas, Nietzsche, Brecht, Celan, and Freud* (New York: Columbia University Press, 1987), p. 2.

2. By "logic" I do not mean some apodeictic necessity, as in the formal sense of *logic*. It would be perhaps better to speak of a highly overdetermined cluster of ideas and associative links that poses itself as self-evident and natural.

3. As a general term signifying the modern study of religion as distinct from theology and from other denominationally specific studies, *history of religion* or *history of religions* seem to be preferred nowadays in North America, whereas the somewhat older designation, *comparative religion,* is more frequently in use in Great Britain.

It is useful to remember, on the other hand, that the two appellations were not considered in any way equivalent earlier in this century, when both *history* and *comparative* were taken in a more literal sense. See, for instance, Louis H. Jordan's characterization of comparative religion in contradistinction from history of religions in *Comparative Religion: A Survey of Its Recent Literature,* vol. 1 (1910; Oxford: Oxford University Press, 1920). Jordan emphasizes "comparison" as an essential aspect of the new study, which purports to be "a comparison of faiths viewed in relation to their entire historical product,—their origin, their gradual expansion, their assimilative functions, their dogmas, their ritual, in fact *every link* in the long chain of circumstances which account for their present features of likeness or unlikeness" [34].

Jordan was also one of the first to insist on the irreducibility of "this new science," which "has a definite sphere of its own to cultivate. . . . Its task consists in framing comparisons—honest, accurate, and comprehensive comparisons—between such *religious* beliefs and practices as it is possible to appraise in the light of their historical development" [40].

4. Mircea Eliade, "The Quest for the 'Origins' of Religion," *The Quest: History and Meaning in Religion* (Chicago: University of Chicago Press, 1969), p. 50.

5. First published in *Zeitschrift für Sozialforschung* 5 (1936); English translation in *Illuminations: Essays and Reflections*, trans. Harry Zohn, ed. Hannah Arendt (New York: Schocken, 1969); subsequent citations to this essay will refer to this English edition, and the page numbers will appear in the text.

6. Let us remark immediately, so as to dispel the specter of so-called crude materialism from the outset, that this is not a presumption of economic determinism in the usual sense. In fact the total effect of Benjamin's essay is that the very notion of causal determination—cause as the origin of an event—becomes problematic. (See Rosalind Krauss on the distinction between developmental history and etiology in *The Originality of the Avant-Garde*, p. 22). The Zohn translation of Benjamin is not always exact in this regard; for instance, *Bedingungen* [conditions] is translated as "causes" [222]. At the same time this is resolutely a materialist analysis in the sense that Benjamin is intent on making his focal point the palpable materiality of life processes, that is, how things are produced and reproduced, how bodies move among them and among one another, the shape of the cities and streets, the way bodies and things are altered, destroyed. It is in the midst of these bodies and things, their movements, exchange, and traffic, that Benjamin locates the conditions of modern art.

183

7. Though seemingly more impressionistic than analytically rigorous, one may surmise that Benjamin derived this idea of the simultaneous rise of the aesthetic and the modern liberal bourgeois society—in the world-historical process of becoming "disenchanted," secularized—from his sustained study of Kant's aesthetic and the post-Enlightenment legacy thereof. The idea that the rise of the aesthetic was an aspect of the advent of modernity—and the concurrent decline of the traditional religious institutions—has been more explicitly discussed in recent years. See, for example, Terry Eagleton, *The Ideology of the Aesthetic* (Oxford: Basil Blackwell, 1990), and Victor Burgin, *The End of Art Theory: Criticism and Postmodernity* (Atlantic Highlands, N.J.: Humanities Press International, 1986).

8. At the risk of some confusion, lacking a better alternative, I will be using the term *originary* as an adjectival form of *to originate*, that is, in the sense of "predicated on the notion of (absolute) origin," and therefore not strictly in the Derridean sense of the term.

9. I extrapolate these reflections based on Molly Nesbit's essay, "Ready-Made Originals: The Duchamp Model," *October,* no. 37 (Summer 1986): 53–64.

10. My discussion will be based primarily on two of Krauss's essays, "Grids" and "The Originality of the Avant-Garde," both in *The Originality of the Avant-Garde.*

11. E. H. Gombrich, *Art and Illusion: A Study in the Psychology of Pictorial Representation* (Princeton, N.J.: Princeton University Press, 1969).

12. In this connection but in a greatly different context, Timothy Mitchell offers an astute analysis of this seemingly paradoxical doubling structure of representation. See his *Colonising Egypt* (1988; Berkeley: University of California Press, 1991), esp. the preface and "Egypt at the Exhibition" (chap. 1).

13. In *Ficciones,* ed. Anthony Kerrigan (New York: Grove Press, 1962).

14. This admittedly triumphalist evaluation of postmodernism invites a problem of its own, the result of which is at once ironic and interesting. For to read postmodernism as a certain awakening from the modernist illusion—thus as something in advance of modernism—restablizes the logic of origination and temporality that has just been called into question. In this regard, the position of Krauss as a *discerning* critic could be cast in a compromising light. To put it differently, her strategic allocation of modern-postmodern begins to seem prepoststructuralist, reliant as it is on certain irreducible dichotomies, rather than the erosion thereof. On the other hand, it seems to me that her employment here of the modern-postmodern dichotomy is essentially a strategic move rather than an indication of her position with regard to the stability or instability of these categories. I am indebted to Richard Shiff for stimulating conversations concerning this aspect of postmodernism debate. See his "Handling Shocks: On the Representation of Experience in Walter Benjamin's Analogies," *Oxford Art Journal* 15; "On Criticism Handling History," *History of the Human Sciences* 2 (Feb. 1989): 63–87; and "Representation, Copying, and the Technique of Originality," *New Literary History* 15 (Winter 1984): 333–63.

15. Eliade, *The Myth of the Eternal Return,* trans. Willard R. Trask (1958; Princeton, N.J.: Princeton University Press, 1971), p. xv.

16. Undoubtedly this explains in part why the implications of the postmodernist critique are so late in coming to the fore. It is all too easy to dismiss it by declaring that this brand of criticism is tantamount to an incidental, allusive, or illusive observation and does not constitute an argument.

17. Marcel Mauss, *The Gift: Forms and Functions of Exchange in Archaic Societies,* trans. Ian Cunnison (New York: Norton, 1967).

18. For extensive probes into the creation of different orders of time in ethnographic writing, see Johannes Fabian, *Time and the Other: How Anthropology Makes Its Object* (New York: Columbia University Press, 1983), and Michel de Certeau *The Writing of History,* trans. Tom Conley (New York: Columbia University Press, 1988). Also illuminating in this connection is Trinh T. Minh-ha, "The Language of Nativism: Anthropology as a Scientific Conver-

sation of Man with Man," *Woman, Native, Other* (Bloomington: Indiana University Press, 1989), pp. 47–76.

19. Eliade, *The Quest*, p. 50.

20. Ibid., p. 51.

21. Ibid., p. 52.

22. See Benjamin, "The Image of Proust," in *Illuminations*, pp. 201–15.

23. Benjamin, "Theses on the Philosophy of History," in *Illuminations*, p. 263.

Chapter Two

1. Dominick LaCapra, *Émile Durkheim: Sociologist and Philosopher* (Ithaca, N.Y.: Cornell University Press, 1972), p. 245.

2. Émile Durkheim, *The Elementary Forms of the Religious Life*, trans. Joseph Ward Swain (1912; New York: The Free Press, 1965), p. 107.

3. See Claude Lévi-Strauss, *Totemism*, trans. Rodney Needham (Boston: Beacon, 1963), and A. R. Radcliffe-Brown, "The Sociological Theory of Totemism," *Structure and Function in Primitive Society* (London: Cohen and West, 1952). **185**

4. Durkheim's notion of the radical dichotomy of the sacred and the profane is often criticized or summarily dismissed on grounds that such a claim is empirically untenable and conceptually confused. See W. E. H. Stanner, "Reflections on Durkheim and Aboriginal Religion," in *Social Organization: Essays Presented to Raymond Firth*, ed. Maurice Freedman (London: Cass, 1967]; Steven Lukes, *Émile Durkheim: His Life and Work* (New York: Harper & Row, 1972), pp. 26–28; and E. E. Evans-Pritchard, *Theories of Primitive Religion* (New York: Oxford University Press, 1965), pp. 64–65. On the other hand some writers suggest certain continuity between Durkheim's sacred-profane theory and more recent anthropological studies. For instance, Ian Hamnett sees a direct connection between Durkheim's "anything can be sacred" thesis and Lévi-Strauss's work. See Ian Hamnett, "Durkheim and the Study of Religion," in Steven Fenton, et al., *Durkheim and Modern Sociology* (Cambridge: Cambridge University Press, 1984), p. 214.

5. "The concept of totality is only the abstract form of the concept of society: it is the whole which includes all things, the supreme class which embraces all other classes" [490].

6. Durkheim contends that the multitude of things venerated in the totemic society are all "sacred in the same way" and that the similarity of the sentiments these varying objects inspire could be due only to "some common principle partaken of alike" palpably contradicting the previous claim just quoted from page 56. In fact, this common principle is now presumed to be the very source of their sacred character; hence, "in reality, it is to this common principle that the cult is addressed" [217].

7. First, an anonymous principle (that is, the "totemic principle") is extracted from the multiplicity of the totemic practices; then this nondescript principle meets its equivalent in the religion of another culture by the name of *mana;* owing to its thoroughly indeterminate nature, this *mana* is further identified as "Power in the absolute sense" [212]. Thus indeterminacy, pervasiveness, sheer energy, extreme affectivity are rounded up in one concept, "absolute Power," awaiting its equation with "collective effervescence" in the next chapter.

8. For Durkheim, magic is only a peripheral phenomenon not properly belonging to the discourse on religion. Although he eventually claims that the essence of magic is primordially the same as that of religion [404–5], he finds the two phenomena so obviously antagonistic to each other that they have to be distinguished [58–59].

9. "The really religious beliefs are always common to a determined group. . . . They are not merely received individually by all the members of this group; they are something belonging to the group, and they make their unity" [59].

10. For instance, he refers to Australian tribes as "Australian societies." See, for instance, pp. 110–11.

11. At one point he asserts that in these primitive societies an individual is most strongly tied to his clan, while his tribal bonds are "much more lax and feebly felt," such that it is the clan, rather than the tribe, that would "express itself in religious symbols" [245]. This does not accord completely with what we are about to hear.

12. See his discussion on the imitative rites [393–405].

13. Hence, what every act of identifying does instead of achieving fusion and merger is to establish rules of exchange—specifications as to what can be interchanged and what cannot. In short, no identity can be *simple* identity; it is always infected by difference and nonidentity; every act of identification is the play of "the different" and "the same." Lévi-Strauss similarly argues that the so-called totemic identity is established by *exchange,* by the play of similarity and difference (*The Savage Mind* [Chicago: University of Chicago Press, 1966], pp. 106–7).

14. This might raise the question as to whether, despite his usual Kantian pretense, Durkheim might have been a crypto-Hegelian, at least in this submerged "thesis."

15. Durkheim attests to this point when he emphasizes that the religious force does not "definitely fix itself" anywhere, and that for this reason man's innermost religious principle—the soul—is "partially external" [363].

16. In each instance, this potentially subversive movement of "absolute difference" is intercepted with an appeal to distinguish religion from magic. With this interjection of yet another duality, Durkheim disclaims his responsibility for accounting for the erosion of just *any* dual distinction. By the same token any phenomenon that goes against the promotion of the social unity (hence against

the promotion of his second thesis) can now be labeled magical rather than religious, and thus dismissed.

17. Except, of course, at "the rite of increase," or *intichiuma,* during which the sanction is lifted for a specific period and the clan members are required to ritually kill, consume, and mourn the sacred animal. The logical mechanism of this rite is ingeniously analyzed by Lévi-Strauss in *The Savage Mind* in terms of the logic of exchange (226–28).

18. "So magic is not, as Frazer has held, an original fact, of which religion is only a derived form. Quite on the contrary, it was under the influence of religious ideas that the precepts upon which the art of the magician is based were established, and it was only through a secondary extension that they were applied to purely lay relations" [404].

19. Durkheim tries to specify the difference by saying that religious interdictions necessarily presuppose the sacred whereas "the interdictions of magic suppose only a wholly lay notion of property" [339]. But *lay* here is simply an antonym of "the religious," which is merely a synonym of "the sacred," so that the whole cycle of terms begs the question.

20. "The faith inspired by magic is only a particular case of religious faith in general . . . it is itself the product, at least indirectly, of a collective effervescence" [405].

21. And they are "facing in opposite directions" because "between the propitiously sacred and the unpropitiously sacred there is the same contrast as between the states of collective well-being and ill-being. But since both are equally collective, there is, between the mythological construction symbolizing them, an intimate kinship of nature" [460].

22. "We have already shown how the rites of oblation and communion, the imitative rites and the commemorative rites frequently fulfill the same function. One might imagine that the negative cult, at least, would be more sharply separated from the positive cult; yet we have seen that the former may produce positive effects, identical with those produced by the latter. The same results are obtained by fasts, abstinence and self-mutilations as by communions, oblations and commemorations. Inversely, offerings and sacrifices imply privations and renunciations of every sort. The continuity between ascetic and piacular rites is even more apparent: both are made up of sufferings, accepted or undergone, to which an analogous efficacy is attributed" [461].

23. This double nature proliferates itself even further. "This duality of our nature has as its consequence in the practical order, the irreducibility of a moral ideal to a utilitarian motive, and in the order of thought, the irreducibility of reason to individual experience" [29].

24. Lévi-Strauss, *Structural Anthropology,* vol. 2, trans. Monique Layton (New York: Basic Books, 1976), p. 5.

25. Quoted by Jacques Derrida, "Structure, Sign, and Play in the Discourse of Human Sciences," *Writing and Difference,* trans. Alan Bass (Chicago: University of Chicago Press, 1978), p. 290.

187

26. Nietzsche, of course, instructs us about the life-threatening danger of all-too-persistent memory in one of his "untimely meditations," *On the Advantage and Disadvantage of History for Life*. In line with this is Samuel Weber's essay, where he speculates on Freud's "failure" to admit his debt to Nietzsche, "The Debts of Deconstruction and Other, Related Assumptions," *Institution and Interpretation*.

Chapter Three

1. Louis Henry Jordan, *Comparative Religion: Its Genesis and Growth* (Edinburgh: T. & T. Clark, 1905).

2. Joachim Wach, *The Comparative Study of Religions*, ed. Joseph M. Kitagawa (New York: Columbia University Press, 1958), p. 3. According to Kitagawa's introductory essay included in the volume, Wach at the time of his death in 1955 was preparing the manuscript of this work.

3. Mircea Eliade, "The 'History of Religion' as a Branch of Knowledge," in *The Sacred and the Profane: The Nature of Religion*, trans. Willard R. Trask (New York: Harcourt, Brace and World, 1959), p. 216.

4. Eric J. Sharpe, *Comparative Religion: A History*, 2d ed. (1975; La Salle, Ill.: Open Court, 1987), p. xi. The Müller quotation in the preface to the first edition is from his 1870 lecture, *Introduction to the Science of Religion*, published in 1873.

5. Most notably in recent years, J. Samuel Preus, *Explaining Religion: Criticism and Theory from Bodin to Freud* (New Haven: Yale University Press, 1987) offers no mention of Max Müller.

6. In *Explaining Religion* Preus retraces a different lineage of the quest for the origin of religion—in a word, a more philosophical lineage—but interestingly he, too, concludes with Durkheim and Freud: "My purpose will be to show how the work of Durkheim and Freud brought to a plateau the explanatory tradition studied here, by extending that tradition into two specialized theories of religion that are different, not wholly compatible as they stand, yet both indispensable and posing still, for those working within the paradigm of the human sciences, the challenge of producing a unified theory of religion" [158].

7. Eliade, "The History of Religions in Retrospect: 1912 and After," in *The Quest*, p. 32.

8. *Rig-veda-Sanhita*, ed. Müller, 5 vols. (London, 1854–74).

9. Among them, *Lecture on Buddhist Nihilism* [delivered before the Association of German Philologists, 1869] (New York: A. K. Butts, 1869?); *Lectures on the Science of Language* [delivered at the Royal Institution of Great Britain, 1861 and 1863], 2 vols. (New York: Scribners, 1884); *Introduction to the Science of Religion* (London: Longmans, Green, and Co., 1873); *On Missions* [lecture delivered in Westminster Abbey, 1873] (New York: Scribners, 1874); *Lectures on the Origin and Growth of Religion as Illustrated by the Religions of*

188

India [delivered in the Chapter House, Westminster Abbey, 1878] (New York: Scribners, 1891); *India: What Can It Teach Us?* (New York: J. W. Lowell, 1883); *Three Introductory Lectures on the Science of Thought* [delivered at the Royal Institution, 1887] (Chicago: Open Court, 1888); *The Science of Thought* (London: Longmans, 1887); *Biographies of Words and the Home of the Aryas* (London: Longmans, 1888); *Natural Religion* [Gifford Lectures delivered before the University of Glasgow, 1888] (London: Macmillan, 1890); *Physical Religion* [Gifford Lectures, 1890] (London: Longmans, 1891); *Anthropological Religion* [Gifford Lectures, 1891] (London: Longmans, 1892); *Theosophy; or, Psychological Religion* [Gifford Lectures, 1892] (London: Longmans, 1893); *Contributions to the Science of Mythology,* 2 vols. (London: Longmans, 1897); *Râmakrishna, His Life and Sayings* (New York: Scribners, 1899); *Last Essays: Essays on Language, Folklore, and Other Subjects* (London: Longmans, 1901); *Last Essays: Essays on the Science of Religion,* 2d series (London: Longmans, 1901); *The Six Systems of Indian Philosophy* (London: Longmans, 1919).

10. *The Encyclopedia of Religion,* 1987 ed., vol. 10, S. V. "Müller, F. Max."

11. "It will be important here not to confound the naturistic theory with [Müller's] controverted postulates; for this is held by numbers of scholars who do not make language play the predominating rôle attributed to it by Max Müller" (Durkheim, *Elementary Forms,* p. 98). **189**

12. Sigmund Freud, *Totem and Taboo,* in vol. 13 of *The Standard Edition of the Complete Psychological Works of Sigmund Freud,* trans. and ed. James Strachey, 24 vols. (London, 1953—74), pp. 110—13. It appears that Freud's acquaintance with Müller was an indirect one, probably through Andrew Lang's polemical renditions.

13. Müller, *Physical Religion,* p. 118; emphasis added.

14. This is not to say that Müller is not always recognized first and foremost as a philologist. However, at least among those interested in him as a contributor to the study of religion, some of the more unusual consequences of his philological statements are often overshadowed by the better-publicized naturist, solar-mythical side of his work.

In this chapter, I will be using the term *linguistic* as the adjectival form of *language,* and not in the sense of "relating to linguistics," that is, a particular school of the study of language which arose expressly in reaction to philology.

15. Of course, Müller is also remembered in India, which he never visited but where he had many friends. I have not made a study of the extremely interesting subject of the colonial and postcolonial reception of Müller's legacy, but if we are to trust the recent Indian biographer Nirad C. Chaudhuri, this remembrance does not amount to much in the way of critical scholarship. Chaudhuri, incidentally, appears to be interested in divesting Müller of his German heritage; for instance, he remarks in an "Important Note": "The fact that Max Müller was German by birth and spent his early life in Germany, has quite unnecessarily fixed the idea that he was a German scholar writing in German." Nor does the author appear very pleased with a recent reappropriation of Müller by the Germans: "It is only very recently that the cultural projection of Western Germany

of today has revived his name by calling its centres in the big cities of India Max Mueller Bhavans or Houses. Through this the Germans have put the memory and prestige of Max Müller behind their cultural propaganda though he was interested only in presenting the rediscovered ancient India, and not Germany, to modern Indians" (*Scholar Extraordinary: The Life of Professor the Right Honourable Friedrich Max Müller, P. C.* [London: Chatto and Windus, 1974], pp. 1–2).

In this connection it may be appropriate to remember that the aforementioned work by Joachim Wach was based on lectures that he gave late in his life but for the first time in India. Wach might have surmised that the recognition at the outset of the famed "Indologist" Max Müller, beloved of many Indian intellectuals, as particularly apposite for the occasion.

16. Jacob Bernays was a classical philologist at the University of Heidelberg, and later at Bonn, known for his work on Aristotle and Joseph Justus Scaliger, among others. He was the younger brother of Michael Bernays, another prominent classicist, and, incidentally, an uncle of Martha Bernays, Freud's wife. Some of the letters exchanged between Müller and Bernays are collected in *Jacob Bernays: Ein Lebensbild in Briefen,* ed. Michael Fraenkel (Breslau, 1932).

17. The book was the second volume of *Chips from a German Workshop* (London: Longmans, Green and Company, 1867). It contains essays on mythology, folklore, and various customs, written in the 1850s and 1860s. The first volume, published simultaneously with the second, was dedicated to Baron Bunsen. See below.

18. In *The Life and Letters of the Right Honourable Friedrich Max Müller,* 2 vols., ed. Georgina Grenfell Max Müller (New York: Longmans, Green, and Co., 1902), 1:360–61. I have depended on these volumes for most of the biographical information pertaining to Müller.

19. His first impression of Oxford (1847) was that of ease of life, beautiful, but "more High School than Universities" (*Letters,* p. 64).

20. Letter to Dr. Rolleston, Apr. 1875, *Letters,* 1:514.

21. This was perhaps truer in Müller's perception and in popular imagination than in reality: "By 1850 the new comparative philology had been known in Britain for a generation. It continued, however, to be thought of as a German discipline, and was for a time popularly identified with a single German émigré scholar: Friedrich Max Müller, who throughout the later nineteenth century was to maintain an interesting contrapuntal relation to the development of British anthropology" (George W. Stocking, Jr., *Victorian Anthropology* [New York: Free Press, 1987], p. 56).

22. This turned out to be an overly optimistic estimate, since the entire project was not finished until 1873–74.

23. Müller, *Chips from a German Workshop,* 1:vii.

24. Virtually all of his publications are in English. Clearly a gifted linguist, he learnt this adopted language as a young adult—interestingly, from a Bengali—while he was a university student in Germany.

25. Sending the first volume of his translation of the Vedic hymns, Müller writes to [Arthur Penrhyn] Stanley, Dean of Westminster: "What I sent you as a first instalment of the *Veda* is real and old—of course no one will read that! Nor do I care. I meant to write an unreadable book, and I believe I have succeeded"; and to William Gladstone (then the prime minister): "The volume which I took the liberty to send to you is hardly meant to be read; I know it is perfectly unreadable, except for Sanskrit scholars. It is, in fact, but the underground foundation on which the pillars are to rest which are to support the bridge on which people hereafter may walk across from the nineteenth century after to the nineteenth century before our era" (*Letters*, 1:388). On the other hand, he expresses his skepticism as to the sale of the German translation of his *Lectures* precisely because it is *not* unreadable, as German academics would expect any serious scholarly work to be (see the letter to Bernays, Mar. 1863, *Letters*, 1:288–89).

26. "In writing [the chips] my principal endeavor has been to bring out even in the most abstruse subjects the points of real interest that ought to engage the attention of the public at large, and never to leave a dark nook or corner without attempting to sweep away the cobwebs of false learning, and let in the light of real knowledge" (*Chips*, 1:viii).

27. Müller had a keen eye for the Victorian collectors' proclivities, and identified a certain necrophilic quality in museums, the institution which was then coming into vogue: "If ever there was an age bent on collecting old things, it is our own. Think only of our museums, brimful of antiquities from all countries and all ages and which, like our cemeteries, will soon become small villages, if they are to hold all that was once young and alive on earth. . . . why should not those who are unable to pay for Roman coins or Greek bronzes, for Egyptian bracelets or Babylonian cylinders, collect antiquities which will cost them nothing, and which are older than the oldest things from any part of the ancient world? The fact is that everybody possesses such a museum of antiquities. Only he does not value it. He does not take the various specimens, clean and label them as he ought, if he wishes to know their real value, and hopes to make them useful to himself and others. That museum is language" (Müller, *Biography of Words and the Home of the Aryas*) pp. 1–2.

28. *Lectures on the Science of Language*, 1:12. There are numerous passages where Müller draws an analogy between philological study and geological or archaeological excavation. Canon Farrar's recollection (in *Letters*, 1:177–78) also testifies to Müller's early fascination with geology and archaeology.

29. In *Chips from a German Workshop*, vol. 2. This lecture, as often as his 1870 lectures on the science of religion, is regarded as the inaugural work of comparative religion.

30. *Lectures on the Science of Language* vol. 2.

31. In *Chips from a German Workshop*, vol. 5 (New York: Scribners, 1881), pp. 53–97.

32. *Letters*, 1:254, 256. Despite the fact that he was born of a famous father (romantic poet Wilhelm Müller) and moved among various aristocratic patrons

191

of learning all over Europe, financial security did not come easily to Max Müller. It appears that it was only after his appointment to the comparative philology chair—and also thanks in no small part to the enormous popularity of his lectures—that he was liberated from constant pecuniary apprehensiveness.

33. See his letter to Charles Kingsley, *Letters*, 1:352.

34. Earlier, around 1850–51 when Müller was slavishly at work on the *Rig Veda* project—in no small part because of the exceptional demands from the then-incumbent Boden Professor of Sanskrit, H. H. Wilson—he was actively seeking a way to return to Germany, possibly to University of Bonn, or else to go to India. Through the 1850s he continued to express his desire to return to Germany, while he lectured at Oxford on such subjects as the "History and Origin of Modern Languages" and the "Niebelungen" as a deputy professor [pp. 122–24].

35. First published in *Kottabos*, no. 5 (1870). The essay is believed to have been written by R. F. Littledale and was reprinted together with, or rather prefacing, Müller's "Comparative Mythology" in the later edition of the essay published as a monograph: *Comparative Mythology*. (London: G. Routlege, 1909).

36. This project, incidentally, was something he took up as an afterthought. Other career options he contemplated at the completion of the *Rig Veda* project included returning to Germany to teach and going to India as a Christian missionary.

37. This edition was not only the first but it remained unsurpassed for a century.

38. Eliade, "Cosmogonic Myth and 'Sacred History'," *The Quest*, pp. 72–73.

39. George Foucart, *La Méthode comparative dans l'histoire des religions* (Paris: Alphonse Picard et Fils, 1909), p. 18.

40. Ibid.

41. After discounting the serviceability of the Hindu and the "primitive" examples for the purpose of theory formation in comparative religions, Foucart goes on to cite the singular advantages of the Egyptian religion, which is to say, not only its antiquity but what he calls "l'évolution normale des idées religieuses s'est accomplie sans interruption, sans réforme, sans introduction de croyances étrangères" [36]. Foucart was therefore of the opinion that Egypt was indeed purer than any other known civilization and, moreover, well documented.

42. "This primitive intuition of God and the ineradicable feeling of dependence on God, could only have been the result of a primitive revelation, in the truest sense of that word. Man, who owed his existence to God, felt God as the only source of his own and of all other existence. By the very act of the creation, God had revealed Himself. . . . This primitive intuition of God, however, was in itself neither monotheistic nor polytheistic, though it might become either, according to the expression which it took in the languages of man" (Müller, "Semitic Monotheism" (1860), review of Ernest Renan, *Histoire générale et sys-*

tème comparé des langues sémitiques, 2d ed. (Paris, 1858) and *Nouvelles considérations sur le caractère général de peuples sémitiques, et en particulier sur leur tendance au monothéisme* (Paris, 1859), *Chips from a German Workshop,* 1:348.

43. Müller, "Comparative Mythology," pp. 11–12.

44. Müller, *Science of Language,* 2:404.

45. The underlying assumption here is that what is essential to the Greek genius is not merely historical or accidental but ultimately providential, insofar as ancient Greece is understood to be the cradle of European civilization, that is to say, *the* human civilization.

The contending images of the Greeks among the philologists and classicists must be seen in the light of the larger context of the European construction of its self-identity throughout the nineteenth century. For an important study of this subject, see Martin Bernal, *Black Athena: The Afroasiatic Roots of Classical Civilization,* vol. 1, *The Fabrication of Ancient Greece, 1785–1985* (New Brunswick, N.J.: Rutgers University Press, 1987), esp. chaps. 1 and 2, "Hellenomania," where the discussion of Karl Otfried Müller (no apparent relation to Max Müller) and George Grote is of particular relevance.

46. Müller, "Comparative Mythology," p. 13.

193

47. Müller, "Philosophy of Mythology" (Lecture at the Royal Institution, 1871), *Chips From a German Workshop,* 5:65.

48. Müller, *Science of Language,* 2nd series, p. 394.

49. Ibid., pp. 375–76.

50. In other contexts, however, Müller concedes that such a stage—when language consisted only of roots—is itself mythic, that is, only speculatively posited rather than historically plausible. See, for instance, *Biographies of Words and The Home of the Aryas* (New Delhi, Madras: Asian Educational Services, 1987; originally published in 1888).

51. See "Comparative Mythology," pp. 70–71.

52. Ibid., p. 63.

53. Müller, "Are There Jews in Cornwall?" in *Chips,* 3:288–89.

54. Müller, *Science of Language,* 2:548.

55. For instance, mythology is "an affection or disorder of language [which] may infect every part of the intellectual life of man," that is, wherever language is used (ibid., pp. 375–76, 432).

56. "Philosophy of Mythology," p. 66.

57. See *Science of Language.*

58. Likewise, it is also noteworthy that Müller emphasized that Sanskrit, though probably the oldest of all known Indo-European languages, is not the "mother" language to all others but something like an eldest sister. "Proto-Indo-European language" remains a speculative construct, and Müller never lost sight of this fact, even though he is regularly accused of assuming such a thing in

the first place. For him, all known languages are already derived, already "corrupt" to some extent.

59. "Philosophy of Mythology," pp. 73–74.

60. At times, Müller redoubles the punning transition by adding another: "At first, the names of God, like fetishes or statues, were honest attempts at expressing or representing an idea which could never find an adequate expression or representation. But the *eidolon*, or likeness, became an *idol;* the *nomen*, or name, lapsed into a *numen*, or demon, as soon as they were drawn away from their original intention" (Müller, "Semitic Monotheism," p. 354).

Chapter Four

1. Primal scene, primal fantasy, primal repression.

2. See "A Note upon the 'Mystic Writing Pad,'" *Standard Edition,* 19:231; hereafter abbreviated *SE*. When the translation is modified or qualified with an addition of the original German phrases, reference will be made to Freud, *Gesammelte Werke*, ed. Anna Freud et al. (Frankfurt am Main: S. Fischer Verlag, 1960); hereafter abbreviated *GW*.

3. *Eines Tages*, which Strachey translates literally as "one day"; the evocation of a fairy-tale quality is inescapable in German.

4. Lionel Trilling, *Sincerity and Authenticity* (Cambridge, Mass.: Harvard University Press, 1972), p. 140.

5. Freud, *An Autobiographical Study, SE* 20:33.

6. Didier Anzieu, "Skin Ego," in *Psychoanalysis in France,* ed. Serge Lebovici and Daniel Widlöcher (New York: International Universities Press, 1980), p. 17.

7. For instance, the three page entry on Freud in the recently published *Encyclopedia of Religion* does not even mention *Totem and Taboo.*

8. Editor's note, *SE* 13:xi.

9. For instance, Freud reports to Sándor Ferenczi concerning *Future* that he already feels at odds with what he has written: " 'Now it already seems to me childish; fundamentally I think otherwise; I regard it as weak analytically and inadequate as a self-confession'" (quoted in Ernest Jones, *The Life and Work of Sigmund Freud* [New York: Basic Books, 1953], 3:138). One might wonder why has he written such a book. According to Jones, Freud told Eitingon something to the effect that the book, though it had "very little value," would be "useful in bringing in some money for the *Verlag*," the ever-tottering publishing house of the International Psychoanalytic Association. As for *Civilization*, his reasons were more pathetic; it was simply something to distract the suffering old man, providing him with a modest means of diversion. He confides in a letter to Lou Andreas-Salomé that the book "deals with civilization, consciousness of guilt, happiness and similar lofty matters, and it strikes me, without doubt rightly so, as very superfluous, in contradistinction from earlier works, in which there was always a creative impulse. But what else should I do? I can't spend the whole day in smoking and playing cards, I can no longer walk far, and the most of what

there is to read does not interest me any more. So I wrote, and the time passed that way quite pleasantly" (28 July 1929, quoted in ibid., 2:448).

If we have learned anything from psychoanalysis, however, we should know that such damaging and dismissive assessments by the author himself do not give us license to dismiss them likewise ourselves. These enormously interesting texts, on the contrary, should command our attention all the more because of the authorial disowning. But that is another matter. The matter to which we should attend in this context is the fact that many contemporary readers of Freud, and many indeed in religious studies, choose to neglect or minimize the importance of *Totem and Taboo* despite the emphatic and tenacious assertion of its centrality on the part of the author.

10. Alfred L. Kroeber, "Totem and Taboo: An Ethnologic Psychoanalysis," *American Anthropologist*, n.s., 22 (1920): 53.

11. The instances of this praise are too numerous to document. Let it suffice to mention that Freud's literary skills have been duly noted both by literary scholars of today and by his fellow analysts: "Only those who have tried can appreciate how very difficult it is to present a long analysis in a coherent and interesting fashion. Few other analysts have succeeded in holding their readers' attention for more than the first pages. Here [in the Wolf-Man case] Freud's unusual literary powers and his capacity for co-ordinating masses of facts made him easily supreme" (Jones, *Life and Work*, 2:274).

12. As we shall see later, Freud repeatedly comes back to this issue especially in the "Wolf-Man" case history.

13. In this same vein, Freud was fond of quoting the following passage, with a connection to Goethe: "Among the writings of the Encyclopaedist Diderot you will find a celebrated dialogue, *Le neveu de Rameau*, which was rendered into German by no less a person than Goethe. There you may read this remarkable sentence: 'If the little savage were left to himself, preserving all his foolishness and adding to the small sense of a child in the cradle the violent passions of a man of thirty, he would strangle his father and lie with his mother.' " Freud quotes this in the original French in both *Introductory Lectures* (*SE*, 16:338) and in *An Outline of Psycho-Analysis* (*SE*, 22:141–207).

14. See Donna Haraway, *Primate Visions: Gender, Race, and Nature in the World of Modern Science* (New York: Routledge, 1989), pp. 3–5.

15. *Dichtung und Wahrheit*, which is translated as *The Autobiography of Johann Wolfgang von Goethe*, trans. John Oxenford (Chicago: University of Chicago Press, 1974).

16. It is also to be observed that some of the most widely read works of Freud (such as "Moses of Michelangelo," essays on Leonardo, Jensen's *Gradiva, Moses and Monotheism*) appeared in one side of these publication branches, where as most of the case histories, papers on technique and on metapsychology were published in the other.

Actually, this business of publication is more complicated than necessary for our present discussion. Were we to account fully for this issue, it would involve all of the political strife within the nascent association, the quarrels with Stekel,

Adler, Jung, and Bleuler, some of which will be touched upon shortly. See Freud, "On the History of the Psycho-Analytic Movement," *SE,* 14:47–48, and the third chapter of the second volume of Jones, *Life and Work.*

17. Literally, "International Journal for Medical Psychoanalysis." Freud mentions in a footnote added in 1924 to "History" that the word *ärztliche* [medical] was dropped as of the sixth volume—that is to say, several years before the publication of his polemical essay, "The Question of Lay Analysis" (1926) and an excerpt therefrom, "Psycho-Analysis and Quackery" (1927).

18. "Journal of the Application of Psychoanalysis to Human Sciences," and later renamed *Zeitschrift für Psychoanalytische Psychologie, ihre Grenzgebiete und Anwendungen.* Jones [2:89] tells us that Freud was initially inclined to name the journal "Eros-Psyche," but owing in part to the fact that it was Stekel's suggestion, it was dropped, and the change of names received favorable response from other members of the association, such as Karl Abraham (see Abraham, letter to Freud, 29 Oct. 1911, *A Psychoanalytic Dialogue: The Letters of Sigmund Freud and Karl Abraham 1907–1926,* trans. Bernard Marsh and Hilda C. Abraham, ed. Hilda C. Abraham and Ernst L. Freud [New York: Basic Books, 1965], p. 109). On the other hand one should also note that—according to J. Laplanche and J.-B. Pontalis's monumental reference, *The Language of Psychoanalysis,* trans. Donald Nicholson-Smith (New York: Norton, 1973), p. 211, the psychoanalytic concept of "imago" was presumably introduced by Jung in his *Wandlungen und Symbole der Libido* (1911), translated into English as *Psychology of the Unconscious: A Study of the Transformation and Symbolisms of the Libido* (New York: Yard and Co., 1916).

19. *SE,* 14:47; *GW,* 10:90.

20. It is according to this mode of thought that Freud himself attempted to draw the line of difference between his and Jung's endeavors. Jones relates Freud's attitude toward Jung's *Wandlungen und Symbole der Libido* in the following terms: "Jung was deriving rather uncertain conclusions from that far-off field [comparative religion and mythological literature] and transferring them to the explanation of clinical data, while Freud's method was to see how far the assured conclusions derived from his direct analytical experience could throw light on the more distant problem of man's early history" [2:351]. The argument is briefly but explicitly restated by Freud in his preface to *Totem and Taboo.*

21. Incidentally, Strachey renders *Seelenkunde* [psychology] also as "mental science"; thus we have the series title of the psychoanalytic monographs, *Schriften zur angewandte Seelenkunde,* as "Papers on Applied Mental Science" [*SE,* 9:248; *GW,* 14:46]. This might have been in order to avoid the word *psychology* in too close connection with psychoanalysis, despite the fact that Freud explicitly stated at one point that "psychoanalysis is a part of psychology *[die Psychoanalyse ist ein Stück Psychologie];* not of medical psychology in the old sense, not of the psychology of morbid processes, but simply of psychology" [*SE,* 20:252; *GW,* 14:289]. We may remember that the controversy over whether psychoanalysis is part of medicine (part of psychiatry) or part of

Geisteswissenschaften, at times appears to be a debate between Freud and the rest of the analysts.

22. This is also a key to the psychoanalytic notion of "regression." In this notion the topographical description of the psyche converges with its temporality, and this temporality encompasses not only the time lived by the individual but also the time traversed by the entire species.

23. See Freud, "Leonardo Da Vinci and a Memory of His Childhood," *SE,* 11:97.

24. See for example this passage from Freud, the so-called case of Dora: "In face of the incompleteness of my analytic results, I had no choice but to follow the example of those discoverers whose good fortune it is to bring to the light of day after their long burial the priceless though mutilated relics of antiquity. I have restored what is missing, taking the best models known to me from other analyses; but, like a conscientious archaeologist, I have not omitted to mention in each case where the authentic parts end and my constructions begin" ("Fragment of an Analysis of a Case of Hysteria," *SE,* 7:12).

25. Freud, "Heredity and the Aetiology of the Neuroses," *SE,* 3:151).

26. Freud, "The Aetiology of Hysteria," *SE,* 3:192.

27. Freud, *Introductory Lectures on Psychoanalysis, SE,* 16:371. Another attestation to the convertibility of the individual and the historical may be found in the fact that, as Rainer Nägele observed, Freud called the psychoanalytic narrative of an individual illness "a case *history [Geschichte],*" whereas the historical course of the Jewish people is ascribed to an individual, Moses. (*Der Mann Moses und die monotheistische Religion* is the original title of *Moses and Monotheism*). See Nägele, "Belatedness: History after Freud and Lacan," *Reading after Freud,* pp. 176–77.

28. Freud, "Findings, Ideas, Problems," *SE,* 23:299.

29. *SE,* 18:3–64.

30. "Note upon a Case of Obsessional Neurosis," *SE,* 10:176.

31. *SE,* 9:7–95. With this new endeavor Freud introduces another line of parallels: between the drama of psychoanalysis and a literary fiction.

32. See note 18 above about the title. This series was later to include Freud's essay on Leonardo da Vinci, Otto Rank's *The Myth of the Birth of the Hero* (1909), Karl Abraham's *Dreams and Myths* (1909), and sixteen other volumes published between 1907 and 1925.

33. See Louis Althusser, "Freud and Lacan," in *Lenin and Philosophy and Other Essays,* trans. Ben Brewster (New York: Vintage, 1971), p. 217.

34. Freud, however, also acknowledges and discusses this element of the improbable, but psychoanalytically ("Jensen's *Gradiva,*" pp. 41–42).

35. Greek is one of the *dead* languages with which he initially attempts to address himself to the apparition, but naturally she asks him to speak German instead.

197

36. Jones, *Life and Work,* 2:341. But Freud himself unusually enjoyed writing it, and he was especially pleased to receive Jung's compliments, as if everyone else had failed to appreciate the essay as it deserved. Freud writes in reply to Jung: "Many thanks for your praise of the 'Gradiva'! You won't believe how few people are capable of doing just that. . . . This time I knew my little work deserved praise; it was written during sunny days and I derived great pleasure from doing it" (Freud, letter to Jung, 26 May 1907, *Letters of Sigmund Freud,* trans. Tania and James Stern, ed. Ernst L. Freud (New York: Basic Books, 1960), p. 252.

37. Editor's note, *SE,* 9:116.

38. In this connection, Michel Foucault's discussion of what he calls "author function" is instructive. He argues that Freud was not merely the founder of a science, but the "initiator of a discursive practice," the point being that the authority and credit of the initiator is entirely of a different sort from that of the founder of a science. See Foucault, "What Is an Author?" *Language, Counter-Memory, Practice,* trans. by Donald F. Bouchard and Sherry Simon ed. Bouchard (Ithaca, N.Y.: Cornell University Press, 1977).

39. Another Zürich native, Protestant pastor and educationalist Oskar Pfister, however, remained Freud's lifelong friend and colleague in psychoanalysis. The most conspicuous among Freud's future dissenters who also worked extensively on the subject of myth and religion is, of course, Otto Rank.

40. That is to say, the analysis was going on even though the writing of the case history was not undertaken until the termination of the analysis in 1914.

41. Freud, letter to Ferenczi, 13 May 1913, quoted by Jones, *Life and Work,* 2:354.

42. Freud, letter to Abraham, 13 May 1913, quoted in ibid, 2:353. Elsewhere, Freud demonstrates by quoting the words of an anonymous patient who formerly underwent an "analysis" by the Zürich school that the school has turned psychoanalysis into something resembling what we now call "religious counseling," or even religious ceremony: " 'Instead of freeing me by analysis, every day brought fresh tremendous demands on me, which had to be fulfilled if the neurosis was to be conquered—for instance, inward concentration by means of introversion, religious meditation, resuming life with my wife in loving devotion, etc. It was almost beyond one's strength; it was aiming at a radical transformation of one's whole inner nature. I left the analysis as a poor sinner with intense feelings of contrition and the best resolutions, but at the same time in utter discouragement. Any clergyman would have advised what he recommended, but where was I to find the strength?' " ("On the History of the Psycho-Analytic Movement," *SE,* 14:63–64).

43. It is noteworthy that Freud's continued interest in the question of religion ultimately culminated in *Moses and Monotheism,* a probe into the origins of anti-Semitism.

44. The *Standard Edition* usefully adds this comment: "The coat of arms represents a ship, and the device may be rendered 'it is tossed by the waves, but does not sink' " (14:7).

NOTES TO PAGES 95–100

45. Freud saw Jung's connection to and direct descent from Protestantism as no mere coincidence: "The theological prehistory of so many of the Swiss throws no less light on their attitude to psycho-analysis than does Adler's socialist prehistory on the development of his psychology." And he judges the preponderant principle of the Zürich school to be "the abstract trains of thought of ethics and religious mysticism" [14:61, 62].

46. Among the five major case histories Freud wrote, only three—including the Wolf-Man case—were based on his own clinical experience. The so-called Little Hans case (*Analysis of a Phobia in a Five-Year-Old Boy* [1909]) was mediated through the little boy's own father who was not himself an analyst, and the Schreber "case" (*Psycho-Analytic Notes on an Autobiographical Account of a Case of Paranoia* [1911]) was, as the title indicates, strictly based on Freud's reading of the autobiography written by the paranoiac himself. Even the cases in which Freud was directly involved are not altogether typical, or "textbook" case histories. The first one, the Dora case, is not an account of a successful analysis, and the title makes no pretention to be otherwise: *Fragment of an Analysis of a Case of Hysteria* (1905). As we shall see presently, the Wolf-Man case is also atypical in that the focus of this history—concerning his own patient, it is true— is about another illness, the one in childhood, that Freud never treated. This leaves the Rat Man case (*Notes Upon a Case of Obsessional Neurosis*, 1909) as the only case history in the proper sense. **199**

47. Freud, "On the Sexual Theories of Children," *SE,* vol. 9.

48. The connection between the ceremonial piety of religion and obsessional neurosis has been a topic of extensive discussion in earlier writings. See especially "Obsessive Actions and Religious Practices," *SE,* vol. 9, and "Taboo and Emotional Ambivalence," the second chapter of *Totem and Taboo, SE,* vol. 13.

49. This interpretation also serves to illuminate another factor at work in the dream production: transposition, or reversal [35]. As we know from other examples of Freud's dream interpretation, reversals are common occurrences in dreams. "Turning into its opposite" is a notoriously regular feature of the working of the unconscious. The reversible pairs of "opposites" tend to be the most psychically primitive kind, such as motion versus rest, active versus passive, subject versus object. It often happens that the dream contains a reversal of some significant sort, which is itself difficult to detect; but alongside it there is also a more conspicuous reversal, as if to signal the presence of the other, less obvious but more significant one. In the present case, the transposition of "opening" from the object (the window) to the subject (the dreamer himself, or his eyes) betokens a series of other reversals: perfect stillness (of the wolves) versus violent activity (of what the child really saw in the primal scene); "intense stare" is transposed from the observing child (witnessing the scene) to the wolves; wolves at the bottom of the tree (in the fairy tale) are transposed upon the tree; the taillessness of the wolf in the fairy tale is overcompensated with the big, foxlike tails of the wolves in the dream [30–34].

50. Apparently this aspect of the case (that the meaning of the dream was shrouded in fairy tales) interested Freud, and he published a brief article on the

matter before the completion of the analytic treatment: "The Occurrence in Dreams of Material from Fairy Tales" (1913), *SE*, vol. 12.

51. A more detailed discussion of the threat of castration and the infant Wolf-Man's reaction to it will be found in the next section.

52. As a matter of fact, the "deferred effect" in the Wolf-Man's case as a whole is considerably more complicated, above all because there is yet another point in time that has to be taken into account: the time of analysis. "At the age of one and a half the child receives an impression to which he is unable to react adequately; he is only able to understand it and to be moved by it when the impression is revived in him at the age of four; and only twenty years later, during the analysis, is he able to grasp with his conscious mental processes what was then going on in him" [45].

53. Whether this saturation reflects an implicit acceptance or expropriation of (probably modified) Freudian theory is another question. As for the opinions on the unconscious, we might have preferred a more restrictive notion of the unconscious than the one psychoanalysis upholds; for instance, the notion of the unconscious as a little extra reserve, as something of which each "I" is ultimately in possession, and thus, in control.

54. I should admit that simply to state this would not be very enlightening vis-à-vis what the actual explanatory power of the constructed primal scene is. Had it been my purpose to give a full account of the case history, a more extensive and thus more convincing rendition of this analytic power would be necessary. I will simply have to refer the reader to Freud's text itself for a more satisfactory version in this regard.

55. This is not to say that language has a role in consciousness only. The unconscious is as much determined by language, yet its role is radically different from the case of conscious mental functions. In the latter, language, or rather words, have what psychoanalysis calls "binding" effect. In the unconscious, words have more thinglike characteristics; rather than having a binding (inhibitive) effect, words in the unconscious are completely under the sway of so-called primary process. See Freud, "Formulations on the Two Principles of Mental Functioning," *SE*, vol. 12.

56. In the introductory remarks, Freud notes the extraordinary difficulty of the case. "The patient with whom I am here concerned remained for a long time unassailably entrenched behind an attitude of obliging apathy. He listened, understood, and remained unapproachable" [11].

57. Although he claims that to reproduce conviction in the reader is not the principal intention of this case history, Freud dramatizes the impact of the key moment of interpretation in the penultimate chapter (before "Recapitulations and Problems"), which he entitled "Fresh Material from the Primal Period—Solution."

58. "It is well known that no means has been found of in any way introducing into the reproduction of an analysis the sense of conviction which results from the analysis itself. . . . So analyses such as this are not published in order

to produce conviction in the minds of those whose attitude has hitherto been recusant and sceptical. The intention is only to bring forward some new facts for investigators who have already been convinced by their own clinical experience" [13].

59. "On the whole [the analysis's] results have coincided in the most satisfactory manner with our previous knowledge, or have been easily embodied into it. Many details, however, seemed to me myself to be so extraordinary and incredible that I felt some hesitation in asking other people to believe them" [12]. "I can assure the reader that I am no less critically inclined than he towards an acceptance of this observation of the child's [primal scene] and I will only ask him to join me in adopting a *provisional* belief in the reality of the scene" [38–39].

60. When he returns to these three questions in a later chapter, he states: "The last question is purely one of fact. Anyone who will take the trouble of pursuing an analysis into these depths by means of the prescribed technique will convince himself that it is decidedly possible. Anyone who neglects this, and breaks off the analysis in some higher stratum, has waived his right of forming a judgement on the matter. But the interpretation of what is arrived at in depth analysis is not decided by this" [48–49].

61. "We know how important doubt is to the physician who is analysing an **201** obsessional neurosis. It is the patient's strongest weapon, the favourite expedient of his resistance. This same doubt enabled our patient to lie entrenched behind a respectful indifference and to allow the efforts of the treatment to slip past him for years together. Nothing changed, and there was no way of convincing him" [75]. Earlier, Freud discussed the significance of doubt in connection to dream interpretation and endopsychic censorship. See *The Interpretation of Dreams, SE,* 5:515–16, and the case history of Dora.

62. He notes with some irritation that this notion of retrospective fantasy was first introduced by none other than Freud himself: "I did not require the contributions of Adler or Jung to induce me to consider the matter with a critical eye, and to bear in mind the possibility that what analysis puts forward as being forgotten experiences of childhood (and of an improbably early childhood) may on the contrary be based upon phantasies created on occasions occurring late in life. . . . I was the first—a point to which none of my opponents have referred—to recognize both the part played by phantasies in symptom-formation and also the 'retrospective phantasying' of late impressions into childhood and their sexualization after the event" [103 n. 1].

63. In the end, Freud takes back these assertions to a degree, on the grounds that we have erred in underestimating "the powers of children," and that, therefore, it would be imprudent to deny them credit in advance for having retrogressive wishes and fantasies [103]. However, this mitigation does not fundamentally change the course of his argument, in which he claims to demonstrate that children are capable of receiving and retaining impressions of a sexual kind from very early years of their lives.

64. It seems that the *Standard Edition* contributes to this confusion to a degree, as it translates Freud's *nachträglich* sometimes as "subsequently" (thus

flattening out the time warp of the belatedness), sometimes as "retrospectively" (thus making it indistinguishable from regression) [94, 95, 96].

65. This was indeed the opinion of the Wolf-Man himself, and, in an interview he gave in the 1970s, he repeated this to a journalist: "There is that dream business. I never thought much of dream interpretation, you know. . . . In my story, what was explained by dreams? Nothing, as far as I can see. Freud traces everything back to the primal scene which he derives from the dream. But that scene does not occur in the dream. When he interprets the white wolves as nightshirts or something like that, for example, linen sheets or clothes, that's somehow farfetched, I think. That scene in the dream where the windows open and so on and the wolves are sitting there, and his interpretation, I don't know, those things are miles apart. It's terribly farfetched" (Karin Obholzer, *The Wolf-Man, Sixty Years Later: Conversations with Freud's Controversial Patient,* trans. Michael Shaw [New York: Continuum, 1982], p. 35).

66. Unless, of course, a whole new course of analysis is undertaken, even at a distance, and a new interpretation is produced in such a new network of signification. This is what Nicolas Abraham and Maria Torok have done to the Wolf-Man case; a laborious and extensive textual analysis—just as Freud did to *Senatpräsident* Schreber's memoir—which resulted in a stunning reinterpretation of the wolf dream. Abraham and Torok begin the introduction to *The Wolf Man's Magic Word: A Cryptonymy,* trans. Nicholas Rand (Minneapolis: University of Minnesota Press, 1986), with the following words: "Five years . . . the average length of an analysis. We have spent them in the company of the Wolf Man. During this entire period, his presence was mediated by Freud, Ruth Mack Brunswick, Muriel Gardiner, and, finally, his own works. He was with us, not in person, like a patient on the couch, but through an immutable collection of documents filling a single volume" [lxx].

67. Peter Brooks, *Reading for the Plot* (New York: Vintage, 1985), pp. 276, 277.

68. Decades after the analysis, the Wolf-Man was offered an opportunity to recall, not without a certain sense of pride and privilege, that "Freud himself" called him "a piece of psychoanalysis." He is recalling the time close to the termination of his analysis with Freud, when he planned to present his physician with a gift, in part to help the dissolution of the transference, in part to commemorate the whole affair: "So we agreed that I would give Freud something as a remembrance. As I knew of his love for archaeology, the gift I chose for him was a female Egyptian figure, with a miter-shaped head-dress. Freud placed it on his desk. Twenty years later, looking through a magazine, I saw a picture of Freud at his desk. 'My' Egyptian immediately struck my eye, the figure which for me symbolized my analysis with Freud, who himself called me 'a piece of psychoanalysis'" ("My Recollections of Sigmund Freud," in *The Wolf-Man by the Wolf-Man: The Double Story of Freud's Most Famous Case* ed. Muriel Gardiner [New York: Basic Books, 1971], p. 150). This celebrated volume, as well as the account of the interview he gave to Karin Obholzer, and countless other publications in recent years further testify to the continuing significance of his "case" to the history and theory of psychoanalysis.

69. One might therefore say that this addendum remains a *Nachtrag*, or *supplément* in Freudian-Derridean sense, rather than succumbing to the effect of "secondary revision" [*sekundäre Bearbeitung; see Interpretation of Dreams, SE, 5:488–508*] and its fantasy of completion.

70. "The action of the two-and-a-half-year-old boy in the scene with Grusha is the earliest effect of the primal scene which has come to our knowledge. It represents him as copying his father, and shows us a tendency towards development in a direction which would later deserve the name of masculine. His seduction [by his sister, in which he assumed the passive role] drove him into passivity—for which, in any case, the way was prepared by his behaviour when he was a witness of parents' intercourse" [94].

71. The term *Freudian* here is meant in the fashion analogous to the way one would speak of a Freudian slip, that is to say, not to suggest that Freud is particularly susceptible to it, but rather in the sense that it was Freud who made us aware of the deeply unconscious determination of these seemingly accidental "errors" and "contradictions."

72. The same holds true, according to Freud, for the case of the prehistoric murder of the primal father.

73. As usual Freud's delineation is based on the model of the *male* child.

203

74. As Laplanche and Pontalis remind us, it was fairly late that Freud came to focus on this notion with discriminating terminology, that is to say, in such a way as to distinguish "disavowal" *[Verleugnung]* from other psychical mechanisms of denial, such as "negation" *[Verneinung]*, "repression" *[Verdrängung]*, and, less clearly, "foreclosure/repudiation" *[Verwerfung]*.

75. Freud, "The Infantile Genital Organization," *SE*, 19:144.

76. This is the course for "sublimation," that is, transformation of the desire from the original, sexual aim to a nonsexual aim.

77. Freud, "The Dissolution of the Oedipus Complex" (1924), *SE*, 19:173–79. In a still later essay, "Some Psychological Consequences of the Anatomical Distinction between the Sexes" (1925; *SE*, 19:248–58), Freud attempts to extend the application of this scenario, *mutatis mutandis*, to the case of female children. As is well known, however, Freud's rendition of female sexual development remains inconclusive at best. Among the legion of critical essays on this subject, I note here one of the most extensive and sustained works: Sarah Kofman, *The Enigma of Woman: Woman in Freud's Writings*, trans. Catherine Porter (Ithaca, N.Y.: Cornell University Press, 1985).

78. Freud's construction also suggests the congenital factor, in the sense that the Wolf-Man's father exhibited his proclivity to anal sexuality by his *coitus a tergo*, the trait which may have been "inherited" by the son.

79. Concerning the question of why the sight of a woman's genitals, particularly those of a grown woman, should be so frightening continues to preoccupy Freud. See "Medusa's Head," *SE*, vol. 18.

80. A fetish is a substitute object standing for the mother's missing penis. As such, it embodies not so much a penis as its lack; or, in other words, it embodies

the ambivalence of the disavowal itself. The object chosen is presumed to be the object seen at the last moment before the sighting of the absent penis: "Thus the foot or shoe owes its preference as a fetish—or a part of it—to the circumstance that the inquisitive boy peered at the woman's genitals from below, from her legs up; fur and velvet—as has long been suspected—are a fixation of the sight of the pubic hair, which should have been followed by the longed-for sight of the female member; pieces of underclothing, which are so often chosen as a fetish, crystallize the moment of undressing, the last moment in which the woman could still be regarded as phallic" ("Fetishism," *SE*, 21:155).

81. It should be remembered once again that the "violence" of the observation, or "encounter" did not really take effect at the time of the primal scene, but some time later, most notably at the night of the wolf dream.

82. Here Freud seems to be speaking of repudiation and repression as equivalent. However, it is evident from the general context even of this work that he considered the two processes to be quite distinct, though by no means mutually exclusive. The present case exemplifies the coexistence of these contrary reactions. The terminological clarification with respect to various mechanisms of defense—"repudiation," "disavowal," "repression"—was never achieved by Freud himself, and the credit for the task goes, as is well known, to Jacques Lacan's elaboration, especially concerning *Verwerfung*.

83. At the earliest stage of development, the demarcation between one's own body and what belongs to another is not clearly drawn; the mother's breast is recognized at this time only as a so-called partial object coupled with the child's desiring organ (mouth).

84. At least this equation seems eminently viable, even though Freud himself offers a different calculation. According to his version, refusal to obey the command is for the purpose of retaining the content of the bowel for one's sheer enjoyment later; in this reckoning, offering/giving up the feces on demand entails diminishing of pleasure.

In addition, it seems that within the structure of anal erotism, even "the horror of castration" is incorporated by the Wolf-Man to the advantage of the incestuous desire. The Wolf-Man's fear of "finding blood in his stool," and his parroting of his mother's lament upon the doctor's departure referred to earlier ("I can't go on living like this") are so many ways of realizing his wish to identify with the mother (thus to take her place); the grounds for this identification was that she apparently suffered from abdominal hemorrhage, which the Wolf-Man interpreted as a result of what his father has done to her [76–78].

85. As an instigating factor for this regression to passivity and anal erotism, Freud also names the sister's seduction, in which the boy was forced to play a passive role.

86. Freud seems to have arrived at a clear notion of these differences in the Schreber case, where he revises the mechanism of projection in the following terms: "It was incorrect to say that the perception which was suppressed [*unterdrückt*] internally is projected outwards; the truth is rather, as we now see, that what was abolished [*das Aufgehobene*] internally returns from without"

204

("Psycho-Analytic Notes on an Autobiographical Account of a Case of Para-noia," *SE,* 12:71). See also Laplanche and Pontalis, S. V. "Foreclosure."

87. I am, of course, adumbrating here what Lacan says about the psycho-analytic view on the "grounding" of the real, as that which comes as (in the guise of?) a chance encounter (*tuché*—Lacan borrows this term from Aristotle) which however is always missed. See Jacques Lacan, "Tuché and Automaton," *The Four Fundamental Concepts of Psycho-Analysis,* trans. by Alan Sheridan, ed. Jacques-Alain Miller (New York: Norton, 1978), esp. pp. 54–55.

88. Here I mean "narrative" in a broader sense that would include not only verbal narrations but also the narrativity implied in the (theatrical) staging of a scene, or in organization of filmic "shots."

89. It is to be remembered that "free associations" have their analytic value owing to the fact, precisely, that these connections are not at all "free" or acci-dental, but unconsciously compelled.

90. Samuel Weber, "Sideshow, or: Remarks on a Canny Moment," *MLN* 88 (1973): 1112.

91. "It is easy to make a unified statement of what was expressed on the one hand by the complaint he made and on the other hand by the single exceptional condition under which the complaint no longer held good, and thus to make clear the whole meaning that underlay the two factors: he wished he could be back in the womb, not simply in order that he might then be re-born, but in or-der that he might be copulated with there by his father, might obtain sexual satisfaction from him, and might bear him a child" [101].

92. This amounts to another "parallel"—between metaphysics and metapsychology—which also ends up by one crossing over to the other. As Laplanche and Pontalis put it, "Freud's reflection upon the relations between metaphysics and metapsychology does not come to an end with this simple par-allel: in a significant passage, he defines metapsychology as a scientific endeavor to redress the constructions of 'metaphysics.' He sees these—like superstitious beliefs or certain paranoiac delusions—as projecting what in reality are the properties of the unconscious on to forces in the outside world" (S. V. "Metap-sychology").

93. Freud, "Formulations on the Two Principles of Mental Functioning" (1911), *SE,* 12:215; *GW,* 8:230.

94. *SE,* 1:283–397. This version was "unofficial" to the extent that the manuscript was discovered among his letters to Fliess, the otorhinolaryngologist who was his only professional confidant of the 1890s. Although it was duly pub-lished in 1950, in the last analysis, the publication was against Freud's own will, perhaps not so much because of its content as because of the disagreeable cir-cumstances under which the friendship had fallen, and it appears that he wished none of the documents of this past—which included, in Ernest Jones's words, "extremely private letters"—to be made public. The circumstance of the discov-ery of these documents during the Second World War, their purchase by Marie Bonaparte, and their subsequent survival despite Freud's wish to destroy them, has been documented by Jones, *Life and Work,* 1:287–318.

95. *SE*, vol. 7. Here Freud attempted for the first time a systematic delineation of infantile sexuality and its later coordination with reproductive function.

96. *SE*, vol. 18. In this publication Freud completely reorganized the theory of the drive, or instinct, by introducing the strangest of drives, or rather, an anti drive—the death drive.

97. *SE*, vol. 18. This treatise took up afresh the problem of identification, which is the psychoanalytic key to understanding *group* psychology in terms of the libido theory.

98. *SE*, vol. 19. This marks a profound change in the psychoanalytic understanding of the mental apparatus; it replaced the "first theory" (explicated in the dream book; in terms of Cs./Pcs. and Ucs. systems) with the "second" theory, which articulates the apparatus in terms of the now-familiar triad of agencies: the id, the ego, and the superego.

99. *SE*, vol. 20. Here Freud significantly altered the psychoanalytic theory of anxiety and its role with regard to repression.

100. In close proximity is another lengthy article of an enormous metapsychological importance, "On Narcissism" (1914; *SE*, vol. 14), published shortly before the date of the original composition of these papers.

206

101. Freud, *A Phylogenetic Fantasy: Overview of the Transference Neuroses*, trans. Axel Hoffer and Peter T. Hoffer, ed. Ilse Grubrich-Simitis (Cambridge, Mass.: Harvard University Press, 1987). It is Freud himself who calls this manuscript "a phylogenetic phantasy," though not as its title but in his private letter to Sándor Ferenczi, whose opinion Freud was soliciting at the time.

102. Freud calls this "the most remarkable feature of the sexual life of man. . . . Of all living creatures man alone seems to show this diphasic onset of sexual growth, and it may perhaps be the biological determinant of his predisposition to neuroses" [20:37].

103. In this connection I am indebted to Teresa de Lauretis for generously providing me with a manuscript version of her paper, "Freud, Sexuality, and Perversion," to appear in *Sexual Discourses: From Aristotle to AIDS*, ed. Domna Stanton (forthcoming).

104. In the *Three Essays*, Freud ventures a more explicit statement on this point: "It seems probable that the sexual instinct [drive] is in the first instance independent of its object; nor is its origin likely to be due to its object's attraction" [7:148]. Also, "The sexual instinct [*Trieb*, drive] has hitherto been predominantly auto-erotic; it now [at puberty] finds a sexual object" [7:207].

105. It is noteworthy that it was in 1924, ten years after the first publication of the *Three Essays*, that Freud inserted an entirely new section entitled "The Phases of Development of the Sexual Organization," in order to present such an overview.

106. Thus Freud continues: "If we look at the attitude of affectionate parents towards their children, we have to recognize that it is a revival and reproduction of their own narcissism, which they have long since abandoned" [14:90–91].

107. Narcissism was introduced as a stage first in connection to the case of Schreber, *Psycho-Analytic Notes on an Autobiographical Account of a Case of Paranoia (Dementia Paranoides)* (1911), *SE*, 12:61.

108. This latter possibility certainly did not escape Freud, who concludes the discussion on the subject with this droll statement: "At the most touchy point in the narcissistic system, the immortality of the ego, which is so hard pressed by reality, security is achieved by taking refuge in the child. Parental love, which is so moving and at bottom so childish, is nothing but the parents' narcissism born again, which, transformed into object-love, unmistakably reveals its former nature" [*SE*, 14:91].

109. Here, as the *Standard Edition* editor warns us, "it should be noted that the 'attachment' (or '*Anlehnung*') indicated by the term is that of the sexual instincts to the ego-instincts, not of the child to its mother" ("On Narcissism," *SE*, 14:87). For a much more extensive discussion of this point, see Laplanche, *Life and Death in Psychoanalysis*, trans. Jeffrey Mehlman (Baltimore: Johns Hopkins University Press, 1976), pp. 8–24.

110. "It must be insisted that the most striking feature of this sexual activity [thumb-sucking] is that the instinct *[Trieb]* is not directed toward other people, but obtains satisfaction from the subject's own body. It is 'auto-erotic,' to call it by a happily chosen term introduced by Havelock Ellis" [*SE*, 7:181].

111. See Laplanche and Pontalis, *The Language of Psycho-Analysis*, p. 288.

112. "The contents of the bowels, which act as a stimulating mass upon a sexually sensitive portion of mucous membrane, behave like forerunners of another organ, which is destined to come into action after the phase of childhood. But they have other important meanings for the infant. They are clearly treated as a part of the infant's own body and represent his first 'gift': by producing them he can express his active compliance with his environment and, by withholding them, his disobedience. From being a 'gift' they later come to acquire the meaning of 'baby'—for babies, according to one of the sexual theories of children, are acquired by eating and are born through the bowels" [7:186].

113. Karl Abraham, "A Short Study of the Development of the Libido, Viewed in the Light of Mental Disorders" (1924), in *Selected Papers* (London: Hogarth Press, 1927).

114. Freud, "The 'Uncanny,'" *SE*, 17:241.

115. Freud, letter to Ferenczi, 12 May 1919; see Jones, *Life and Work*, 3:40.

116. The essay itself testifies to its own protracted birth, which took place in the span of nearly seven years. Based upon internal evidence, James Strachey infers that "the subject [of the uncanny] was present in [Freud's] mind as early as 1913" [*SE*, 17:218], the year of the publication of *Totem and Taboo*; on the other hand, it is announced in the essay that at the time of its (final) writing, *Beyond the Pleasure Principle* was "already completed" [17:238]. Whereas *Totem* elaborates on the return of the dead, belief in ghosts and the like phenomena which haunt the most ancient stratum of human memory, *Beyond* locates the phenomenon of return *[Wiederkehr]* at the most fundamental level of life, and

identifies repetition *[Wiederholung]* as something constitutional (that is, instinctual) to all organisms; in fact, the book introduces something extraordinarily strange—an idea wearing the mask of the Hereafter (Beyond, *Jenseits*)—the death drive. "The uncanny" is an unexposed trade route between the prehistoric and the hereafter, traversing the unmistakable region of death.

117. Editor's preface to the original edition, in Freud, *A Phylogenetic Fantasy,* p. xvi.

118. Quoted in ibid.

119. Grubrich-Simitis further relates that the trunk full of papers was given by Ferenczi to Michael Balint, his compatriot and junior colleague.

120. The temporality of human cultural history, however, is not the most comprehensive or global of the temporalities Freud entertained. In fact, he sees a correspondence between the ontogenetic formation of the ego and the phylogenetic "history" of the vertebrates: "One thereby gets the impression that the developmental history of the libido recapitulates a much older piece of the [phylogenetic] development than that of the ego; the former [that is, libido] perhaps recapitulates conditions of the phylum of vertebrates, whereas the latter [the ego] is dependent on the history of the human race" ("Overview," p. 12). The similar speculation is repeated, as is well known, in *Beyond the Pleasure Principle.* Sándor Ferenczi furthers this speculation in his *Versuch einer Genitaltheorie* (1924; translated as *Thalassa, a Theory of Genitality*) and gave it a name, "bioanalysis."

121. Previously Freud drew another kind of chronology upon this nosographic chart: "The order in which the main forms of psychoneurosis are usually enumerated—Hysteria, Obsessional Neurosis, Paranoia, Dementia Praecox [later to be called "schizophrenia"]—corresponds (even though not exactly) to the order of the ages at which the onset of these disorders occurs. Hysterical forms of illness can be observed even in earliest childhood; obsessional neurosis usually shows its first symptoms in the second period of childhood (between the ages of six and eight); while the two other psychoneuroses, which I have brought together under the heading of 'paraphrenia,' do not appear until after puberty and during adult life. . . . The characteristics peculiar to both of them [paranoia and schizophrenia] . . . have obliged us to conclude that their dispositional fixation is to be looked for in a stage of libidinal development *before* object-choice has been established—that is, in the phase of auto-erotism and of narcissism. Thus these forms of illness, which make their appearance so late, go back to very early inhibition and fixations" ("The Disposition to Obsessional Neurosis: A Contribution to the Problem of Choice of Neurosis" [1913], *SE,* 12:318). The same point is repeated two years later in the unpublished "Overview," p. 12.

122. "Perversions" and "actual neuroses" are located in the margins of psychoanalysis; they are within view, and within the theoretical concerns of psychoanalysis, yet outside its therapeutic responsibility or efficacy. This in turn brings into sharper focus what is located squarely in the domain of psychoanalytic practice proper, psychoneuroses. These are certain mental disorders that are

clearly felt as suffering or perceived as pathological, and that have their source in some infantile experience. In 1924 Freud wrote that "the etiology common to the onset of a psychoneurosis and of psychosis always remains the same. It consists in a frustration, a non-fulfillment, of one of those childhood wishes which are forever undefeated and which are so deeply rooted in our phylogenetically determined organization" ("Neurosis and Psychosis," *SE,* 19:151). In contradistinction from actual neurosis which has its etiological source in the current psychosomatic conditions (resulting from frustration, nonfulfillment of a *current* desire or wish), psychosis and neurosis originate in memory. What causes disturbance in the case of these latter, in other words, is a reactivation of repressed memory.

"Transference Neurosis in the narrow sense" refers to the condition produced in, and thus specific to, the analytic situation.

123. "Overview," p. 13.

124. The "idea" is a *representative,* or proxy, of the drive: "An instinct *[Trieb]* can never become an object of consciousness—only the idea *[Vorstellung]* that represents the instinct can. Even in the unconscious, moreover, an instinct cannot be represented otherwise than by an idea" ("The Unconscious" [1915], *SE,* 14:176). In some earlier contexts Freud speaks of the drive *[Trieb]* itself as a representative *[Repräsentant* or *Repräsentanz]* of the stimuli originating in the organism. The editor's note to "Instincts and Their Vicissitudes," *SE,* 14:111–13, negotiates this ambiguity in some detail. For the present discussion concerning the vicissitudes of a frustrated wish/desire (that is, processes of introversion, repression, introjection, and projection), more relevant is the notion of the drive as represented by an idea and its attendant quota of affect.

As Freud goes on to elaborate, insofar as this idea remains in the unconscious, it is a thing representation *[Ding-* or *Sachvorstellung],* whereas when it is conscious, the thing representation is coupled with word representation *[Wortvorstellung].* See "The Unconscious," 14:200–202.

125. If we are to be precise about the nature and mechanism of repression *[Verdrängung],* it must be admitted that the matter is considerably more complicated than this version (which Freud himself utilizes often) might suggest. The complication is due above all to the extremely obscure nature of the so-called primal repression *[Urverdrängung],* which has to be presupposed in order to account for repression proper. (This latter, Freud suggests, is most accurately described as *Nachdrängung,* "*after*-pressure.") In "Repression" (1915) Freud writes, "a *primal repression* [is] a first phase of repression, which consists in the psychical (ideational) representative of the instinct being denied entrance into the conscious. With this a *fixation* is established; the representative in question persists unaltered from then onwards and the instinct remains attached to it. . . . The second stage of repression, *repression proper,* affects mental derivatives of the [primally] repressed representative, or such trains of thought as, originating elsewhere, have come into associative connection with it. On account of this association, these ideas experience the same fate as what was primally repressed. Repression proper, therefore, is actually an after-pressure" [*SE,* 14:148]. In effect, an idea is repressed in part by being repelled by con-

sciousness, and in part by being drawn to some element of the primally repressed.

126. In the conversion hysteria, therefore, it is the substitute formation that is felt as a symptom, as an ailment.

127. *"Unter dem Zeichen der Energie"* seems pregnantly obscure. It is not clear to me exactly what Freud had in mind with this phrase, or *Energie* in particular.

128. It may be surmised that this emergence of speech is the point where the most rudimentary psychic differentiation—some form of demarcation of inside/outside, or perhaps incipient separation of agencies, conscious/unconscious—took place. For according to psychoanalysis it is words that "bind" certain flow of energy to constitute the unique system or agency, preconscious/conscious. See *Project, SE* 1:360–76.

129. This intrapsychically split condition of the obsessional neurotic is commensurate with what may be called the defining characteristic of this neurosis, ambivalence. Of course, ambivalence itself cannot be considered an ailment. As a matter of fact, in the case of obsessional neurosis, neither the fact of repression nor the reaction formation is perceived in itself as a symptom. For, in a way, the obsessional neurotic has *solved* the problem of repression; it is the secondary reaction to this solution that eventually comes to be recognized as pathological.

At first, repression appears to be almost completely successful: the idea *[Vorstellung]* is entirely rejected, and the quota of affect seems to disappear. There is no bodily organ cryptically (that is, hysterically) expressing the repressed idea. What emerges as a substitute formation here is a sort of increased conscientiousness, which is hardly regarded as an illness. And yet the pathogenic source lies in the recourse taken initially to deal with the inadmissible desire, regression. This latter refers to a return to the libidinal structure of an earlier, pregenital sexual organization; or, more specifically in the case of obsessional neurosis, regression to the anal-sadistic phase. This recourse is particularly well-suited for the profound ambivalence—libidinally charged attitude of both love and hate simultaneously—which is characteristic of the obsessional neurotic.

Thus, the exaggerated degree of conscientiousness on the part of the obsessional neurotic is in reality an overcompensation for the aggressive, hateful attitude that is vigorously repressed and yet remains strong in the unconscious. Eventually, the quota of affect returns as social anxiety, and in the form of the unbearable severity of self-reproaches. As in the case of phobia, the repressed idea, too, will return by relaying its irrepressible meaning through an interminable series of substitutes, which are in themselves utterly trivial, and which are acknowledged as such by the very patient herself. The result, therefore, is equally interminable attempts at flight—avoidance, prohibitions, precautionary "rituals," all contrived to prevent one from coming into contact with the forbidden idea. It is this last form that gives the obsessional neurotic her characteristic symptom: compulsive thoughts and acts, which are recognized by the patient herself as, precisely, senseless.

NOTES TO PAGES 154–55

130. As will be evident presently, what is in question here is not entirely or purely chronological order. The "time" of psychical "development" is as structural as temporal, and it has a way of regressing as well as progressing.

131. Freud also observes that the same individual may suffer from phobia or hysterical symptoms as a very young child, become an obsessional neurotic later in youth, and manifest signs of paranoia as an adult (for example, the Wolf-Man); while there is no case known to him where this succession of illness is manifested in reverse order.

132. "The difference between paraphrenic affections and the transference neuroses appears to me to lie in the circumstance that, in the former, the libido that is liberated by frustration does not remain attached to objects in phantasy, but withdraws on to the ego" ("On Narcissism," *SE*, 14:86).

133. At the same time, as compensatory attempts at recovering the lost tie to the external reality, the schizophrenic psyche construes and reinvents "external reality" in its own terms, subjecting it to its own laws (primary process); the result is a marked alteration in speech, and hallucination. Freud comments elsewhere that in psychosis the words themselves become subject to primary process, rather than function as a "binding," controlling devices. See "The Unconscious," 14:197–99.

134. Freud comments here that "the youthful individual" suffering from this disorder "behaves as though he had undergone castration. In fact, self-castrations are not uncommon with this disorder" [17]. It is also to be remembered that, as in the case of obsessional neurosis, some of the symptoms of this disorder are in fact reaction formation, combating the total loss of object cathexis; "the speech alterations and hallucinatory storms" [ibid.] are so many desperate attempts to recover the tie with outside reality, at the cost of fabricating such reality.

135. Between dementia praecox (schizophrenia) and paranoia there is something of a transposition. The order here corresponds to the "chronology" of the prehistoric phases (to be discussed shortly), but in terms of the ontogenetic chronology, the fixation relevant to schizophrenia (autoerotism) is supposed to be more primitive than the fixation relevant to paranoia (homoerotism). For Freud's discussion of the affinity and difference between paranoia and schizophrenia, see for example the last chapter of the Schreber case, *Psychoanalytic Notes, SE*, 12:76–77.

136. As the case of the *Senatpräsident* Schreber stunningly testifies, through multiple reversals (love into hate, subject into object), "I (a man) love him" is transformed into "he hates/persecutes me." Given the general atrophy of the external reality and the concomitant overestimation of the ego, the persecution theme takes on a global outlook—"the whole world is against me"—while the attention continues to be fixed upon the personage with respect to whom the repressed desire is current.

137. Of course, as we already know from *Totem and Taboo,* this religious festivity is a derivative form of what is a far more faithful representation of a

211

"prehistorical event." The prototype of these festivals, in other words, is the "more primitive" rite of totemism.

138. The melancholic identification differs from hysterical identification in that in the latter, the object cathexis is not abandoned but rather manifests in some isolated actions and innervations. On the other hand, melancholia has in common with obsessional neurosis a strong element of ambivalence; the loss of the loved object becomes an occasion for acting out this love-hate emotional charge. See "Mourning and Melancholia," *SE*, 14:250.

139. Here the love withdrawn from the external world does not result in the ego-aggrandizement, but it is the hidden object in the ego that absorbs it entirely; in the melancholic phase, therefore, the ego surrenders to this unconscious mourning—which no amount of "work of mourning" *[Trauerarbeit]* can finish, since the object is kept intact in the unconscious, and its libidinal endowment is never assimilated, absorbed, and dispersed in the process—and the ego is utterly impoverished.

Chapter Five

1. Victor Turner, foreword to Eliade, *Australian Religions: An Introduction* (Ithaca, N.Y.: Cornell University Press, 1973), p. v.

2. Turner, foreword to Nancy D. Munn, *Walbiri Iconography: Graphic Representation and Cultural Symbolism in a Central Australian Society* (Ithaca, N.Y.: Cornell University Press, 1973), p. viii.

3. Turner, foreword to Eliade, *Australian Religions*, p. vi.

4. Furthermore, the author's preface as well as the bibliographical fine print informs us that the book was based on the seminar given at the University of Chicago in 1964, and it was first published as a series of five articles in the journal *History of Religions* (1966–67), the foremost publishing venue of this "discipline."

5. Called "Arunta" in earlier literature, including Spencer and Gillen, Durkheim and Freud.

6. In this regard, Eliade quotes W. Lloyd Warner: " 'the personality before birth is purely spiritual; it becomes completely profane or unspiritual in the earlier period of its life when it is classed socially with the females, gradually becomes more and more ritualized and sacred as the individual grows older and approaches death, and at death once more becomes completely spiritual and sacred' " [84]. The quotation is from Warner, *A Black Civilization: A Study of an Australian Tribe* (1937).

7. "Though the women are not admitted to the male secret ceremonies, they do play a subsidiary role in some of them. For instance, they observe the prescribed taboos while the men are gathered for the secret rituals, they dance and chant in many preliminary stages, they answer ritual calls, and they are even present at some final episodes" [120].

8. From of old, these women's practices are classified as "magic," rather than as "religion proper." Although Eliade scrupulously avoids traditionally derogatory terms such as "superstition" and "magic" except in quotation marks, it is evident that he does not fundamentally challenge the powerful association underlying the traditional magic/religion distinction, namely, the oppositional groupings of women's practice, sexuality/biology, private, individual, *oikos* on the one hand and men's practice, culture/philosophy (theology), public, societal, *polis* on the other. In discussing the prevalent myth that asserts that the most sacred ritual objects were originally in women's possession and subsequently either stolen by or given to men, Eliade describes the gist of this tradition thus: "All these sacred objects and secret rituals have something in common: they are *powerful,* somehow 'magical' instruments, for they can incorporate or represent supernatural forces (e.g., bull-roarers), or, more precisely, they can *compel* the incarnation of such supernatural forces (e.g., the masks). They are all related to the epiphanies of life (blood, sex, fertility) or to the power deriving from them. However, *no important religious doctrines—and no significant cosmological myths—are said to have been discovered by, or to have been the original property of, women"* [125–26].

9. More recently, based on her fieldwork in the 1970s, Diane Bell has challenged not only the traditional ethnography but more recent ones, including Munn's, on this point. Bell takes issues with the more traditional understanding of the gender differentiation as regards the knowledge/power over native geography, and argues that the women's practices she observed demonstrate greater association with geography than previously assumed. See her *Daughters of the Dreaming* (Melbourne: McPhee Gribble, 1983).

10. "As is the case with all other 'primitive' religions, to understand the Australian religion ultimately means to know what happened *in illo tempore,* that is to say, what type of Primordial Beings made their appearance at the very beginning, what kind of activity they carried out—and to what purpose—and what became of them afterward" [2].

11. This designation, "archaic," is actively and regularly in use in all of Eliade's works, despite its association with the notion of certain stagnation or petrification, the state of being "antiquated," a "living fossil," and so on.

12. There is a delicate negotiation of notions such as "development," "creativity," and "progress" here. On the one hand, Eliade considers "development" an antithesis of what is "static and 'monolithic'" or stagnant; in this sense, "primitives" are of course said to be "developed"—they "not only survived but prospered and developed"—and the evidence of this "development" is above all seen in their "religious creativity." On the other hand, he also has another kind of development in mind when he mentions "all other cultures, [whether] 'primitive' or highly developed"; in this latter sense, "development" must refer to some other kind of "progress," such as a technological one.

13. I regard this presumption on the par with the equally well-meaning arrogance of the "religionists" of the Tillichean era, and their assumption that

213

religion is "the depth dimension" of just about everything humans do. A hardly disguised presupposition here is that whether one investigates the political systems, economy, kinship rules, arts, or literature, insofar as one does not see these phenomena in relation to the religious/spiritual outlook of the people concerned, one will fail to know the *meaning* of these phenomena, "what they are about," their core essence, so to speak. This assumption conveniently accords the "religionists" a position of absolute privilege, which is difficult to contest because it is utterly dogmatic. But such a position can be maintained only at the expense of abdicating the privilege of being impacted by those very studies—sociological, political, literary—that the "religionists" consider exterior or preliminary to "the ultimate concern."

14. The point is quite plainly put in another text: "the scholar has not finished his work when he has reconstructed the history of a religious form or brought out its sociological, economic, or political contexts. In addition, he must understand its meaning—that is, identify and elucidate the situations and positions that have induced or made possible its appearance or its triumph at a particular historical moment" (Eliade, "A New Humanism," *The Quest,* p. 2).

15. The end of this preface informs that it was initially published in 1967 under the title "On Understanding Primitive Religions," in *Glaube und Geschichte: Festschrift für Ernst Benz.*

214

16. Eliade alludes to "the innumerable and extravagant theories, before and after Freud, grounded on the supposed antiquity of circumcision" [192]. I cannot evaluate this statement here because the allusion is too vague. He may have had Gezá Róheim in mind. As far as Freud is concerned, the antiquity or lateness of circumcision has no visible impact on his admittedly "outrageous theory" of religion and religious origins. In fact, in *Moses and Monotheism,* against the traditional presumption of its antiquity among the Jews, Freud suggested that the custom was not original with those people who later came to be known as Jews but rather externally imposed by the Egyptians. Whether or not he was right on this matter, it has no direct implication to the case of the Australian aborigines.

Eliade also lists other "results of the last thirty years of comparative ethnological research," historical knowledge concerning, for instance, relative antiquity of the megalithic cultures in Australia, late introduction of fertility cults from Melanesia, and a greater than previously assumed degree of interpenetration and cultural exchange among different societies on the Australian continent.

17. Eliade, preface to *The Quest,* n.p.

18. Munn, *Walbiri Iconography: Graphic Representation and Cultural Symbolism in a Central Australian Society* (1973; Chicago: University of Chicago Press, 1986), pp. 23–24; this is a reprint of 1973 Cornell University Press edition, with a new afterword by the author.

19. Munn notes that the narration at first sounded to her ears as singing, although she was to learn that Walbiri "singing" is quite distinct from this style of diction used in sand storytelling [61].

20. Munn relates that "to live on the ground" is an important factor in Walbiri's identity of themselves in contrast to the white settlers, who do not. "My residence in a camp rather than in a house on the European settlement was, I believe, the most important single factor in establishing a satisfactory role for me in my work with the Walbiri" [xiv]. "Men constantly remarked on my new living quarters (a tent), pointing out that I now lived 'on the ground' as did the Walbiri" [xvi].

21. If this is puzzling, it is no more so than, say, the exact location of a murder in Sherlock Holmes: it usually takes place in some nameable location, yet it takes place nowhere, but, of course, it does take place between two covers.

22. This provides an opportunity to raise a question which was never so much as mentioned explicitly by Eliade in his book on Australian religions: why, in the century-old tradition of European ethnography, is the all-important epoch of mythical ancestors and high gods called the *dream*time. In the context of the Walbiri, there is at least one immediate answer: because *djugurba* means— among others—just that.

23. "Designs are thus channeled from men to women, *via* the marital relationship, but there are no designs that women teach to men for the latter to use in their rituals, an asymmetrical feature that is undoubtedly due to the relatively low ritual status and power of women" [38].

24. It must be admitted also, however, that in certain other respects her structuralism limited her analysis. She adds this self-critique in her 1986 afterword.

25. I have chosen to use this little fortuity of 1973 as a way of illuminating one of the stakes facing "our field," not because I took the two authors to be necessarily representatives of different "methods" or interpretive strategies (of course, there certainly is this difference between them) or champions of certain "schools."

Hier und Jetzt, Benjamin's notion of, 17, 32–33
Historicism, 33
History, non-teleological notion of, 5, 177–79
History of religion(s), 4, 14, 66, 162, 166–69, 178, 182n.3. *See also* Comparative religion; *Religionswissenschaft*

Infantile sexuality, 11, 77, 136, 139–48; Freud's disputes with Jung over, 11–12, 94–97; Wolf-Man's Case as an evidence for, 106–7, 116, 132–33
Intrauterine experience, fantasy of, 132–36. *See also* Rebirth fantasy

220 James, Henry, 22
Jones, Ernest, 92, 158, 194n.9, 195nn. 11, 16
Jordan, Louis Henry, 58, 182n.3; *Comparative Religion: Its Genesis and Growth,* 58; *Comparative Religion: A Survey of Its Recent Literature,* 182n.3
Jung, Carl Gustav, 11–12, 92–97, 133, 195n.16, 196n.20, 198n.36; and Aryan religiosity, 93–94, 105, 198n.42, 199n.45, 201n.62

Kofman, Sarah, 203n.77
Krauss, Rosalind, 21–25, 27, 182n.6, 183n.6; as a postmodern critic, 184n.10, "Grids," 23–25, 184n.10; "The Originality of the Avant-Garde," 22, 184n.10; "Poststructuralism and the Para-literary," 182n.6
Kroeber, Alfred L., 79–80, 156

Lacan, Jacques, 10, 120, 130, 205n.87; on *Verwerfung,* 123, 130, 204n.82
LaCapra, Dominick, 185n.1

Laplanche, Jean, 157; and J.-B. Pontalis, 10, 196n.18, 203n.74, 204n.86, 205n.92
Latency (sexual), 122, 141, 148
Lévi-Strauss, Claude, 35, 55–57, 75, 186n.13, 187n.24
"Little Hans," case history of *(Analysis of a Phobia in a Five-Year-Old Boy),* 199n.46
Lukes, Steven, 185n.4

Magic, 213n.8; as primitive habits of thought (Freud), 153; derivation from religion (Durkheim), 46–47, 51; difference from religion (Durkheim), 39, 186nn. 8, 16; gender economy of, 213n.8
Mana, 56–57, 186n.7
Marx, Karl, 20
Mauss, Marcel, 27, 55–57
Max Müller, Georgiana Grenfell *(The Life and Letters of the Right Honourable Friedrich Max Müller),* 64, 65
Melancholia-Mania. *See under* Psychoneurosis
Metapsychology, 10, 130, 137–61, 205n.92; analogy with metaphysics, 137; publication of Freud's works on, 137–39, 148–50
Mitchell, Timothy, 184n.12
Müller, Friedrich Max, 6, 8–9, 58–75, 88, 177, 179; as exponent of nature myth theory, 8–9, 60, 66, 69, 189n.11; as the first Chair of Comparative Philology, 64–65; and the Boden Chair of Sanskrit, 64–65, 192n.34; lectures on the science of language, 64; legacy of, 58–61; on Greek myths, 67–68; and Oxford, 8–9, 59, 61–62, 64–65, 190n.19; principal works by, 60, 188n.9; publication of *Chips from a German Workshop,* 63; public lectures of, 61, 63; *Rig*